THE GOOD RICH AND WHAT THEY COST US

THE GOOD RICH AND WHAT THEY COST US

Robert F. Dalzell, Jr.

Yale UNIVERSITY PRESS
New Haven & London

Yale University Press books may be purchased in quantity for educational, business, or promotional use. For information, please e-mail sales.press@yale.edu (U.S. office) or sales@yaleup.co.uk (U.K. office).

Set in Galliard Roman and Copperplate 33bc type by Integrated Publishing Solutions.

Printed in the United States of America.

Library of Congress Cataloging-in-Publication Data

Dalzell, Robert F.
The good rich and what they cost us / Robert F. Dalzell, Jr.
   p. cm.
Includes bibliographical references and index.
ISBN 978-0-300-17559-2 (alk. paper)

1. Wealth—United States—History. 2. Rich people—United States—History.
I. Title.
HC110.W4D35 2013
339.40973—dc23   2012022382

A catalogue record for this book is available from the British Library.

This paper meets the requirements of ANSI/NISO Z39.48–1992 (Permanence of Paper).

10 9 8 7 6 5 4 3 2 1

For Lee, again and always

CONTENTS

CREATING THE PARADIGM

1

PARADOX

"Man must have an idol—the amassing of wealth is one of the worst species of idolatry."[1]

So wrote Andrew Carnegie in 1868, and not for publication, but scrawled across a list of his current financial holdings. Only thirty years old, with assets of $400,000, he had about decided to abandon what he saw as the soul-crushing business of perpetual profit seeking. Instead, over the next thirty years he built in the steel industry one of history's greatest fortunes, the lion's share of which he then spent on a multitude of projects designed to help his fellow human beings. Thus did he escape making wealth his personal idol. Nor was that all he escaped. His years in business had been marked by brutal ruthlessness toward anyone who challenged his will—including his workers, most notoriously in his battle to crush the Homestead strike of 1902, which cost sixteen lives. But there too money had its uses. As one of his biographers wrote: "He did not die disgraced; he had given it all away."[2]

So once heartily disliked by his fellow countrymen, Carnegie lived to see his reputation sponged clean—to become one of America's "good rich." Indeed for many people his life would stand as the founding model of everything it took to belong to that fabled fraternity, a view Carnegie himself eagerly promoted, though in reality he was following a tradition stretching back to the earliest days of British settlement in North America. And if his fortune had for a while seemed uniquely large, in time John D. Rockefeller would earn far more than Carnegie ever had. The two differed in other ways as well. But they remained united—as do we all—by one venerable strand of American culture, and that is the abiding paradox at the core of our attitudes toward wealth and democracy.

That paradox is the subject of this book.

Broadly speaking, my approach has been shaped by three propositions, one obvious, the other two hardly less so, although they are easily taken for granted. The first is that from the beginning ours has been a capitalist society; the second, that the chief function of capitalism is to create wealth; and the third, that even at its most successful, left unmediated, capitalism does nothing to ensure the equitable distribution of that wealth. In fact it usually does just the opposite: under its aegis a small number of people become rich, leaving the rest of the population to arrange themselves on the downward sloping terrain below.

Wealth and inequality, then. But if that is what capitalism appears to bring, people can and do imagine very different outcomes, as the brilliant young aristocrat Alexis de Tocqueville discovered on his travels in the United States during the 1820s. Nothing more impressed him about the nation he saw than the extraordinary degree of equality that prevailed throughout it. As he declared in his magisterial *Democracy in America,* "Men are there seen on a greater equality in point of fortune and intellect or, in other words, more equal in their strength, than in any other country in the world, or in any age of which history has preserved the memory."[3] He also noted how deeply attached Americans were to this "equality of condition" or "the democratic principle"—phrases he used interchangeably. Yet at the same time he took care to qualify his assertions in one crucial respect: "I do not mean that there is any lack of wealthy individuals in the United States. I know of no country, indeed, where the love of money has taken stronger hold."[4]

A passion for equality paired with widespread wealth and a love of money—truly this was a paradox, and perhaps to soften the incongruity of the combination Tocqueville went on to suggest that money circulated so rapidly in the United States that it seldom landed anywhere for very long, thereby making large private accumulations of wealth only a fleeting affair. As he put it, "Experience shows that it is rare to find two generations in full enjoyment of it."[5] But even as Tocqueville wrote, John Jacob Astor and Cornelius Vanderbilt were building fortunes that two hundred years later still support their descendants, and scores of similar examples could be cited. (Of those appearing on *Forbes* magazine's 2011 list of the four hundred richest Americans, fully 29.8 percent inherited all or part of their wealth.) So the paradox stands. Regardless of our democratic ideals, wealth can last for generations in American families.

On the other side of the balance it must be noted that our love of money does not always extend to its possessors, as the steady drumbeat of recent headlines about "obscenely large" Wall Street bonuses shows. On the contrary, in myth and legend some of our nastiest villains have been rich—mean-hearted plutocrats consumed by greed—figures like Jay Gould, Samuel Insull, and, more recently, Bernard Madoff.

Ultimately, though, making villains (or heroes, as we more often do) of the rich tends to say as least as much about us as it does about them, for it is we who fashion those characterizations: the emotions that lie behind them are ours, not theirs. Nor is it enough to recognize how strong those emotions can be, or how widely they sometimes diverge. To understand them we have to search for their origins—to uncover the sources of our complex and often contradictory feelings about the rich.

With this in mind, in the first part of the book I have focused on the lives of five Americans—all of them rich—to see not only what gave direction and meaning to their lives but also, and more importantly, what has shaped our attitudes toward them and the role our democratic values have played in that process. Also for the reasons noted above, I have not included Andrew Carnegie in the group, though he will make an important cameo appearance later.

Listed in chronological order the five are:

> *Robert Keayne*, a Puritan merchant in seventeenth-century Boston who ran notoriously afoul of his fellow citizens for charging too much for his goods and spent the rest of his days disputing the case against him and planning a series of impressive benefactions for the town that had treated him so harshly.
>
> *George Washington*—planter, land speculator, slave owner, victorious general of the American Revolution, and first president of the United States—who began life wanting nothing so much as wealth and the power it brought, yet lived to renounce both.
>
> *Amos and Abbott Lawrence*, brothers, merchants, and, later, manufacturers who built a great fortune in the cotton textile industry and

who also became noted philanthropists, though they disagreed completely about what form their generosity ought to take.

John D. Rockefeller, who parlayed iron-willed determination and a genius for business into unimaginably vast wealth, while at the same time pursuing a parallel career in philanthropy, using business principles to organize what he called "the difficult art of giving."[6]

Next, moving forward in time, I shall examine what later generations of the Rockefeller family did with the money they inherited. Then, to bring all this up to date, I have chosen a source already mentioned: *Forbes* magazine's annual list of the four hundred richest people in America—billionaires all—to see how they became so rich and what they do with their money, particularly that part of it set aside for philanthropic purposes.

I chose these individuals for several reasons. First, because of the sheer magnitude of their wealth. During their lifetimes each of them stood at the pinnacle of wealth in American society. The pride and glory of free-market capitalism, these were the richest of the rich. Second, all of the initial five and at least some of the others did choose to commit a sizable part of their fortunes to helping others. In them we see wealth and generosity joined to an impressive degree. And something else that drew me to them was that at one time or another many of them faced formidable public criticism. Selfish, heartless, greedy, cold, cruel, and criminal: the epithets hurled at them could be all too angry—and disturbing.

So what can we learn from such lives? To begin with, a sense of where great wealth has come from in the United States—the economic, social, and cultural factors that generate it, no less than what it takes in personal terms to drive certain people to accumulate a disproportionately large share of whatever passed as wealth at the time. Then there are the costs and benefits of that achievement, including what has led the rich or, at any rate individuals like these, to devote time, energy, and money to acts of generosity.

Fully as significant, too, is the question of how such people see themselves and also how their fellow countrymen have seen them, which brings us back to the paradox with which we began. Six decades before Tocqueville visited the United States, Abigail Adams—in words almost identical to his—playfully asked in a letter to her cousin Isaac Smith: "Don't you think this little spot of ours better calculated for happiness than any you have yet seen? Would you exchange it for England, France, Spain or Italy? Are not the people here more upon an Equality in point of knowledge and of circumstances—there being none so immensely rich as to Lord it over us, neither any so abjectly poor as to suffer from necessaries of life?"[7] Like Adams, too, most of us to this day resolutely persist in believing that the nation's identity is indissolubly linked to democracy, to equality, and that includes every one of our subjects. Being rich was never something they could take for granted. Indeed, for many it proved to be a source of genuine anxiety.

Put succinctly, what we have, then, is a group of people who won great wealth, tended to anger their fellow Americans in the process, and out of conviction, or guilt, or a desire to improve their images—or some combination of those impulses—have chosen to give away a lot of money. But while in broad terms this thumbnail narrative might seem to describe the lives in question well enough, it leaves out vital facts. Details do matter. The wealth that distinguishes these individuals was earned in different ways. Their generosity has also taken different forms, and it began at different points in their lives: some were generous from the start, others waited until very near the end, which John D. Rockefeller, a lifelong philanthropist, dismissed as behaving like "the man who plans to do all his giving on Sunday."[8]

Yet however they managed their generosity (and in no small part because of it), in the end they have succeeded in endearing themselves to us, just as Andrew Carnegie did. Even in cases where we once thought only of selfishness and greed when we saw their names or faces, we now perceive upstanding public benefactors—indeed, "the good rich."

Also crucial, along with their philanthropy, in winning our good opinion are the narratives they themselves construct to convey to the world their own sense of their motives and achievements. Several wrote autobiographies. Two left wills that went well beyond what is usually found in such documents. In addition, we have letters to and from some, as well as public statements made by many of them about themselves. And taken together, what these narratives constitute is a powerful argument proclaiming, if not the innocence of their creators, then at least their earnest desire to explain themselves to us. Implicit in them, too, is an invitation to complete the stories they tell: to add the essential dénouement ourselves, by choosing to forget just how angry such individuals can make us, which by and large we have done, in spite of our democratic ideals.

So the narratives are ours as well as theirs, and what they express on both sides appears to be a serious, indeed a heartfelt, desire to forge an accommodation between wealth and democracy, to blend the two in a way that not only affirms our democratic faith but also accepts a corresponding affirmation from the rich—or at any rate from those of them who care about such things.

Yet there is also another reaction we have had to lives like these, one that unlike the first would not at all have pleased the individuals in question. In telling their stories they invariably worked at making clear how different they were from the great majority of the "merely" rich—those who spent their money living opulently and preserving whatever remained for their descendants. Ironically, however, we tend to assume that precisely the opposite is true: that to be both rich and generous is par for the course in America, a broad pattern, endlessly repeating itself across time. The result of that assumption, in turn, is a unique national consensus that simultaneously applauds the creation of wealth and adds a moral dimension to it by assuming that—whatever their transgressions—its creators will invariably both seek our forgiveness and share with us a substantial portion of their gains. In short, the paradox disappears, and in its place wealth, democracy, philanthropy, and absolution are joined together in a single, harmonious whole, which has come to stand as one of the defining paradigms of American culture.

Still, like all such visions this one has to be measured against reality if it is to do more than simply make us feel good. Certainly one question we need to ask is whether the rich really are as generous as we seem to want to think they are. And the evidence on that point, as we shall see, is not unambiguous, but a short answer would appear to be that while some are, others definitely are not. (In 2009 the editors of *Forbes* magazine reported that only ten people on their annual list of the four hundred richest Americans—whose average wealth was $3.6 billion and in some cases rose to more than ten times that amount—had given away as much as $1 billion, prompting one of their number to remark, "It's a shame there aren't a lot more.")[9] And if the record is uneven, it would also seem to be worth asking what we gain by believing otherwise, as well as what we lose as a result. If the rich can not reliably be counted on to "give back"—if doing so is not the norm—where does that leave us?

That question, too, becomes particularly pressing in light of the current trend toward steadily rising levels of inequality in the distribution of wealth and income in the United States. If in fact we are becoming less equal, and therefore less democratic as a nation, what can we say of a narrative that has long been offered as a kind of counterweight or antidote to the presence of inequality among us? Indeed, even if the rich did give back at the rate we imagine they do, would it be enough to matter—to truly make a difference? This and other issues will be considered at length in the conclusion of the book. Before then, however, we must meet the characters described in the chapters to come. And happily, most of them turn out to have led fascinating lives, full of odd twists and turns and even a memorable cliff-hanger or two.

For the rest, while reading those chapters it may be helpful to keep in mind a statement Andrew Carnegie made to Britain's William Gladstone and later repeated in his famous essay "Wealth" (or "The Gospel of Wealth," as it is usually known): "The man who dies rich dies disgraced."[10] A skeptic might well reply: "Disgraced, perhaps, but doesn't history show that in all likelihood the man's wealth will live on, secure in the hands of his heirs?" Certainly there is ample evidence for such a view. And failing Carnegie's opinion in the matter there is always the much-quoted exchange between F. Scott Fitzgerald and Ernest Hemingway—the one that has Fitzgerald remarking, "The rich are different from you and me," to which Hemingway is supposed to have replied, "Yes, they have more money."[11] The story is almost certainly apocryphal, but true or not it conjures up, in a crisp and entertaining way, two very different attitudes that invariably buzz around even the briefest encounters with the American rich.

2

ROBERT KEAYNE'S CONTRACT WITH BOSTON

An ocean away from "home," the first English settlers in North America had no choice but to build their lives anew. They were not completely isolated, however. Trade with England would be an essential part of their experience—and indeed the driving force behind the developing American economy. Thus the ragtag English settlement at Jamestown, in Virginia, achieved stability only after its inhabitants discovered in tobacco a commodity that could be marketed profitably abroad. In Puritan New England ocean-borne commerce was equally vital.

Yet as they imported goods from abroad to sell wherever they could find buyers, New England merchants, in addition to the usual dangers of their calling—shipwrecks, falling profits, the lack of a reliable currency—also faced, looming around every corner, a dense thicket of religious beliefs that saw service to the community as the proper goal of all human activity. And in Boston during the early years those beliefs proved strong enough to land at least one wealthy merchant in court for charging what his fellow colonists saw as too much for his wares. In that position he had—or should have had (for he was convicted as charged)—two options. He could either leave Massachusetts and settle elsewhere, or he could stay, make a decent show of contrition, and content himself with lower profits.

Robert Keayne—for that was his name—did neither. Instead he remained in Boston and was still arguing his case twenty years later, knowing full well that the difficulties he faced were formidable. Because what he was calling for was a freer, more open society that accepted the fundamental fairness of a market economy and the wealth it produced.

Nothing about the story would ever seem simple, not to him, not to those confronted with his explanations of it in years to come. A successful London merchant, in 1635 he had joined the decadelong Puritan immigration to New England and settled in Boston, where he added to his wealth, trading in goods imported from London—useful items the townspeople had serious need of, if they were to have any chance of living as they had in England. Yet before long those same people fell to grumbling about his prices and the interest he charged for late payment of them. In the end he found himself tried, censured and fined, and, more troubling still, made to confess his "sins" in church. For the rest of his life he would brood over those events. His cascading thoughts, justifications, and quarrels with his accusers and judges even made their way into his final will and testament (his "Apologia," as it has come to be called), stretching it out to more than fifty thousand words.

His hope was that he might thereby erase the blot on his reputation, a goal that had stubbornly eluded his grasp through the years. In time he left trade behind and invested most of his wealth in land and cattle, a change that no doubt raised his standing a bit. He also held various offices in both the town and the colony and was even appointed to a judgeship. But by then he had begun drinking heavily and was forced to step down from the bench. Privately, too, he was offered the opportunity to have the fine he paid rescinded, but apparently he wanted a more public form of exoneration. He refused the offer, though in his will he did instruct his executors to see whether they could get the money back, charging them, if they succeeded, to donate it to Harvard College, thereby adding to the already sizable portion of his estate set aside for charitable purposes.

So ran the life of Robert Keayne, one of America's first entrants into the ranks of the very rich. Like many who came after him, he saw himself as a self-made man and took pains to point out in his will that he had received "no portion from my parents or friends to begin the world withal."[1] Yet his father was a butcher and had managed to secure an apprenticeship for him in London. After that he operated as a merchant tailor, earning, he claimed, "£2,000 or £3,000 in good estate" by 1635, when he left for Boston.[2] While that amount of money hardly placed him in the forefront of Britain's commercial elite, it was a more than respectable sum, winning him status enough to become a member of both the Merchant Tailors' Company and the Honorable Artillery Company of London, a pair of organizations that mixed military practice with a lively calendar of social activities. In Boston he participated in creating a similar company and later left part of his wealth to it.

Although in many ways life in Boston differed profoundly from the one Keayne had known in London, there were some similarities between the two. The names of several of the streets were the same as those in London's Cheapside—the teeming center of its commercial life—including Cornhill, Boston's main thoroughfare, where Keayne lived and worked near a dozen or more other merchants, some of whom he doubtless knew from London. And just as they had done there, those merchants would have scanned the water constantly, looking for incoming ships, and on their arrival hurried to see what cargoes and news they carried. From such sightings grew the tenuous lifeline that ensured not only the survival of the colony but also—if all went well—the profits earned by those same merchants.

In Massachusetts, however, something far outweighed merchants' profits in importance, and that was the sacred covenant the colony had entered into with God. "A Citty vpon a Hill," that was how the colony's first governor, John Winthrop, had described what the place was meant to become— a shining example of lives truly and completely lived according to God's will.[3] On some points Puritan theology could seem quite abstruse, but on this subject it was crystal clear: in Massachusetts one owed one's first allegiance to that holy mission, always.

Presumably Robert Keayne understood this, and it was bound up with his decision to leave England for the New World. He was in fact a deeply religious man. His brother-in-law, John Wilson, was a respected minister in Boston, and he counted several other clergymen among his friends, as evidenced by his will, which fairly bristled with bequests to men of the cloth. Always, too, he carefully credited God for his success as a merchant. Yet good Puritan that he was, he well knew how problematic it would be to imagine that such blessings proved anything at all about the state of his soul. Was he destined for salvation? Only God knew the answer to that question, for He alone determined it, proceeding according to His own lights, which no mortal could ever fully see or fathom. To believe anything else was heresy.

But if the inner reaches of God's mind were sealed, his scriptures were not, and Keayne spent untold hours poring over the Bible. He also carefully recorded his thoughts on what he found there, as he said in his will, "in 3 great writing bookes, which are intended as an Exposition or Interpretation of the whole Bible . . . [and] a 4th great writing booke which is an exposition on the Prophecy of Daniel, of the Revelations and the Prophecy of Hosea," which volumes he so valued that "till my sight or life should be taken of me I should not part from them."[4] Three "great writing bookes," plus another! Did anyone else in Massachusetts, except for the clergy, write as much about the Bible as Keayne did? Surely not. And what of his particular interest in the prophets of the Old Testament? Is it possible that he saw himself in the same role—one more voice crying in the wilderness? Unfortunately his volumes have not survived, so we shall never know the answer to that question, or what other subversive thoughts might have enlivened that huge cache of private musings.

For clearly Keayne's conduct as a merchant was not the only point on which he differed with the Puritan orthodoxy espoused by the colony's leaders. In the same sermon made memorable by Winthrop's vision of the city on the hill, for example, he presented as God's design for society a rigid order of descending ranks, stretching from rich to poor, rulers to ruled, without the least suggestion that such matters would be any differently arranged in the New World. But to someone like Keayne, who had risen to wealth from well down the socioeconomic ladder, this championing of the existing social order could hardly have seemed appealing.

What Winthrop also stressed, however, was the need to infuse that social order with compassion and charity by building a loving community—one where the rich would do everything in their power to aid and succor those below them in the hierarchy, or, as he put it, "wee must be knit together in this worke as one man, wee must entertaine each other in brotherly Affeccion, wee must be willing to abridge our selues of our superfluities, for the supply of others necessities, wee must vphold a familiar Commerce together in all meekenes, gentleness, patience and liberallity, wee must delight in eache other, make others Condicions our owne, reioyce together, mourne together, labour, and suffer together, allwayes haueing before our eyes our Commission and Comminity in the worke."[5]

But even this presented problems for Keayne, again in his role as a trader. How in such a setting was a merchant to behave? For sellers and buyers alike, trade was quintessentially about securing individual, personal advantage in transactions that had little if anything to do with selfless love. The world of commerce was a world of clear-eyed, rational calculation; the loving community drew its sustenance from radically different sources.

All of which had become clear in the events that brought Keayne into court and before his angry fellow church members. By then he was well established in Boston, selling work-a-day items like bridles, buttons, and nails. As it happened, too, it was nails that became the source of all his woes, for as lowly and plain as they seemed, few commodities were more important during the colony's early years than nails.

In England most of the forests had long since been stripped from the land, and buildings were made of stone or brick or small amounts of wood combined with stucco in the "half-timbered" construction that subsequent generations would find so romantically appealing. In North America, however, wood abounded. In many places it had to be cleared from the land before crops could be planted, and everywhere sawmills were set up to turn it into lumber for building. The result was hundreds and eventually thousands of wooden structures both cheaply and quickly built, a crucial factor with so many people needing houses, barns, and churches, not to mention docks and serviceable ships for fishing and trade, all as soon as possible. And while the heavier timbers supporting such structures were joined together with wooden pegs, for everything else stout, iron nails—which had to be imported from England—were essential. As religious faith brought New England's communities together in a spiritual sense, in material terms they depended no less completely on nails.

Thus overcharging for nails—as Keayne was accused of doing—cut to the heart of Puritan New England in two ways. It literally thwarted the all-important process of community-building, and it promoted his profits at the expense of his neighbors' vital needs, thus undermining the moral basis of community. But if his prices were too high, what should he have charged? Theoretically Massachusetts held to the medieval doctrine of the "just price." Under it, profits were permitted, provided they were kept within reasonable limits. As the colony's leading clergyman, the Reverend John Cotton, put it, the goal was to arrive at "such a price as is usual in the time and place," meaning what a knowledgeable buyer would pay for the item "if he had occasion to use it."[6] The exception was where there was "a scarcity of the commodity." In that case, Cotton argued, "men may raise the price for now it is the hand of God upon the commodity, and not the person."[7]

Putting all this together, it still seems hard to say exactly what the price of nails should have been in Massachusetts in 1639. In any case, Keayne was brought to trial and fined £200 (later reduced to £80) for "taking six-pence in the shilling profit; and some above eight-pence; and in some small things above two for one" in a case that began with a sack of nails.[8]

The story, as he told it in his will, was that his accuser had sent to him for "two or three thousand" six-pennyweight nails, whereupon Keayne supplied him with a bagful just as they had come "from Mr. Footes in London," charging eight pence per pound.[9] The buyer, however, found the nails he had ordered too small for the job and returned them, asking for larger ones in exchange. Keayne then sent him a bag of eight-pennyweight nails at ten pence per pound, and at the same time—in a fateful move—he changed the numbers in his account book to reflect the larger size nail and higher price. As events proved, it would have been far better to have written out an entirely new entry, but he presumed the buyer would pay promptly. Yet after two years he had still not done so, and the hastily altered figures in Keayne's ledger could easily enough be made to suggest that he was either charging excessively high prices or improper rates of interest on his customers' unpaid balances, or both, and probably fiddling with his books to boot, all of which the court appeared to conclude when it censured him.

In his will Keayne did claim that after his trial a third party surfaced who confirmed his version of events. He also depicted his accuser as a scoundrel, who later went into trade himself and charged much higher prices than Keayne ever had. In addition he brought a second charge against Keayne, accusing him of failing to pay a long-standing £200 debt. In that instance a frantic search finally produced a receipt proving Keayne had paid the debt. But when he set out to sue his "enemy" for slander, the Reverend John Cotton persuaded him to forbear because, according to Keayne, "of my late troubles and that it was no time for recriminations."[10]

Together, Cotton's argument and the general tone of Keayne's account of the entire saga—nails, unpaid debts, and all—suggest that a good part of the community believed he was indeed guilty as charged. Also, the members of the court, though they disagreed about the amount of his fine, voted unanimously to censure him. Was justice served by their verdict? It was John Winthrop himself who later offered to have Keayne's fine returned. Perhaps he was innocent after all, perhaps not. At this distance it is impossible to tell.

Whatever the truth, Keayne never stopped questioning the *logic* of it all. "Now I leave to the world or to any impartial man," he declared in his will, "whether this was a just offense or so crying a sin for which I had such cause to be so penitent."[11] In other words, even if the facts were as his accuser represented them, should he have been punished as harshly as he was? "I confess still, as I did then," he continued several hundred words later, "that the newness and strangeness of the thing, to be brought forth into open court as a public malefactor, was both a shame and an amazement to me."[12] But as novel and upsetting as he found the proceedings, he stopped short of arguing that what the court and his church had done was wrong, for as he said, "I know it is not lawful to speak evil of dignitaries nor to revile the rulers of the people."[13] Rather he chose to accept the burden laid upon him and work "patiently to bear the indignation of the Lord, because I have sinned against Him."

And so Keayne lived out his life in Massachusetts—angry, never fully reconciled to the community's judgment of him—yet believing that all things rested finally in God's hands. There was, however, a different way to look at the matter and another line of action he might have pursued. For in the years just before Keayne's troubles, the colony, and particularly Boston, had been sharply split over a series of religious issues that bore directly on Keayne's situation.

At the center of the controversy was Anne Hutchinson, that charismatic figure whose robustly unflinching exploration of religious matters led her to a number of arresting conclusions, which she began sharing with a small group of acquaintances that grew steadily larger as the time passed. The particular issue she addressed was the most difficult one of all in Puritan theology: how an individual might come to know whether he or she was destined for salvation. The church's position was that only through an unceasing struggle to act according to God's will could someone come to even the most tentative sense—which was all that was possible—of whether salvation awaited. For Hutchinson, on the other hand, the answer lay within each individual; it had little or nothing to do with external signs, including one's behavior, however exemplary (or sinful) it might appear to the world at large.

For all the care that Hutchinson took to state her opinions only at meetings in her own home, as the number of her followers grew, the colony's leaders became increasingly anxious about her activities. In their view, elevating individual authority to the position she wanted to give it threatened to divide—ultimately even tear apart—the community, ending all hope of fulfilling its mission in the New World. To meet that threat, Winthrop and others decided Hutchinson had to be brought to trial and made to see the error of her ways. As hard as they tried, however, she refused to relent, ultimately going so far as to claim that she was acting in response to divine revelation. At that point her judges concluded their only recourse was to banish her from the colony.

Later, she was killed by Indians while living in New York, an ending the court had by no means intended. In its eyes her beliefs were plainly heretical, but if she was not condemned to death—as, from time to time, other heretics in Massachusetts were—the judges had good reasons for treating her with a measure of leniency. She was an impressive person in her own right, and she had powerful supporters. Her husband and brother-in-law were prominent traders in Boston, as were many of her other followers. For merchants precariously placed in a world where profit-seeking could all too readily be interpreted as exploitation of the godly community, a theology that rejected behavior as a mark of salvation seemed tailor-made. So strong was the attraction of Hutchinson's ideas, in fact, that after her downfall many of her leading supporters among Boston's merchants chose to abandon the colony altogether.

But Robert Keayne remained in Massachusetts while so many others were leaving (most of them, it turned out, for Rhode Island). He also does not seem to have been among Anne Hutchinson's followers, and even when his own tribulations with the court and the church arose two years later, he resisted whatever temptation there may have been to leave the colony. Why? What prevented him from joining the dissidents' ranks, and what kept him in Massachusetts?

In truth there was little in Hutchinson's theology to attract Keayne.

Quite the reverse. If she and her supporters saw inner spirituality as the one true sign of God's blessing, the evidence Keayne cared about was all external. Let others shrink from the battle; he meant to confront his accusers on their own ground. In his will he wrote constantly about behavior—his own and everyone else's. He also wrote endlessly about the special favor God had shown him through his success as a merchant and his various victories over his enemies. Thus had God, as Keayne reported time and again, "blessed me with a large and comfortable estate."[14] And while some people saw his wealth as "my great hurt, yet God had been pleased to turn it to my good."[15] Similarly, at the time he was falsely accused of not paying off that old £200 debt, "by a singular providence of God I found a clean and full receipt in one of my books."[16] And though, during his years as a merchant, he often saw himself struggling under a burden of debt "sufficient to have broken the back of any one man in the country," he was proud to say that "God carried me through it beyond my own expectation or foresight."[17]

Indeed, so eager was Keayne to make clear the constancy with which God prospered his ventures that it is hard not to feel he hoped to demonstrate even more by it, to prove what he knew better than to say: that God's favor in such matters could after all be taken as a sign that he was in fact destined for salvation. His decision to remain in Boston may also have been something that he hoped—and calculated—would argue in his behalf.

There was, too, yet another piece of evidence in his favor that he could point to: the large portion of his wealth ultimately set aside for charitable purposes. Would someone not touched by divine grace have bequeathed to his community between a quarter and a third of his entire worldly estate? For that was what Keayne did. And lest anyone miss the point, he put it all at the beginning of his otherwise rambling and disjointed will, right after a short summary of his major bequests to his family.

The funds were to be used for a variety of purposes: building a "Conduit" to bring water to the center of Boston, plus a "market house"—adjacent to the town's marketplace—containing a meeting room, a gallery, a library, a granary, and an armory. There was also a separate provision for a firing platform and "Butt" for the Ancient and Honorable Artillery Company, as well as corn and cattle to be managed "for a stock from year to year," with the proceeds to be used for "the training up of some poor mens' children" in the Boston free school and for the relief of the town's poor generally. And if any of these projects were not carried out for some reason, Keayne directed that the money should go instead "to the sole use of the College in Cambridge," and in particular "for the use and help of such poor and hopeful scholars whose parents are not comfortably able to maintain them there."[18]

College scholarships, teaching poor children to read and write, improving the town's water supply and military defenses, and erecting a commodious, multipurpose Town House (as it came to be called)—worthy causes all. If this was to be Keayne's legacy he could be proud of it, and obviously he was. The Town House, especially, caught his fancy. Flowering in his imagination "as a great ornament to the town," it would be a place where "country people that come with their provisions for the town [could] sit dry in and warm both in cold, rain, and dirty weather." The courts and "the commissioners of the town" could meet there. So could "the elders and deacons . . . the divines and scholars," and of course "merchants, masters of ships, and strangers . . . to confer about their business."[19] A prime gathering point, it would thus draw together in a single structure not only the political, religious, and commercial activities of the town, but also the leading figures in each of those areas, and all in what Keayne chose to call (as opposed to the name later given it) a "market house." Trade playing host to the entire public life of Boston and the power structures that managed it—or so he seemed to have envisioned it.

As for the formal rationale behind his benefactions, he had saved that for later in his will, declaring there: "In point of disposing a man's outward estate, especially if it were of any value and his children not very numerous, I look at it as a great oversight and evil to give all or the most part . . . only to wife and children to make them great and rich in the world and to leave little or nothing to friends or to any public or charitable use."[20] As God had given Keayne wealth, so too did He have a just claim on part of it, as did the community Keayne was a member of: "the commonwealth or place where we live and where we have got more or less of that estate is also to be considered."[21]

He had in mind, as well, an appropriate formula for determining who got what. In general, he believed, "God and the country should come in for a child's part of our estates."[22] In his case, with only a wife and one son to provide for, that suggested a simple three-part division, but it turned out to be more complicated than that. There were items beyond the strictly calculated third that Keayne wanted to leave his wife: a silver bowl and his "second or next to best" bed (the best one went to his son). He also wanted to provide a dowry of £300 for his only grandchild, Anna, and there were small bequests to other relatives as well as to several friends, plus those to clergymen, though presumably they counted as part of God's share. To further complicate matters, Keayne had overestimated the size of his estate. In his will he put the total at "four thousand pounds or thereabout,"[23] whereas following his death in 1656 it was officially appraised at £2,569. Using that figure, his bequests to God and "the country" did come close to a third of his wealth: using his figure for the total, the share was lower.

Yet the amount of money involved was still quite substantial. Because the figures were so high, too, Keayne suspected that some ungrateful souls would wonder why he had not contributed more to the community during his lifetime, but he had a ready answer: to have done so might have been dismissed simply as an attempt to win public approval. As it was, he would be dead before his generosity became known, thereby making it clear that he sought nothing for himself, or as he said: "If a man did look after outward applause and the praise of men more than of God it were a great inducement to do all while he lived and nothing when he died."[24] As he saw it, he had chosen the better, purer path.

And along with providing for his family, God, and the community, and defending yet again his conduct as a merchant, Keayne also took occasion in his will to exclude explicitly from his largesse certain individuals, among them his son's wife, Sarah. The daughter of Thomas Dudley—who served for a time as governor of the colony—she must have seemed like a good catch, but sadly for the Keaynes it turned out otherwise. One of those restless souls who steadfastly resisted Puritan discipline, she fell into "Irregular prophecying" and worse still, "odious, lewd, and scandalous unclean behavior with one Nicholas Hart, an excommunicated person of Taunton."[25] Divorced by her husband and banished from the First Church of Boston, not only was she expressly cut out of Keayne's will, but he also charged his executors to be sure that she was denied any possible benefit from the funds that would eventually come to her child, his granddaughter.

The unending totaling up of what was due him and what was due others, the innumerable ledgers he described in his will so his executors could find them all: he could not help it. There was a cast to Keayne's mind that operated relentlessly whatever the subject at hand. With identical precision he labored to calculate exactly where he stood in God's favor. And the same attitude would govern what he feared might be the most difficult part of his will, which came near the end and involved two particularly thorny issues.

The first had to do with the sheer size of his estate. Mindful of the fact that it was widely thought he had begun life with nothing, he was afraid some people would conclude that such prodigious wealth could only have come from oppressing others and would once again, as he said, "load me with diverse reproaches and long to lay me under a dark cloud."[26] His answer was to do the arithmetic, which showed that if his estate was divided by the "40 or 50 years" he had been in trade, it came to less than £100 a year, an amount, he argued, any "tradesman or merchant that hath a full trade" could easily earn "very honestly without hurting his own conscience or wrong to those that he deals with at all."[27] And if anyone doubted his figures, his own books would prove the truth of his claim.

The second issue that he suspected could lead to fresh attacks on him was more difficult to handle, for Robert Keayne had systematically cheated on his taxes. His method was to under-report the value of his assets. He could have chosen to say nothing about it in his will, but once his estate was appraised, what he had done would become obvious. Best, then, to accompany the damaging evidence with an explanation. The problem was, he did not have much of a defense, just a grab bag of excuses that sputtered on and on: he was never sure what his true net worth was, everybody else did it, and of course the taxes were too high. "Neither God nor any Christian state in policy would have their inhabitants crushed or weakened by continued [taxation]." On the contrary those inhabitants should "be nourished and preserved in a thriving condition, that they may live well and still be able to do good [to others]."[28] And so it had worked out in his case—after a fashion. In effect he had gone ahead and cut his own taxes, but the money the colony lost as a result would be amply returned to it in the form of his many charitable bequests. He owed nothing to anyone on that score.

Still, he could not stop worrying. What if, after his death, someone "should complain to the Court" about his various transgressions, de manding that a fine be levied on his estate? He doubted that anything would come of it, but how could he be sure? "I know not how strangely things may alter nor who may get into power,"[29] he fretted. So whatever might happen, he wished to make one thing absolutely clear: if any action against his estate were to be attempted and the authorities took it seriously—"entertained or countenanced" it, were his words—there would be consequences, serious consequences.[30] In such a situation, he wrote: "I do hereby declare it to be my will and full mind, that all and every gift or legacy that is mentioned in this will to be laid and disposed of for any general or public use . . . save only that hundred and twenty pounds that I have given to the school and poor in Boston and what other legacies that I have given to particular friends or persons . . . shall utterly cease and become void."[31]

"Utterly cease and become void." He could not have made his wishes plainer. And with that dictum he also turned his "Apologia" into something that went well beyond a mere set of instructions for dispersing his assets or even a defense of his conduct as a merchant. What he had done, in effect, was transform his will into a contract with that world he had entered all those years ago when he first stepped ashore in Boston. Convinced that he was a good man much favored by God, he wanted that fact acknowledged, or at least not formally disputed by the officials of Massachusetts Bay Colony ever again. In return he was prepared to finance important improvements in the quality and convenience of life in Boston. That was the deal he offered. After his death it would be up to the colony's leaders to either accept or reject it.

In the event, they accepted it. Over the years there were to be several legal suits involving Keayne's estate but none brought by angry citizens challenging the way he had done business or even his failure to pay his fair share of taxes. For through his generous benefactions, if nothing else, he appeared to concede that after all the community had won; that it had persuaded Keayne to acknowledge, however reluctantly, its claim to a significant share of his wealth. If there was less love and more calculation behind his generosity than some might have wished, it was still an unassailable fact.

In due course, too, the handsome Town House he had left money for rose in the center of Boston, built very much as he had imagined it, with an open area surrounded by pillars below, where merchants gathered to do business, and a commodious room above where the courts met, as well as a library and an armory for the Artillery Company. And from that building, as historian Bernard Bailyn has said, "radiated a large part of the commercial cords that laced New England to the other coastal ports, to the West Indies, the Wine Islands, Spain, and especially to England. . . . It was the exact pivot point of the primary orbit of Atlantic Trade in New England."[32]

Keayne could also take credit for helping to forge that steadily expanding commercial network, for he had been one of the first merchants with transatlantic ties trading in Boston. In his will he chose not to give himself much credit in that regard, but he did note with something approaching glee that where once there had been few merchants in Boston, now there were many, charging prices compared to which his own were "cheap pennyworths," and that as a result the community at large, as he said, "hath got better experience in merchandise."[33]

The private matters Keayne's will touched on also seemed to come to a happy conclusion, and one not without a larger significance of a different sort. Despite the fact that his estate proved smaller than he had supposed, his widow, Anne, managed to remarry and live on comfortably in Boston. His son, Benjamin, had left for England soon after the breakup of his marriage to Sarah Dudley and did not return, but their daughter, Anna, who had been raised by her grandparents, spent much of her life in Massachusetts, and a colorful life it turned out to be.

Though Keayne's will had made Anna an heiress, initially it did her scant good. She was duped into marrying a man named Edward Lane, who proved to be impotent. First divorcing, then remarrying and living with Lane for a time, she gave birth to two children and soon afterward left on a trip to England. During her absence Lane died, and when she returned to Boston she had a new husband, Nicholas Paige. In the interim her fortune had been awarded to two shady friends of Lane's. There was also a question about whether she had married Paige before or after Lane's death, and rumors began to circulate that Paige, not Lane, had fathered her children. Weighing all this, and influenced no doubt by the scandalous lives of both her mother and grandfather, a Boston grand jury proceeded to indict Anna for adultery. When the case came to trial the court failed to reach a verdict, which might have let her off the hook. Instead, however, the whole business was referred to the General Court of the colony, the body that ordinarily functioned as its legislature, but which occasionally heard cases. Once again no clear-cut verdict emerged, yet the consensus was that—at a minimum—the accused had committed "much wickedness."[34]

There was a time when such a finding would have cast Anna Keayne Lane Paige forever beyond the pale in Boston, but happily for her sake, those days were gone. Also, her luck had turned. Her second husband, Nicholas Paige, prospered as a merchant and artfully managed to parlay his run of good fortune into growing political influence. As a result he and Anna were able to recover the portion of Keayne's estate that had been taken from her, which by then included not only his property in Boston, but also the spacious house he had built on his extensive landholdings in Rumney Marsh. And there "Madam Paige"—rich, the "sumptuous" dinners she gave much admired, as were her coach and liveried black servants—would live until she finally breathed her last on June 30, 1704. On hearing the news of her death the governor of the colony, in her honor, prorogued the General Court "till the 16th of August"—fully six weeks.[35] Robert Keayne would have been proud, had he lived to see it.

As Anna Paige's sparkling success in the role of great lady suggested, Boston was changing during those years and would continue to change, becoming finally not so very different from half a dozen other prosperous, provincial English cities. In such a place—with the market every bit as central to life as once the Puritan covenant with God had been—Robert Keayne would surely have felt, as his granddaughter obviously did, quite comfortable. Unfortunately it had been his lot to live in difficult, more challenging times.

Yet out of the turmoil of those times Keayne did manage to produce at least one other notable legacy. Shortly before the trial involving the nails, he had become locked in a dispute with "Goody" Elizabeth Sherman over a pig. The animal in question had been running loose in Boston, and Keayne, as was his right, impounded it. If he wished to keep the pig the law obliged him to search for its owner, which he did, and when the search failed to unearth any candidates he went ahead—as was also his right—and slaughtered the pig and ate it. Soon afterward Goody Sherman, having lost one of her pigs, appeared at Keayne's house and asked to see whatever pigs he had on hand. Finding that hers was not among them, she proceeded to claim that the one he had killed and dined on actually belonged to her. Suits and countersuits followed, dragging on for years, with Keayne generally getting the best of it. Still, his other troubles helped keep the case alive, and eventually it came before the General Court, where the two legislative branches split over it.

At that point a question arose as to whether the two branches could operate independently of one another in the matter or ought to vote instead as a single body. An extraordinarily complicated debate ensued, which was finally resolved in favor of maintaining—as a permanent arrangement—the division between the branches. Massachusetts thereby acquired what it has had ever since, a bicameral legislature, with John Winthrop arguing strongly in favor of the division as a protection against "democracie." Thus in Puritan New England did momentous outcomes flow from matters of little apparent consequence: worldwide trading networks from disputes over six-pennyweight nails, bicameral legislatures from runaway pigs.

Beyond such outcomes, too, lay another set of protean links: namely, those between Keayne's tangled life and what would become a series of perennial questions about the place of wealth and the wealthy in American life. In the half-medieval world where neighbors quarreled for years over a missing pig, Keayne's maverick, hardheaded trader's rationality won him few friends, but it turned out to be prophetic in multiple ways. His relentless drive to become rich, the corners he cut in doing so, and the mistrust and dislike he encountered among his fellow Puritans as a result would all find parallels in many personal odysseys in his adopted homeland.

But so too (if less often) would his decision to return to his society a significant portion of his wealth. In every subsequent generation there would be Americans who did the same. And like Keayne, most would want their generosity appropriately acknowledged, though few were as openly insistent on the point as he had been. For he was, to the end, a pioneer traversing uncharted ground. If he believed only the strictest imaginable account-keeping would suffice, that was a lesson he had learned at great cost. Those who followed him could afford to be more relaxed about such matters. Ironclad contracts were not always necessary. On the contrary, our inclination has been to accept such gifts gratefully—to right old wrongs, settle old scores.

3

GEORGE WASHINGTON, REVOLUTIONARY

The tobacco trade that rescued the starving Jamestown settlement in Virginia from extinction also became the colony's future. While Robert Keayne battled with his neighbors in Boston over the price of nails, tobacco growing was spreading throughout the Tidewater. And in time it would lead to the rise of a distinct elite, the members of which raised "tobac" on plantations of hundreds—sometimes thousands—of acres. Politically they dominated the colony's government; socially they dedicated themselves to living lives that followed as closely as possible English aristocratic models. They copied English fashions, aped English manners, and embraced English ideas. Yet beneath the fragile scrim of gentility they wove around themselves, their power depended on a gritty amalgam of three things: the money they made growing tobacco, the land on which it grew, and the African-American slaves who did the work.

To live in Virginia was to be ranked routinely by the amount of land and the number of slaves you owned. To acquire slaves, money was essential. Land could be procured through either purchases or grants from the colony's government. For those who lacked money and large numbers of acres and slaves, it was all but impossible to find a place in the upper reaches of the colony's elite. Yet that was precisely George Washington's position before he began the spectacular rise which ultimately brought him both great wealth and worldwide fame, as he fought and won a revolution, presided over the creation of a new national government, and became the first president of the United States. That ascent would also challenge, and finally change completely, the values with which he began life.

In the pantheon of American heroes, no one stands taller than George Washington, yet few people reflecting on his life stop to consider how rich he was. For he was rich, very rich. To accompany the final version of his will he left a "Schedule of Property," listing roughly a million dollars in assets.[1] In today's currency that equals more than $100 million, making him one of the wealthiest citizens in the new American nation he had done so much to create and certainly the richest person (in constant dollars) ever to have served as president of the United States—this, too, despite his constant complaints about being short of funds. What he actually lacked at such moments was cash, as was true of so many Virginia gentlemen of his day. In that world honor dictated that to be too flush with money smacked of crassness, if not outright greed. Yet deep in his heart Washington harbored a great fondness for money—getting it, keeping it, and making sure that no one took more of it from him than he owed.

Nor are the reasons for his feelings hard to discover. A younger son born to a family of modest standing in the colony's planter elite, he lost his father when he was eleven and, having inherited only a small amount of land and a few slaves, had to face—from then on—the necessity of acquiring for himself whatever wealth and standing he was to have. He was also fiercely ambitious and meant to rise in life far beyond any of his forebears.

Yet happily in this, as in so many other campaigns he fought in life, luck was with him. It began with a set of old surveying instruments he happened to find in a storeroom at his mother's house. If land was synonymous with wealth in Virginia, here was a key which could help unlock that treasure chest. He would become a surveyor. And as it turned out he could not have chosen a better occupation. Surveying kept him outdoors and on the move, he genuinely liked the work, and out of his earnings he was soon making modest loans to friends and family members. More important still, surveying gave him a firsthand look at how the land game was played in Virginia. Because tobacco rapidly exhausted the soil, the demand for fresh land was insatiable, making it a prime commodity for speculation, as well as a means of accumulating wealth and holding it for future generations. In a world without banks, stocks and bonds, or insurance companies, large landholdings functioned as all three. They also brought access to political power, which in turn brought more access to land.

Surveying also introduced young George to some of the key players in the land game, a result reinforced by yet another stroke of good fortune. In material form it was represented by a newly built, impressively grand brick mansion located on property adjoining the plantation his older half-brother, Lawrence, had inherited from their father and renamed Mount Vernon (and which George himself would one day inherit). What made the new house significant was the fact that it belonged to Colonel William Fairfax, whose cousin—Baron Thomas, Lord Fairfax—had the distinction of possessing the largest single landholding in Virginia.

A staggering five million acres, stretching for hundreds of miles inland to the west, the property had come to Lord Fairfax by a circuitous route beginning with a grant from King Charles II. And therein lay an unimaginable multitude of opportunities. In a single year—acting as Fairfax's agent—Robert "King" Carter had succeeded in patenting almost ninety thousand acres of land for his children and grandchildren, and over the next several years he added another one hundred eighteen thousand acres to that total.

No doubt with such examples in mind, Lord Fairfax—who visited his immense domain only occasionally—decided to turn the management of it over to someone with whom he had closer ties, which was what brought Colonel Fairfax to Virginia as his lordship's agent and Lawrence Washington's neighbor. Over the next several years, too, Lawrence had the good fortune to marry Anne Fairfax, one of the colonel's daughters. Meanwhile young George, who idolized his brother, was spending as much time as he could at Mount Vernon.

He also continued his surveying, yet increasingly his time was taken up with military matters—a new career he owed to William Fairfax's influence with Robert Dinwiddie, the governor of the colony, on whose Council Fairfax sat. After several informal, and by no means glorious, forays against the French on the frontier, he next joined General Braddock's disastrous attempt to take Fort Duquesne. And though the British were soundly beaten Washington helped manage the retreat with striking skill, as a result of which he concluded that he deserved a regular commission in the King's army. Unfortunately (though happily for the future United States of America) the British didn't see it that way, so he had to settle for command of the colony's Virginia Regiment, where he performed useful service protecting the colony's western frontiers from French and Indian raids. Which was all well and good—even admirable—yet it did little to increase Washington's financial resources, beyond giving him enough money to rebuild Mount Vernon on a rather grand scale, with nothing left over to support such an elaborate establishment. But then once again luck appeared on the scene in the person of Martha Dandridge Custis, an amiable woman who was also reputed to be the richest widow in the colony.

Beneath the Virginia elite's patina of gentility, marrying for money had long been one of the most reliable means of rising—when it could be managed. Up to then, Washington's only known romantic attachment had been an almost certainly platonic flirtation with Sally Fairfax, the wife of his close friend and neighbor, George William, the son of Colonel William Fairfax. While this was hardly a satisfactory substitute for matrimony, Washington's chances of actually marrying into one of the colony's leading families were slim, for most such marriages united individuals of comparable wealth and standing, a game to which he brought little. At six feet three inches he was blessed with an imposing physical presence, and in Virginia he was considered a genuine war hero, yet neither asset had any monetary value.

Conveniently for both their sakes, however, the widow Custis's wealth came in a form that trumped the usual rules of the marital sweepstakes. In addition to its sheer size, it had the great virtue of having come to her by way of inheritance from her first husband, Daniel Parke Custis, rather than through her own family, who thus were in no position to dispute her choice of a second mate. Nor was anyone else: she could pick whomever she chose. As for Washington's feelings about her, on more than one occasion he would describe her as "agreeable," which she certainly was, as well as wise and discreet, and while he may not have been passionately in love with her, their marriage proved to be a remarkably happy one.[2] Plainly, too, had he not married Martha his career as it unfolded over the next thirty years would have been unimaginable. From the beginning her money made possible what could never have happened without it.

There were strings attached, however. Since Daniel Custis had died without a will, his estate was divided, as common law required, into thirds, with one-third going to Martha and the other two-thirds to her children, Jackie and Patsy Custis, though Martha (and therefore Washington) had the right to draw on the children's share for their support. Also, as nearly as possible the estate's assets had to remain intact. Thus only the income from them could be used to cover expenses. But considering the enormous size of the property—17,438 acres of land in Virginia, plus personal property valued at £20,000 sterling, including £8,958 worth of slaves—Washington could well afford to live luxuriously at Mount Vernon and, within reason, do whatever else he wanted.

The resulting change in his standing was dramatic. Overnight he became part of the small circle of men whose wealth and power made them, perforce, the colony's leaders. Wisely, he spent the first several years learning the ropes of that heady world. He entertained often and handsomely at Mount Vernon and attended without fail the meetings of the House of Burgesses, to which he had been elected near the end of his military service. Uneasy about speaking in public, he remained silent most of the time there but gradually acquired a reputation as a solid and thoughtful member, with valuable knowledge of military affairs, as well as of the colony's western lands.

Yet sitting in the House of Burgesses was hardly a full-time occupation. As rich as his marriage had made him, Washington still had to fill his days in other ways, so he elected to do what most Virginians—rich and poor—did: he grew tobacco. And to that end he began spending a good part of Martha's income buying land adjacent to Mount Vernon when he could and adding to the plantation's slave labor force. With more land and more slaves he could grow more tobacco to send off to England. Also, because Mount Vernon's soil was only moderately fertile, he spent a significant amount of time experimenting with ways to improve it, even mixing with it mud laboriously dug up from the bottom of the Potomac River.

Running a plantation, too, involved a multitude of other tasks beyond simply growing crops. There was livestock to tend to, along with everything required to prepare the crops for shipment abroad. There was also building and keeping in good repair dozens of structures of all kinds, including miles of wooden fencing. And most important and difficult of all, there was managing the plantation's laborers, both black and white: housing them, feeding them, and organizing them to perform as efficiently as possible the tasks expected of them.

"A penny saved is a penny got." To work for Washington was to be peppered incessantly with such aphorisms, reflecting his passion for saving money, as well as using with the utmost effectiveness what money bought, above all his workers' time. As a young planter struggling to make Mount

Vernon pay, he described in his diary what amounted to a time and motion study of two of his slaves hewing wood. Sitting, pocket watch in hand, he observed each of them hew twenty feet of logs in the space of an hour and twenty minutes, whereas over the entire previous day a crew of four slaves had hewed only one hundred and twenty feet, a fraction of the pace they worked when he was there watching them. This was money wasted on a truly distressing scale, and it was only one among countless examples of the inefficiency of Mount Vernon's labor force. Of the plantation's carpenters, who were among the best trained and most privileged of his slaves, he would write later: "It appears to me, that to make even a chicken coob [*sic*] would employ them all a week: Buildings that are run up [in Philadelphia] in two or three days (with not more hands) employ them a month or more."[3]

Part of the problem was poor management. Mount Vernon had a full complement of overseers, including a skilled artisan hired to supervise the slave carpenters and "hurry and drive them" in their work, but all too often the overseers proved even less satisfactory than the slaves they were in charge of. John Askew, one of the many individuals hired at various times to manage the carpenters, missed so many days his first year that he had to work another five months to make up for lost time. To help cover his debts he even pawned his tools to Washington, yet his absences only continued, and when ordered to fix a particular gate he dallied for weeks, which resulted in the ruin of an entire field of peas by unrestrained livestock roaming about. "I then asked him if he did not think himself one of the most worthless and ungrateful fellows that lived for his treatment of me," wrote Washington, adding, "I never desire to see his face again."[4] But five years later Askew was still at Mount Vernon, presumably with his debt to Washington still unpaid. Equally problematic was Thomas Green, another overseer of the slave carpenters, who continually, as Washington said, "trifles away that time for which he is paid"—behavior, he told Green, that amounted to robbery, and "robbery of the worst kind, because it is not only a fraud but a dishonorable, unmanly and deceitful fraud."[5]

Fortunately for his sake Washington had better luck filling the most important position at Mount Vernon—the plantation's overall manager. On average they did well, but the best of them was his cousin, Lund Washington, who served throughout the Revolution and was also charged with overseeing the extensive rebuilding of the main house, which was going on at the same time. Forced both to run the plantation and to find workmen and supplies for the building project under the worst possible circumstances, he could not have done better.

Yet even Lund, as hardworking and loyal as he was, sometimes angered Washington. Among his other wartime duties was collecting the various rents and debts owed "the General," which meant riding for miles from place to place to get the funds, then carefully recording the proceeds. The time and effort required were substantial, or would have been, if Lund had done what was asked of him, which plainly he did not. "You seem to have an unconquerable aversion to going from home, one consequence of which is, I expect I shall lose all my rents," wrote Washington.[6] Lund's usual excuse was that with so many other urgent matters demanding his attention he simply could not get away to collect the funds due his employer. Softhearted by nature, he also balked (though this he barely mentioned to Washington) at dunning people for money in wartime, when almost no one had any cash to spare. Nor did he keep proper accounts or communicate regularly, as he was supposed to, with Washington on the subject. Lamely, he pleaded "an aversion to writing," which in turn drew from Washington a torrent of outraged abuse. "These are but other words for saying 'as I am not fond of writing . . . it is *quite* immaterial whether you have any knowledge or information of your private concerns!" To drive home the point he continued, with withering sarcasm, "It is not to be supposed, that all the avocations of my public duties, great and laborious as they have been, could render me totally insensible to the *only means* by which myself and family and the character I am to maintain in life hereafter is to be supported."[7]

But happily for Lund's sake such storms invariably passed, to be replaced by expressions of heartfelt gratitude: "Nothing but that entire confidence which I reposed [in you]," Washington wrote with war at last over, "could have enabled me . . . to have given not only my time but my whole attention to the public concerns of this country."[8] There was also never the slightest hint that Lund cheated Washington, unlike so many people he dealt with, who all too often seemed bent on helping themselves to as much as they could of what was rightfully his.

A prime example there was Robert Cary, the British merchant responsible for selling Washington's tobacco and purchasing the London finery with which he clothed himself and his family and filled the rooms at Mount Vernon. In theory those transactions were straightforward enough. The tobacco was shipped off to England, where Cary was supposed to dispose of it for the highest possible price. The proceeds were then credited to Washington's account, and against it was charged the cost of the myriad items—most of them unobtainable in Virginia—for which he sent requests once or twice a year in lists many pages long. As agents went, Cary appears to have been of above average diligence and honesty. Yet characteristically Washington came to think he did badly everything he was paid to do, and though nothing was ever said in so many words about his honesty, plainly Washington had doubts on that score too.

The problem with his handling of Washington's tobacco shipments was that he rarely if ever got as much as Washington expected for his crop. Virginia planters liked to brag about the prices their tobacco brought in England, and Washington invariably found himself on the losing side in that competition. "I am at a loss to conceive the reason why Mr. Wormsley's, and indeed some other Gentlemen's Tobacos should sell at 12 d. last year and mine . . . fetch 11/12," he complained to Cary, adding, "No person in Virginia takes more pains to make their tobo fine than I do and its hard then I should not be as well rewarded for it."[9] But the truth was that, despite all Washington's attempts to improve Mount Vernon's soil, it would never yield more than modest amounts of tobacco, and that of a quality well below what brought top prices in London. In time Washington realized this, but until then he laid the blame squarely on Cary.

And the difficulties grew even greater when it came to the goods Cary shipped to Mount Vernon. Had Washington required less, the job would have been simpler, but he wanted a truly staggering number of things: hats, coats, shoes, cloth and lace for ladies' dresses, books, bridles, writing paper, cups, dinner plates, wine glasses by the dozen, chairs, tables, sofas, rugs, oil paintings, and tools of every kind. One list alone specified, among many other items, twenty-two pairs of men's stockings, half a dozen pairs of men's shoes with high heels, half a dozen pairs of men's gloves, two beaver hats and a red morocco sword belt, six pounds of snuff and the same amount of perfumed powder, four pounds of green tea, twenty-five pounds each of raisins and almonds, fifty pounds of candles, twenty loaves of sugar, twenty sacks of salt, and an extensive selection of medicines, including six bottles of "Greenhouse's Tincture."[10]

Cary's assignment was to find all of these things, supervise their packing and stowing on board ship, and send them off to Virginia, an assignment demanding the utmost care and attention to detail, which he claimed he provided. Still, hardly ever did a shipment arrive at Washington's wharf without producing some sort of complaint. Invariably the goods came later than he expected (one shipment actually went to the wrong river in Virginia). Upon occasion, too, Cary was simply unable to find what Washington wanted, as when he asked for eight busts of military figures to adorn the hallway at Mount Vernon. And even when the items ordered did come, some were damaged or spoiled, while others were of notably poor materials and workmanship. Then there were the prices Cary charged. "Mean in quality but high in price," Washington fumed, "for in this they excel indeed far above any I have ever had."[11] The charge for a wooden case holding twelve large glass decanters particularly infuriated him. "As great an imposition as ever was offered by a Tradesman," he howled to Cary, "a ridiculous price!"[12] The same item, he claimed, could have been made in Virginia for less than a quarter of the £17.17 Cary charged for it.

Washington also continually asked that the items Cary sent meet the highest standards of London taste—that they be, as he put it, both "neat and fashionable."[13] And it was there that Cary's goods most disappointed him. For all too often they were out of date, out of style, the kinds of wares that came from the dusty back shelves of merchants' shops. "Instead of getting things good and fashionable in their kind we often have articles sent us that could only have been used by our forefathers in days of yore," Washington wrote Cary early in their relationship, no doubt hoping that his new agent—forewarned—would do better than his predecessors, yet there is no evidence that he ever felt Cary did.[14]

Routinely overcharged for goods of inferior quality, with little if any claim to being stylish or fashionable—at least as he saw them—Washington obviously felt he had ample cause for complaint. But there was yet another, even more disturbing aspect to his relationship with Cary. For year by year the financial balance between the two of them kept tipping further in Cary's favor, to the point where the amount Washington owed his agent reached £1,800. In theory the debt ought to have been made up by tobacco sales, but thus far that had not happened, nor did it seem likely to anytime soon. Concerned, Cary wrote Washington suggesting that he reduce his balance.

In turn, expressing surprise that someone "so steady & constant as I have proved" should be thus reminded of his obligations, Washington—in what amounted to the verbal equivalent of drawing himself up to his full height, nostrils flaring—replied that he could not, at least "in a manner convenient and agreeable to myself," make payments any faster than his crops would "furnish me with the means."[15] Though this could hardly have satisfied Cary, soon afterward the master of Mount Vernon did begin shifting the plantation's principal crop from tobacco to wheat, which could be turned into flour and sold at a profit in the West Indies. At the same time, he was exploring what his labor force could do to produce items that would reduce the size of his annual orders for British goods, and though the outstanding balance was not reduced, at least it rose at a slower rate.

However little Washington liked corresponding with Cary on the subject of his unpaid balance, one fact, which, if he had not already learned it, did become clear. As rich as Martha was, her wealth was not infinitely elastic; it could be stretched only so far. To be truly as wealthy as he wanted to be, therefore, he had to find another source to tap, which in time he did. Though a great deal of hard work had to be done before he achieved that goal.

In 1754, when troops were first being raised to assault the French and their Indian allies, Governor Dinwiddie, in order to increase the disappointingly slow trickle of volunteers, decided to sweeten the recruiting pot by adding a promise of western lands to it. According to his proclamation, those who served could look forward to sharing in a grant of two hundred thousand acres—a great windfall, especially for the officers, who were likely to receive larger portions owing to their rank, with the largest one of all going to Colonel George Washington.

The problem was how to make it all happen. When the grant was announced, it included no procedures for fulfilling Dinwiddie's promise, and more than a decade passed before—thanks to Washington's efforts—a proper proposal for doing so was brought before the House of Burgesses and the colony's new governor, Norborne Berkeley, Baron Botetort, who, happily, was sympathetic to the project. By then Washington had found the lands to be distributed and arranged to have them surveyed and equitably divided among those entitled to receive them. Every step in the process, too, had to be formally approved by the Governor's Council.

By the end of 1772, several large tracts of land were ready for division and distribution, with the remainder of the full two hundred thousand acres to be added soon afterward. And all told, Washington himself netted 24,100 acres of prime land. Such was the reward for his efforts to secure for himself and his fellow veterans "the bounty lands."

Yet inevitably the question arises: had he pressed too hard, especially where his own interests were at stake? He had personally picked the land for the grant on a trip to the west made specifically for that purpose, which put him in a unique position to choose for himself the very best acres available, thereby feathering his own nest at the expense of his comrades. Yet the regulations expressly stipulated that if that were to occur Washington would have "to give up all interest under his patent . . . [and] submit to such regulation as the Board saw fit."[16] In other words, if he played too fast and loose with the process he stood to lose everything.

It is hard to imagine him taking such a risk, but in later years he did claim that he had gotten "the cream of the country."[17] It was also a fact that he violated the rules at least once by taking more river frontage relative to the depth of the land behind it than was permitted. And one of his biographers quotes a remark, made in London in 1779, asserting that so eager had Washington been to lay hold of large tracts of land for himself that he acted consistently "under the specious appearance of disinterestedness," which the biographer concludes "apparently had considerable foundation."[18] In sum, Washington had masked in public the full extent of his personal interest in the matter.

On the other hand "the specious appearance of disinterestedness" his London critic referred to was in fact endemic to Virginia politics, the very warp on which its time-honored procedures were woven. Annually, gentlemen from all over the colony gathered in Williamsburg to conduct the business of government and also see to their own affairs, convinced that the two—public business and private interest—could somehow be seamlessly knit together. And in the case of the bounty lands that seamlessness did seem to have been achieved, for none of Washington's fellow veterans ever formally challenged the fairness of the division he had crafted. Afterward, however, one intrepid soul—though he lodged no formal complaint—did approach the great man in person, in front of other people, claiming to have been cheated, only to find himself met with an icy stare and dismissed as an "ungrateful & dirty fellow."[19]

But if the London critic (and perhaps the ungrateful dirty veteran) missed the point of the exercise, one thing the critic got right was just how eager Washington was to produce the result he had. What drove him so? As he declared in a letter to his fox-hunting friend and neighbor, John Posey, "The greatest fortunes we have in this Colony were made . . . by taking up and purchasing at very low rates the rich back lands which were thought nothing of in those days"[20] He meant to win one of those fortunes himself, and honorably or not he spent every bit of energy and guile he could muster doing so.

Soon after he received his uncommonly large share of the bounty lands, too, his affairs took yet another step upward, though the event that prompted it was anything but welcome. In June of 1773, Martha's sixteen-year-old daughter, Patsy, suffered a seizure, as she often had in the past, but this time she suddenly and inexplicably died. Martha's grief was boundless, and Washington too was deeply affected. But it was also true that Patsy's inheritance from her father's estate—which under Washington's careful management had grown to over £16,000—would now come to Martha and, through her, to him. Here was a way to settle at last his debt to Cary (though Cary did not see it that way). Washington also began planning a second full-scale rebuilding of Mount Vernon. But increasingly during those years he was shifting his attention to something that before long would claim all of his energy: the steadily deepening quarrel between Great Britain and its North American colonies.

History records that the opening gambit in what amounted to a concerted effort by Great Britain to redefine the colonial relationship was the Stamp Act, which was passed in 1765 and greeted from the start with fierce opposition in the colonies. In Boston, mobs rioted and Governor Thomas Hutchinson's house was robbed and set ablaze. In Williamsburg, Patrick Henry spoke eloquently in the House of Burgesses against Parliament's decision to tax the colonies directly. Yet Washington took no part in the debate and very likely had already left for Mount Vernon, so we have no way of knowing what he thought.

But four years later the Townshend duties moved him to propose with George Mason a ban in Virginia on imports of all taxed items. And by August of 1774 he was writing his friend Bryan Fairfax that "an Innate Spirit of Freedom" told him Britain's determination to have its way with the colonies was "repugnant to every principal of justice," and for Virginians to submit to it would make them, he claimed, "as tame and abject slaves, as the blacks we rule over with such arbitrary sway."[21] Then came the Battle of Lexington and Concord in Massachusetts and the Second Continental Congress, which Washington attended as he had the first (only this time in military uniform), and which, in one of its most fateful acts, unanimously chose him to lead the forces gathered around Boston as "Commander-in-Chief of the American Armies."

Thousands of pages have been written about what had brought Washington to that moment. Yet to take him at his word, one point that remained central to his thinking was the issue of taxation. In the context of the imperial system, as he understood it, for Parliament to tax the colonies, when they had legislatures of their own to do that, was to rob them not only of a crucial right but also of their most basic liberties and in the end to make "slaves" of them. A good deal of British political philosophy reinforced the point, but very little if any of it had Washington read. As he said, at the heart of his thinking lay "an Innate Sense of Freedom." And if that seemed a trifle airy, it was backed by half a lifetime's experience of Virginia politics.

As a young man, backed by the Fairfaxes and dealing with the politics of Williamsburg, Washington had learned many lessons, but the most important of them was that making one's way in Virginia required making a friend of the governor, which depended in turn on a reciprocal exchange of favors. Every year from England governors received long lists of items they were expected to accomplish, including raising money to pay the cost of the colony's government. To carry out those instructions they had to win the approval of the colony's legislature and the men who controlled it. Hence the exchange of favors: to win the support of those men, an astute governor learned to satisfy their private requests, and in return he could expect to find them opening the purses he wanted opened.

While this system satisfied most Americans, it had come to seem woefully slow and inefficient to the British. They also believed it gave too much power to colonial legislatures and their leaders. Hence the decision to remake colonial government by giving the whip hand to Parliament, particularly in matters involving taxation, which at the seat of power in Whitehall seemed a relatively simple matter. Yet to someone like George Washington, such a change was bound to appear disastrous. Everything he had become in life—plus any additional benefits he might hope to win in the future—depended on preserving that system as it was.

Ultimately, too, around that issue patriot leaders like Washington succeeded in building a much broader case for their position—one in which they argued that the liberties of all Americans stood at risk, not just the favors coveted by the rich and powerful. If the King's ministers had their way over taxation, quite ordinary people—or so ran the argument—could expect to have their freedom, their homes, their very lives taken from them, as Washington's letter to Bryan Fairfax claimed. And when push came to shove in April of 1775, at Lexington and Concord, in a move of astonishing stupidity, the British did exactly what Washington and his fellow patriots had predicted they would do, and thereby lost an empire.

Not all at once, however. It took eight years for Washington and his ragtag army to defeat the British—years as well in which some of his attitudes changed significantly.

The most important thing the Revolution taught Washington was patience. By instinct he was bold, daring, and eager to fight, always. Yet the Revolution compelled him to wage war with an army that hardly ever totaled more than a third of the British forces it faced. And to risk battle against the combined might of those forces would almost certainly turn out disastrously, as he learned early in the war when a devastating defeat on Long Island left him on the brink of despair. "I see the impossibility of serving with reputation, or doing any essential service to the cause by continuing in command," he wrote his cousin Lund at one point, "yet I am told that if I quit the command inevitable ruin will follow . . . I never was in such an unhappy, divided state since I was born."

For five long years after that he struggled to hold his army together, using it to fight only when he faced a limited number of British troops, often with the element of surprise on his side. But fight he had to, for he also needed victories to keep patriot spirits up, and there were just enough of those—beginning with Trenton in the winter of '76—to do that. But to win the war, he continued to believe there had to be at least one great battle against the British, and the opportunity for that seemed never to come. Then suddenly, with all his troops and the French army and navy perfectly aligned, came the miraculous victory at Yorktown. At long last independence had been well and truly won.

But if that was the great issue confronting Washington during the war, there had been others. His correspondence with Lund, for example, had also addressed a subject which—for the first time—seemed to be giving him genuine concern. And that was slavery. Before the Revolution the only aspect of the institution that seemed to trouble him was its chronic inefficiency. Yet early in the war he wrote Lund a letter in which he mentioned his "Negroes" and then, immediately afterward, put in parenthesis, "Whom I every day long more and more to get clear of."[22] Also a while later, when the two wrote back and forth about the possibility of selling some of Mount Vernon's slaves to raise money, Washington stated emphatically that he would do so if it did not mean separating children from their parents or husbands and wives from one another.

Believing slavery was inefficient and refusing to divide slave families represented two very different responses to the subject. The first dealt with its economic aspects; the second was a question of moral principle and altogether unlike anything Washington had said previously about slavery. As for what accounted for the change, it is tempting to imagine it was the Revolution itself. The timing was right, and during the war he witnessed black enlistees fighting every bit as bravely as white troops (though initially he had not wanted to accept them in the ranks). There was, too, of course, Thomas Jefferson's ringing statement about human equality in the Declaration of Independence. Had it led Washington to see slavery differently?

He simply did not say enough to support definitively such a conclusion. Two things do seem to lend weight to it, however. One is the fact that his desire to "get clear" of slavery grew steadily stronger after the Revolution. The other is the way he chose to explain the inefficiency of the system in a letter to Arthur Young, the noted English agricultural reformer. His point was that the slaves—having no opportunity, as he put it, "to establish a good name"—lacked any incentive to do good work because they earned nothing as a result.[23] In turn, this implied that it was slavery itself which accounted for the slaves' lack of ambition, not any inborn characteristic or incapacity of theirs. Since, too, nothing acted more powerfully on George Washington himself than his own need "to establish a good name," he was in fact equating the slaves' inner lives to his own, thereby embracing something very like the principle of human equality.

But any personal views he held in this regard had to be weighed constantly in the balance against other issues, some of them far more important than slavery, at least as he saw it. Soon after the war Lafayette, his great good friend and comrade in arms, had written proposing that the two of them undertake to settle freed slaves on farms in Virginia, in what amounted to a demonstration project that Lafayette hoped would eventually contribute to freeing all the slaves in America. "I would be happy to join you in so laudable an effort," Washington replied and then did nothing about it.[24] The following year Lafayette visited Mount Vernon, and no doubt Washington explained to him that as little as he liked slavery, his greatest concern was the weakness of the national government and the resulting threat to the federal union itself. On that front any move against slavery had the potential to worsen an already precarious situation and, if he was involved, undermine whatever influence he might have in addressing the problem.

Year by year after the Revolution, too, his anxiety about the weakness of the national government continued to grow. Nor was he alone in those feelings, as shown by the convention held in 1787 in Philadelphia—with Washington presiding—to revise the Articles of Confederation, the instrument which had called that government into being. Then, instead of simply revising the Articles, the convention took the extraordinary step of deciding to create an entirely new national government, with Washington's complete agreement. Neither was there ever any doubt that however little Washington might have wanted the honor, he would be chosen as the first president of the United States in that government.

His last great public role in national life, it did not turn out to be a particularly happy experience. The brilliant individuals he chose as his advisers were soon at one another's throats—with Thomas Jefferson and

Alexander Hamilton leading the way—in a contest that led eventually to the emergence of a full-fledged two-party system, a development Washington deplored. Eventually he sided with the Hamiltonians, only to have the editors of the Jeffersonian press heap abuse on him. Nevertheless, a great deal was accomplished during his two terms as president. The new national government was established and proved to be far stronger than its predecessor. America's financial credit was restored, the nation remained at peace, and work was under way on a new "federal city" to be known (though no one spoke of it yet) as Washington.

Washington's greatest concern, however, would remain the survival of the federal union. And on that score the constitutional convention had left open two especially vexing questions: one was where ultimate sovereignty would lie in the new system—with the national government or with the states—and the other was slavery. With regard to slavery, the delegates had tried to craft a compromise, providing on the one hand for the return of fugitive slaves and allowing the South to count three-fifths of the slave population in determining electoral districts for the House of Representatives and, on the other hand, mandating the end of the slave trade after a certain date. To those items, too, the new congress added—after a heated debate—a declaration that it had no power to abolish slavery in the states where it already existed. But regardless of his personal feelings on such measures, Washington watched in silence as slavery worked its way deeper and deeper into the fabric of national life. Yet if the union was as fragile as he believed it to be, nothing seemed more likely to shatter it than a protracted clash over slavery, or an airing of his own views on it.

Others felt differently, however. In 1785 Robert Pleasants, a Virginia Quaker who had freed his own slaves, wrote Washington, trying to goad him into doing the same. How, Pleasants asked, could the great leader of the Revolution continue to hold "people in absolute slavery, who were by nature equally entitled to freedom as himself?"[25] Although Washington did not answer Pleasants's letter, the following year he wrote his friend Robert Morris: "There is not a man living who wishes more sincerely than I do, to see a plan adopted for the abolition of it."[26] Yet this was a private communication; he knew he could trust Morris to say nothing about it. Meanwhile never once, as president, did he publicly state his opinions about slavery, or, by so much as a single word or deed, let the veil slip.

There was another place where he could express his views more can-didly, however, and that was in the weekly letters he wrote home to Mount Vernon throughout his presidency. And along with the usual drumbeat of comments about the slaves' poor work habits, there were signs that his attitude toward them had continued to change since the Revolution, as, for example, when he wrote of their health care: "It is foremost in my thoughts, to desire you will be particularly attentive to my Negroes in their illness . . . for I am sorry to observe that [most overseers] view these poor creatures in scarcely any other light than they do a draught horse or ox; ne-glecting them . . . instead of comforting and nursing them when they lye on a sick bed."[27] He became increasingly sensitive, too, to complaints from the slaves about their treatment. On the subject of their food he wrote in 1793: "In the most explicit language I desire they may have plenty; for I will not have my feelings again hurt with complaints of this sort."[28]

Yet it was not playing the benign patriarch—a role he seemed doomed to perform more and more every year—that Washington most wanted. What he continued to long for was being free of slavery altogether, but was such a thing even imaginable? How was he to operate a six-thousand-acre plantation without slaves? Who would do the work, raise the crops, tend the livestock, keep the gardens in order? Also, who was to wait on the flood of visitors his fame brought to Mount Vernon in ever-increasing numbers? To further complicate matters, only half the slaves at Mount Vernon actually belonged to him; the other half were Martha's, and over the years the two groups had frequently intermarried. If Washington did decide to free his slaves, what would become of those family ties, since under the terms governing the Custis estate, Martha was not at liberty to free her slaves?

The fact was that Washington had constructed for himself a life utterly dependent on slavery. Still, he kept hoping that somehow a way to at least reduce the number of Mount Vernon's slaves could be found. He also de-veloped several concrete ideas for moving in that direction. One was an innovative round barn, the design for which, done in his own hand, he sent off to Mount Vernon. Its purpose was to provide a place for thresh-ing and storing wheat, using a minimum amount of labor (and providing maximum protection against theft).

A second idea, to which he became passionately wedded, was what he called "live fences," which the English refer to as "hedgerows." Few tasks at Mount Vernon took more time and effort than building and maintaining fences. If it was possible to replace them with something that simply grew on its own into stout barriers that livestock could not penetrate, the savings would have been tremendous. "Nothing is nearer, both to my interest and wishes . . . because it is indispensably necessary to save timber and labour," Washington declared to his overseers. "There is no time to lose."[29] And with great care the seeds he sent home were duly planted for several years. Yet each summer dense thickets of faster-growing weeds overwhelmed the tender shoots, consigning them to oblivion.

Still, Washington refused to give up the search for ways of limiting his involvement with slavery, and if relatively minor changes did not work, he was prepared to try more sweeping ones. In 1793 he took the surprising step of putting parts of Mount Vernon up for rent, privately explaining to his friend Tobias Lear that his intention was to use the proceeds, as he said, "[to] liberate a species of property which I now possess very repugnantly to my own feelings."[30] Unfortunately, the only prospective tenant who materialized—a knowledgeable Englishman of exactly the type Washington hoped to find—turned him down after examining the farms, explaining that the soil was too poor for the kind of farming he had in mind. (His father, he said, produced ten times the wheat per acre Washington did.)

Meanwhile, his second term as president ended, bringing him back to Mount Vernon, where despite all his efforts, slavery remained as entrenched as ever. Nonetheless, he threw himself into refurbishing the place, repairing and repainting everywhere, indoors and out. As usual he found it no easy matter to manage the slaves and the workmen he hired. "Workers in most countries, I believe, are necessary plagues," he wrote. "In this, where entreaties as well as money must be used to obtain their work . . . they baffle all calculation."[31] A revealing example of what he meant involved his latest plantation manager, James Anderson, who usefully instituted the large-scale distilling of rye whiskey at Mount Vernon, which proved quite profitable. Anderson was also a man who knew his worth and insisted on it. When Washington criticized him at one point, he responded by threatening to leave. After negotiations lasting several days, he finally agreed to stay on, provided his workload was lightened. Along with his usual grumbling Washington even came up with an apology.

An apology! Was he losing his grip? Actually he was, though not in the usual sense of that phrase. For after four dozen years of purposeful, self-confident mastery, George Washington was in fact in the midst of rethinking in fundamental ways his beliefs about how society should be structured—and the proper place in it not only of slaves, but also of people like James Anderson and even himself—all of which he would shortly make clear.

In 1799, at the age of sixty-seven, George Washington was still in excellent health and could have been expected to live a good while longer, yet in December of that year he contracted a severe throat infection, which rapidly worsened. Two days later he died, and one of his last conscious acts was to have his "new will" brought to him. Less than six months earlier he had drafted it himself, with no legal advice at all, then copied it carefully on fine paper. Now he wanted to be sure those present at his deathbed understood that it contained the true expression of his final wishes. He did not add that there was much in the document which was likely to surprise people, but they would learn that soon enough.

Twice before at key points of transition in his life Washington had taken the opportunity to share, by gesture and word, his thoughts with his fellow citizens: first in 1783 when, with the war finally over, he returned his commission to Congress, then rode off to Mount Vernon in time to arrive on Christmas Eve. The second time was in 1797, when, as his second and last term as president was drawing to a close, he delivered his instantly and forever famous Farewell Address. In both cases he was relinquishing power, and each time there were lessons he wished to teach. In his will—the last and in some ways the most interesting of his grand farewells—he was relinquishing what would remain after life itself ended, and once again there were lessons he wanted to teach.

He well knew that after his death the contents of the will would quickly become public knowledge. He also knew what the world would see as the single most striking feature of it. For twenty-five years the question had hovered over his head like a dark cloud: how could the hero of the American Revolution possibly remain a slaveholder? Here at last was his answer. Laying aside all the sundry complications, both public and private, that might have kept him from acting, he did what he long wanted to do, becoming, incidentally, the only one of the slaveholding Founding Fathers to do so: he freed his slaves. And while this may not have been philanthropy in the usual sense, what Washington gave his slaves was the greatest gift anyone could have—lives of their own.

To underline the importance of that portion of the will, too, he put it at the beginning, immediately after directing his executors to pay his debts and a brief statement conveying to Martha, as long as she lived, the use of his estate, including his slaves. But once she was gone they could go wherever they wished, do whatever they wanted. In addition, Washington provided support for all those unable to manage without it: for the old, regular payments as long as they lived; for the young, enough education to be able to read and write as well as training "in some useful occupation." (Forty years later his estate was still making payments to several former slaves.) Sadly, Martha's slaves would remain in bondage, but he refused to let his dreams shatter on that particular rock.

But if all of this was clear in the will, one thing about it would seldom be noticed. And that is the extent to which freeing the slaves also functioned as a kind of preface to everything else that followed in the will. For having begun boldly, Washington meant to press on in the same spirit, which in fact he did, making the later sections of the will the most interesting and significant part of it.

At stake were the tens of thousands of acres of prime land he owned, his livestock, his stocks and bonds, as well as Mount Vernon itself, plus the whole array of possessions that filled it: all those things Washington had spent a lifetime struggling to acquire and hang on to. Presumably, if he and Martha had had children of their own the largest share of everything would have gone to them, but the Washingtons had remained childless. In that situation the usual solution, at least in Virginia, would have been to choose some relative—generally a nephew, if one was available—and leave most of the estate to him, thereby keeping it intact. In Washington's case this would have been simple, for he had almost a score of nephews and nieces, plus Martha's four grandchildren, to choose among.

In the end, however, he settled on a radically different strategy. Instructing his executors to divide the greater part of his property into twenty-three equal shares, he ordered that they should be parceled out to *all* of his nephews and nieces or to their heirs, if they had died. Martha's grandchildren were also to receive shares. But a modest competence was all any one individual would inherit.

Nowhere in the will did Washington explain why he had arranged matters this way. At a minimum it offered an answer to the characterizations of him by the Jeffersonian press. At various points he had been described as the dupe of a corrupt cabal of stockjobbers, dismissed as a lover of aristocracy, or, worse still, as a secret monarchist who, as one newspaper article put it, "holds levees like a king, receives congratulations on his birthday like a king, employs his old enemies like a king, shuts himself up like a king, shuts up other people like a king."[32] Plainly, to see Washington in such terms was absurd, but for anyone who doubted that, his will offered powerful evidence to refute such charges. At least he would not die like a king.

Equality and the impermanence of wealth and power: those were the points the will stressed, and they could as easily be applied to society as a whole as to a single family. The society that embraced them, too, was bound to be utterly unlike the one into which Washington had been born and grew to maturity. Inequality, money, and status perpetuated across time, privilege and power as the prerogatives of a fortunate few, favor and patronage as the glue that held it all together and determined who would rise and who would not: such were the hallmarks of that society, and with relentless drive and more than a little good luck Washington had managed to maneuver his way to the top of it. But successes like his were rare. Who could say what would happen if the barriers he had to surmount were lifted, if the familiar imperatives were cast aside?

For that, by extension, was the future Washington pointed to in his will. Disparities of wealth and power there would always be, but they did not have to be treated as structures of stone built to dominate the social landscape through all time. Rather, they should be created anew in every generation. Equality of opportunity: that was the point. A nation of people who, like James Anderson, knew their own worth and who were prepared to fight for it.

Also of a piece with this message, and in some ways an even more arresting expression of it, was the future to which Washington consigned Mount Vernon, his beloved, much-altered home of almost half a century. In his hands (for he was his own architect, always) it had become unmistakably the sort of place wealthy Virginia families built to stand generation after generation. Its carefully positioned outbuildings, its symmetrical plan and spacious rooms, its extensive use of classical architectural detail inside and out, its handsome mahogany furniture and tastefully done family portraits—all announced, as they were meant to, that this was not just a house, but a true family seat—anchoring its owners' position in a social order as hierarchically arranged as Mount Vernon's façade was, rising upward to its crowning cupola. Yet if that was the language he had designed the place to speak, the treatment of it in his will spoke in an altogether different tongue.

Mount Vernon was not included in the twenty-three-part division. Instead its land was to be divided into four separate pieces, each of them left to a different person. The house itself would go to Bushrod Washington, one of his nephews, who at that point was serving as a Supreme Court justice. Yet, as he had nothing more than a modest income, no slaves, and only part of the land, it was far from clear how he was to maintain his inheritance.

Better than anyone, Washington knew the enormous outlay of time, energy, and money that went into maintaining Mount Vernon. If he had wanted the place preserved as it was, certainly he could have made arrangements to do so. Failing that, what was likely to happen was exactly what did: decade by decade the place slipped further into disrepair and decay, until by the 1850s it was dangerously close to collapse, which appears to be precisely what Washington intended. Whatever was true of the public realm, private life—he seemed to be saying—ought not be about permanence or trying to inscribe on what should be the blank slate of the future old barriers, old divisions, even, if it came to it, old triumphs and the monuments meant to celebrate them.

As a military commander Washington had always dreamed of the dashing stroke, the decisive battle with its great victory, though of necessity he had learned to proceed more cautiously—to shepherd his resources. But in composing his will he could be as daring as he wished. The fatherless boy who so desperately wanted to be rich; the young groom so eager to cram into his newly rebuilt house all the luxurious trappings he could lay his hands on; the war hero and later ex-president always willing to welcome anyone who appeared on his doorstep; the gracious gentleman and dedicated public servant who lived for most of his adult life with over two hundred slaves at his beck and call: Washington had been all of those, but in his will he elected to present himself as someone engaged in a massive act of renunciation.

And unlike Robert Keayne, he did it with a minimum of preaching. As was so often true of Washington, the act and its meaning were meant to be inseparable—what you saw was designed to speak for itself. The only place in the will where he included anything approaching an explanation was among his charitable bequests—which all had to do with education. The last of them consisted of fifty shares of Potomac Company stock to go toward creating a national university in the District of Columbia. His hope was that such an institution would both help overcome what he called "local prejudices and habitual jealousies" and keep American youths at home instead of sending them abroad, where they too often acquired, he felt, "not only habits of dissapation & extravagance, but principles un-friendly to Republican Government, and to the true and genuine liberties of mankind."[33]

There was a time when George Washington wanted nothing so much as the opportunity to acquire "habits . . . of extravagance," but that time had long since passed. And if his will was any guide, what replaced it did indeed amount to a dedication to the principles of republican government, and   using his words in a different context—"to the true and genuine lib-erties of mankind." He had seen young men with little or no property—including black freemen—battling against all odds for independence. They deserved, for their bravery and persistence, a better world than the one they had been born into. Here indeed was a vision of a new American fu-ture. And in that sense Washington was not so very different from Robert Keayne, after all. To both men it was the future that mattered most, and both saw it in terms of liberation.

Like Keayne's will, too, Washington's was the product of a long and complex—if more subtle—negotiation with his society. No one had done to him what had been done to Keayne. Except for his ties to slavery—an institution that had become abhorrent to many Americans—he had little else to apologize for or defend. If a handful of Jeffersonian editors thought otherwise, most of his countrymen took him to be a model of all that was noble and hopeful about the United States of America. What they saw was a great and good man steadfastly committed to what the Revolution had wrought: to liberty and independence, to a republic with no monarchy, no titles of nobility, no established church, just ordinary individuals elected to office by their peers.

But had Washington really come to embrace those ideals (Jefferson had his doubts), or was it all just an artfully concocted piece of theater designed to portray him as someone he was not—a set of hollow gestures that signified nothing? In his will, acting as a private citizen, George Washington answered that question once and for all. He chose to become, truly, the person his fellow Americans wanted him to be, indeed needed him to be.

4

THE BROTHERS LAWRENCE

When the world of factories and machines came to the United States the consequences were less dire than many people (most famously Thomas Jefferson) feared they would be. As in England, cotton textile manufacturing led the way, with technology that was also largely British. Yet the wrenching social dislocation that accompanied England's "Industrial Revolution" was largely absent in America, at least at first. Factories filled with machines there were, as well as laborers working long hours in unhealthy conditions. But Britain's "dark satanic mills," which so appalled observers like Charles Dickens, were few and far between in America. Wages were higher, and a majority of the early textile workers seem to have spent only a few years as mill "operatives," before using the money they were able to save to move on and start new lives elsewhere.

Mostly American, too, was the capital that paid for the mills and the machines. It came from many different sources, with no clear pattern, except that initially the mills tended to be quite small, requiring an investment of only a few thousand dollars. There was one notable exception, however. Starting in 1814, at Waltham, Massachusetts, and continuing at Lowell, thirty miles away on the Merrimack River, some very large cotton mills, employing hundreds of workers and costing hundreds of thousands of dollars, were built. The investors who financed those enterprises were also unusual, for contrary to the standard stereotype, most were already rich and had no great desire to increase their wealth. They also were eager to avoid the problems factories and machines had caused abroad: the exploitation of the poor and the overcrowded cities, and the misery and squalor everywhere in them.

By mid-century the core group of investors in Waltham-Lowell-type mills had grown to nearly eighty individuals, who together controlled the largest pool of industrial capital in the United States. And the largest single share of that capital—America's first great manufacturing fortune—belonged to a pair of brothers named Amos and Abbott Lawrence.

He was the luckiest of the lucky few. Among the legions of eager young men flocking to Boston to make their fortunes, Amos Lawrence would conquer the field. Born in Groton, Massachusetts, where his ancestors had lived since the seventeenth century, he was twenty-one years old when he arrived in the city Robert Keayne had tried so hard to make safe for modern commercial enterprise. It was April 29, 1807, and he came with $20 in his pocket but feeling, as he wrote later, "richer than I had ever felt, or have felt since."[1]

Appearing at the end of this sentence it is the "since" that was meant to catch our eye. What is it doing in a statement written by a man who by then had become one of Boston's two or three richest citizens? How could he have felt rich with only $20 in his pocket? It turns out Lawrence's words were actually about his state of mind, not the concrete items—the ships' cargoes, the stocks and bonds—that would eventually constitute his wealth. He felt rich because he had well and truly earned the $20. It came to him for serving as an apprentice/clerk in a store in Groton; it had not been borrowed from anyone, or pledged as security for someone else's loan, or sent out across an ocean that might at any moment swallow it up, or invested in some corporate enterprise with scores of other stockholders. The money was his alone. He could do whatever he wished with it, so he blithely decided to spend part of it in an act of charity. He gave the man who rode with him to Boston $2, as he said, "to save him from any expense, and insure him against loss by his spending two days on the journey here and back (for which he was glad of an excuse)."[2]

Making money and giving it away to people who often were not only delighted but also quite surprised to receive it: Amos Lawrence's busy and fruitful life would be largely composed of those two activities. Yet never again would he feel so anxiety-free, as happy-go-lucky, as he did that April day in 1807.

There is one other interesting detail in the story Amos Lawrence told of his arrival in Boston. When he and his companion traveled there they did so thanks to the loan of his father's horse and chaise. Later, too, when he was getting started in business in Boston, his father lent him a thousand dollars. In other words Amos's rise was not the rags-to-riches story that Robert Keayne liked to think his had been. Amos's father was a prosperous farmer, "comfortably off," as his son described him, "with perhaps four thousand dollars"—a tidy sum in those days.[3]

Given his father's circumstances, Lawrence could have chosen to stay home and farm. But he did not, nor did his younger brothers, William, Abbot, and Samuel, who also went off to Boston to make their fortunes. And in each case it seems to have been less the push from Groton than the appeal of the big city that drew them there. Also, in pursuing the main chance as they did, they were following something of a family tradition. John Lawrence, the first of the clan to settle in Groton (and who, in the town history, is listed as "probably" having come from England in the company of John Winthrop in 1630), made his mark by taking the extraordinary step of adding two acres of the town common to his own property. Finding him determined to hold on to what he had appropriated, the town voted to let him keep the two acres, but then—in the interests of preserving "the love and peace" of the place—granted all other property holders a similar amount of land, in addition to what they already owned.

It was not, in short, a happy beginning. And perhaps for that reason two of John's sons left Groton to settle elsewhere in Massachusetts. Yet later at least one of his descendants moved back to Groton, and it was a descendant of his, Samuel, who fathered Amos and his brothers. Samuel also sallied forth to join the American forces at the start of the Revolution, though after fighting at Bunker Hill he remained in the army for only a while longer before returning to Groton, where he lived to become one of the town's leading citizens and, among other worthy deeds, helped found Groton Academy (academies in those days provided roughly the equivalent of a high school education).

Despite Samuel Lawrence's interest in education, practical experience remained the cornerstone of the family's preparation for life. Amos went through the standard seven-year apprenticeship as a storekeeper in Groton, and according to his later recollections the most important lesson he learned was "that restraint upon appetite was necessary to prevent the slavery I saw destroying numbers around me."[4] Every day he and the other apprentices would prepare a bowl of punch, supposedly for the customers, but the boys drank it too, and often far too much of it, except for Amos, who, by his own account, soon decided to forgo drinking the punch and never again touched alcohol or tobacco. As an apprentice he also acquired "the knowledge of every-day affairs" that stood him in good stead in Boston, where he soon found work as a clerk in a "respectable" merchant house and almost as quickly was offered a partnership in the firm.[5] But instead of accepting the offer he decided to go into business by himself.

As it turned out, he chose a moment full of peril to strike out on his own. Twenty-five years earlier, in the aftermath of the Revolution, the nation's economy—and particularly its overseas trade—had passed through a devastating depression, as American merchants found themselves shut out of British markets and had to scramble for whatever scraps of business they could find around the Atlantic and the seas beyond it. Then war exploded in Europe as a consequence of the French Revolution, and everything changed. Suddenly American cargoes were welcomed by the belligerents on both sides, and neutral trade became a great cornucopia, spilling out fortunes to traders up and down the New England coast. At the same time, however, both France and England were working to suppress American trade with their enemies, making it increasingly hard for Americans to maintain their neutrality. Finally in 1807—just as Amos Lawrence was arriving in Boston—in a bold stroke to cut through the tangled snarl of contending forces, the American government under Thomas Jefferson declared an embargo, temporarily suspending all trade with the belligerents. And when that failed to work, in 1812 the United States declared war against Great Britain.

Together the embargo and the war again brought New England's commerce to a standstill, though with the coming of peace, transatlantic trade sprang to life again. And that would remain Amos Lawrence's principal business for the next twenty-five years. He imported a variety of goods but chiefly textiles with his brother Abbott, who had arrived in Boston in 1808 and would eventually join him in establishing the firm of A. & A. Lawrence. Before that, however, Abbott had to serve the usual apprenticeship with his brother, and "a first-rate business lad" he proved to be.

Legally, the partnership was established in 1814, with Amos, as he said, "putting fifty thousand dollars that I had earned, into the concern."[6] The fact that he had accumulated such a hefty nest egg in only seven years—especially given the treacherous business conditions of the time—was striking, though occasional letters published in his *Diary and Correspondence* provide some clues as to why he and his brother were so successful. In 1815, with the war at last over, Abbott Lawrence was on the first ship leaving Boston for England and once there immediately acquired and shipped home new merchandise, prompting Amos to write his wife: "I suspect there are few instances of a young man leaving this town and sending out goods, and having them sold within ninety days from the time of his departure."[7] Writing Abbott himself he was even more rapturous: "You are as famous among your acquaintances here for the rapidity of your movements as Bonaparte."[8]

Speed: that was one of the chief ingredients in successful merchanting, especially for Americans operating, as they did, outside of any established commercial network. Opportunities arose in a flash. One had to be perpetually ready to take the plunge or sacrifice all hope of profit, for idle mercantile capital earned nothing. And at every step along the way the risks multiplied. Ships sank, cargoes could be ruined even if the ships remained afloat, and prices rose and fell in an endless, dizzying whirl.

In time Amos Lawrence would come to feel acutely the tensions he lived with day in and day out. Never physically strong, he became ill and took several long trips—to New York, to Canada, to Washington, D.C.—which removed him, at least for a time, from the pressures of business. Meanwhile he grew richer year by year. "I am the richest man, I suppose, that there is on this side of the water," he noted with pride in 1817.[9] Yet a decade later he was complaining unhappily of his "*overengagedness*" in business. "I now find myself so engrossed with its cares, as to occupy my thoughts, waking or sleeping, to a degree entirely disproportionate to its importance . . . property acquired at such sacrifices as I have been obliged to make this past year costs more than it's worth, and the anxiety in protecting it is the extreme of folly."[10]

A year later, having significantly reduced the risks he took in business, Lawrence wrote, in a happier vein: "The principles of business laid down a year ago have been very nearly acted upon. Our responsibilities and anxieties have greatly diminished as also have the accustomed profits of business."[11] Just how long Lawrence was prepared to continue earning "greatly diminished" profits was unclear. Almost certainly his brother and partner, Abbott—who was always more comfortable with risk than Amos—would have opposed making a permanent thing of that year's regimen. In any case it all became moot four years later when Amos suddenly fell ill again, this time with an ailment that would remove him from business for the rest of his life.

The precise nature of his illness was never specified. From the description of its symptoms he appears to have been suffering from stomach ulcers, and he himself viewed the illness as closely linked to business anxieties. Eventually he recovered enough to spend several hours a day riding through Boston on horseback. He also, during those years, carried on a program of personal philanthropy that took at least as much energy and time as his business ever had.

The money that underwrote both Amos's retirement and his generosity came from his share of the profits of A. & A. Lawrence, which as senior partner he continued to receive. During those years, however, the nature of the firm's business was changing, and in ways that did indeed diminish risks while continuing to return a comfortable margin of profit. "Manufacturing stocks": that is what Lawrence recommended to someone who wrote asking for advice about where to invest money. There alone could one have "a *reasonable assurance* that the investment would not," he continued, "be worth less than cost, allowing 6%, and deducting dividends for the next five or seven years."[12] A. & A. Lawrence, he might have added, sold the products of various manufacturing companies and was also investing heavily in their stock. In addition, the firm would become engaged in establishing new manufacturing enterprises—all of this, too, in the same industry: cotton textiles. Nor were the Lawrences alone in shifting the bulk of their business activities from commerce to manufacturing. A good many other merchants they knew were doing the same.

What began the process was the establishment of the Boston Manufacturing Company, at Waltham, Massachusetts, in 1813. Backed by a small group of investors, it was the brainchild of Francis Cabot Lowell, who, in the midst of a successful career as a merchant had suffered a series of health problems sufficiently serious to send him to England and Scotland for two years with his wife and children to recuperate. While there, he

Andrew Carnegie, 1913.

Alexis de Tocqueville, 1850,
by Théodore Chassériau.

Drawing of Robert Keayne's "Market House," built and renamed the Boston Town House in 1657, by Charles Lawrence, 1930. (Courtesy of the Boston Views Collection, Massachusetts Historical Society)

Aquatint of Mount Vernon, by Francis Jukes (after Alexander Robertson), 1800. (Courtesy of the Chapin Library, Williams College, Williamstown, Massachusetts)

George Washington as Colonel in the Virginia Regiment, 1772, by Charles Willson
Peale. (Courtesy of the Washington-Custis-Lee Collection, Washington and Lee
University, Lexington, Virginia)

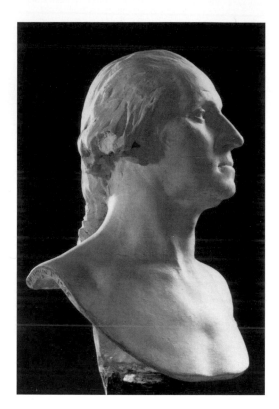

Bust of George Washington
from a life mask, 1789, by
Jean Antoine Houdon.
(Courtesy of Mount Vernon
Ladies' Association)

Photograph of Mount Vernon in the 1850s before its rescue by the Mount Vernon Ladies
Association of the Union. (Collection of the author)

Engraving of Amos Lawrence, based on a portrait by Chester Harding, 1846.
(Source: *Extracts from the Diary and Correspondence of Amos Lawrence* [Boston: J.
Wilson and Son, 1855])

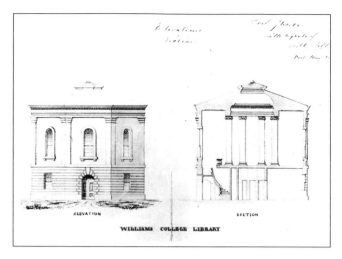

Drawing of Lawrence Hall, Williams College, by its architect,
Thomas A. Tefft. (Courtesy of the Williams College
Archives and Special Permissions)

Engraving of Abbott Lawrence, based on a portrait by Chester Harding, 1846.
(Source: *Extracts from the Diary and Correspondence of Amos Lawrence*
[Boston: J. Wilson and Son, 1855])

John D.
Rockefeller,
1875, by Eastman
Johnson. (Courtesy
of the Rockefeller
Archive Center)

Forest Hill, the Rockefeller family's summer home in Cleveland.
(Courtesy of the Rockefeller Archive Center)

John D. Rockefeller, 1904. (From Ida M. Tarbell, "John D. Rockefeller: A Character Sketch," *McClure's Magazine*, July 1905)

The two John D. Rockefellers, junior and senior, in New York, early twentieth century. (Courtesy of the Rockefeller Archive Center)

Newlyweds John D. and Abby Aldrich Rockefeller. (Courtesy of the Rockefeller Archive Center)

Kykuit, final version of the entrance front. (Courtesy of the Rockefeller Archive Center)

The third generation: the five Rockefeller brothers with their father shortly after the end of World War II. From left to right: Laurance, Winthrop, Nelson, Junior, John III, and David. (Courtesy of the Rockefeller Archive Center)

Large Spiny, by Alexander Calder, commissioned by Nelson Rockefeller in 1966 for the gardens at Kykuit. (Courtesy of the Rockefeller Archive Center)

A helicopter is enlisted at Kykuit to move into place a piece of sculpture acquired by Nelson Rockefeller. (Courtesy of the Rockefeller Archive Center)

Warren Buffett and Bill Gates at Buffett's favorite diner in Omaha, Nebraska.
(Photograph by Mark Peterson/Redux)

Steve Jobs doing what he did best—introduce an Apple innovation, on this occasion the MacBook Air. (Matthew Yohe via Wikimedia Commons [Creative Commons Attribution 3.0 Unported])

Oprah Winfrey, undated, by Chris Hopkins. (AA Reps Inc.)

Occupy Wall Street demonstration, September 30, 2011.
(Photograph by David Shankbone)

Benozzo Gozzoli, *Three Wise Men,* fresco panel in the Magi Chapel of Palazzo Medici-Riccardi, Florence, 1459–61. Cosimo de' Medici is in the left foreground, mounted on a donkey. His various relatives appear in the crowd behind him. (Photograph by Samuel Y. Edgerton, Jr.)

made a point of visiting several textile mills in Manchester and studied the operation of the power loom—the crown jewel of Britain's industrial technology—closely enough to be able to reproduce a version of it on his return to America, thus evading British laws prohibiting the export of either the machine or any models or drawings relating to it.

Along with this stunning piece of industrial piracy, Lowell subsequently initiated half a dozen other features that distinguished the Boston Manufacturing Company from existing cotton textile firms on both sides of the Atlantic. Up to then the two processes involved in mechanized textile production—spinning the yarn and weaving it into cloth—were routinely carried on in separate establishments. At Waltham, however, they were combined in a single "integrated" mill, where literally the raw cotton entered at one end of the factory and the finished goods exited at the other. Also, from the beginning the company was organized as a joint stock corporation, with individual stockholders purchasing shares giving them the right to elect a board of directors and divide, pro rata, any and all profits. The principal reason for using the corporate form was that it facilitated the pooling of the very large amounts of capital ($400,000, which quickly rose to $600,000) needed to build the Waltham company's integrated mill—and also to create its unique system of labor.

In England the textile manufacturing workforce consisted of adult men and women plus large numbers of children, many of them paupers. In America the prevailing system was "family labor," which also brought adults and quite often their children into the mills to work together. At Waltham, on the other hand, the labor force was made up primarily of young, unmarried women (we would call them "teenagers"). And since there were not nearly enough of them in the area to meet the company's needs, it recruited its "mill girls" from dozens of other locations around rural New England. It also built—as accommodations for its workforce— handsome boardinghouses presided over by respectable older women. Standards of proper dress and behavior as well as regular church attendance were strictly enforced. Thus were upstanding Yankee farmers persuaded to part with their daughters. For the girls, however, what counted most was the chance to earn cash wages, which a great many of them saved, enabling them, after only a few years in the mills, to leave and make whatever use they wished of the financial independence they had gained thereby.

Or such was the hope, and for a substantial period of time it was actually fulfilled. So when Amos Lawrence bought "manufacturing stocks," he was also subscribing to a highly innovative social experiment, and one that had the virtue of being much admired and frequently praised. No less a person than Charles Dickens, comparing the results to the woeful industrial conditions he was familiar with in England, described the difference as tantamount to that "between the Good and Evil, the living light and deepest shadow," adding that he had seen "not one young girl whom . . . I would have removed from those works if I had had the power."[13]

The mills Dickens saw were in Lowell, Massachusetts. Named in honor of Francis Cabot Lowell, the place had been founded under the leadership of Nathan Appleton, another wealthy Boston merchant, in order to create a site for a whole string of new textile manufacturing concerns. To accomplish this the Merrimac River had been dammed and an elaborate system of locks and canals constructed to provide water power for the individual mill sites. When Dickens saw the place it had already become the second largest city in Massachusetts. In time, too, it would have many imitators, including Lawrence, Massachusetts, founded nearby by Abbott Lawrence.

Presumably what drove all this expansion was the amount of money to be made in textile manufacturing. Yet money-making in this case has to be rather carefully defined. Profits at first ran high, but between 1838 and 1861 a sample of eleven Waltham-Lowell-type companies shows an average of only 7.9 percent in profits (net earnings)—and paid out dividends (as a percent of paid in capital) at exactly the same rate. Also, even the high profits of the early years amounted to less than what wealthy merchants like Nathan Appleton and Amos Lawrence could hope to earn in a single, well-managed trading venture, which typically ranged from 30 to 50 percent and in some cases rose even higher.

Clearly these figures suggest there had to be factors aside from simple money-making that drew so much New England capital from commerce into textile manufacturing, and there were, as was hinted at in a passing remark made later by Nathan Appleton in his brief *Introduction of the Power Loom and Origin of Lowell*. He knew Francis Cabot Lowell well, and from the first his ideas about textile manufacturing intrigued Appleton, who agreed to invest $5,000, a sum he was prepared to lose without complaint. Meanwhile he described himself as being, at that point in his life, "content with a moderate fortune" and wishing "not to perform any part of the labor of carrying on the business."[14]

Precisely the same combination of investment in the textile industry and a desire to curtail active involvement in business would occur later in Amos Lawrence's case. And indeed it would become common in Waltham-Lowell-type enterprises, with large initial investments generally coming from a small circle of wealthy individuals, many of whom had earned their fortunes in commerce and were eager to leave behind the pressures of business. If the profits were lower, they were both steady and reliable, and nothing more was required than purchasing the stock and collecting the dividends. As it turned out, Appleton did not retire from business; he spent the rest of his life involved in the textile industry and related enterprises. Amos Lawrence, on the other hand, left entirely to his brother the management of his very considerable investment in the industry— including the development of the city of Lawrence—and devoted his time and energy to what he plainly found far more interesting and satisfying than business: giving his money away to help others.

From Robert Keayne's day on, Boston had produced more than a few dedicated philanthropists, and the first half of the nineteenth century saw their ranks growing more rapidly than ever. In part this was because more money was available to use for philanthropic purposes. Also, with thousands of newcomers crowding into Boston every year many of whom ended up living in grinding poverty—there was an urgent need for money to help them. Equally vital were less tangible means of support. Or as a letter appealing to the "wealthy inhabitants of the town" for funds to establish what became the Massachusetts General Hospital put it: "When in distress every man becomes our neighbor."[15] That sense of neighborliness had roots running deep into the region's past. When Robert Keayne was censured and fined in Boston, it was because he had put his interests above those of the community. Similarly in Groton, when John Lawrence offended his fellow townspeople by taking two acres of the common for his own use, "the love and peace" of the place had to be restored and in a way that left no one feeling unfairly treated. For there as well, the community had been violated.

How did one create a sense of neighborliness, of community, in a city filled with newcomers unknown to one another or anyone else? Conceived as a way of meeting that problem, the hospital was, in its very creation, organized as a community effort. The rich were appealed to in thoughtfully composed letters, while a door-to-door campaign carried on throughout the city over three days brought in $78,000. Of the 1,189 donations received up to 1843, fewer than three hundred were for $100 or more, while 556 amounted to $10 or less. Here truly—as Josiah Quincy, Sr., the city's mayor, would proclaim at the laying of the hospital's cornerstone—was a philanthropic project that saw "all classes of . . . citizens combining and concentrating their efforts" toward a common goal.[16]

The drive for funds for the Massachusetts General Hospital began in 1810, just three years after Amos Lawrence had arrived in Boston, and in due course he took his place as one of the hospital's trustees. Among the various duties of the position, he particularly enjoyed visiting the patients, though after he became ill himself he felt that he could no longer continue as a trustee and resigned. But the number and variety of his philanthropic activities continued to grow year by year. And most of them had two characteristics in common: they were intensely personal, and all of them were designed to draw people together in one way or another.

In the early years, the project that he cared most deeply about was the completion of the Bunker Hill Monument, in Charlestown, across the river from Boston. A massive granite obelisk that would eventually stand 221 feet tall, it was begun in the 1820s to commemorate the first full-scale battle of the Revolution. For several years it rose steadily upward, then the money ran out and work stopped. Yet Lawrence, whose father had fought in the battle, was determined to see the monument finished, and not simply as a personal memorial. Rather it was meant to act, in his words, "as a nucleus for the affections of people," perpetually reminding them of their shared heroic past.[17] For that to happen as many people as possible had to contribute—freely and above all unselfishly—to the project. Hence Lawrence's anger when the directors of the Bunker Hill Monument Association applied to the state for permission to raise the necessary funds by holding a lottery, which as he saw it was all too likely to attract people interested only in making money for themselves. "I opposed the measure in all its stages and feel mortified that they have done so," he remarked in disgust.[18]

Happily for Lawrence's sake, the lottery scheme failed, at which point he stepped in and offered to contribute $5,000—an amount he later doubled—if the rest of the money could be raised through individual donations. And eventually, after three tries, that was how it was done. As he wrote afterward, "Three Appletons, Robert G. Shaw and us three Lawrences could have raised the entire amount without saying by your leave to the public."[19] But the whole point was to make it a community effort; if that took more time and trouble, then so be it.

On other projects Lawrence was content to act alone, especially if they involved what increasingly became his primary philanthropic interest: education. He was a loyal and generous supporter of Groton's academy, which his father had helped to establish. He also became the largest single donor Williams College had ever had up to that point. Founded in 1793 and tucked away in the northwestern corner of Massachusetts, Williams had originally benefited from having no rivals nearby, but that soon changed, and by the mid-1840s it was struggling to survive. Fortunately in the person of Mark Hopkins it had a resourceful and charismatic president, who in his religious convictions hewed a decidedly conservative line, which was what first brought him to Lawrence's attention.

In 1844 Hopkins was invited to give a series of lectures at the Lowell Institute in Boston, and so taken was Lawrence with what he heard at the opening lecture that he immediately sent his son to Hopkins's hotel with an offer of a $5,000 contribution to Williams. That was followed over the next several years by a second $5,000—donated to end the college's indebtedness—plus a gift of $10,000 the following year, and the year after that a contribution to cover the entire cost of building a new library, which amounted to $7,000. Over the years there were other, smaller gifts: for enlarging the college's grounds, providing it with a new telescope, and establishing scholarships for graduates of Lawrence Academy (as the Groton school had been renamed to acknowledge the family's generosity to it).

Coming from someone who had himself never been to college, Lawrence's generosity to Williams might have seemed surprising, but in Mark Hopkins he would always feel he had found both a spiritual mentor and a true friend. His own Unitarian faith had long since come to seem cold and uninspiring to him, especially in its tendency, as he said, to "sink" Jesus "to the level of a mere human teacher."[20] Hopkins stuck steadfastly to the divinity of Christ, which alone was enough to win Lawrence's heart. In addition he was a kind and caring individual who valued not only the money Lawrence gave Williams, but also the spirit in which he gave it. His fondest hope was, as he explained to Hopkins, that "our places of education be sustained, as supplying the pure and living streams that shall irrigate every hill and valley of this vast empire, and train men to do their duty."[21] Fully as appealing, too, was the *way* Lawrence gave money—particularly, as Hopkins said, "the personal attention and sympathy which he bestowed with it."[22]

A generous and thoughtful donor to half a dozen worthy causes: that would have been enough to satisfy most people, but not Lawrence, for he truly longed to make a daily practice of his philanthropy, and the way he found of doing it proved, for him at least, ideal. Using one or sometimes two or three rooms in his house, he kept large supplies of dozens of different items, from which he would take, by the armful, piles of assorted things to bundle up and send off to various people, many of whom were total strangers. Often they were clergymen or teachers, but anyone who attracted his attention for whatever reason could suddenly be favored with a package containing, as one did, "a dressing gown, vest, hat, slippers, jackknife, scissors, pens, neck-handkerchiefs, pantaloons, cloth for coat, 'History of Groton,' lot of pamphlets"; or as another parcel, sent to a college president, did, "a bundle of books, with broadcloth and pantaloon stuffs, with odds and ends for poor students when they go out to keep school in winter."[23]

Lawrence also made a practice of keeping in his carriage a large supply of books which he distributed during his drives around the city, again to people who for the most part were strangers. He delighted in handing out shiny coins to children too. When asked why he did these things he replied, "Remember where it is written 'Cast thy bread upon the waters, for thou shalt find it after many days.'"[24] And once, writing more broadly of what he saw as the proper mission of philanthropy, he remarked, "Our first duty is to those of our own household, then extending to kindred, friends, neighbors (and the term 'neighbor' may, in its broadest sense, take in the whole human family), citizens of our state, then of our country, then of other countries of the world."[25]

The point was that if you began at your own doorstep and moved resolutely outward from there, it was impossible to know where the road might take you. So Lawrence started, always, with what he knew and understood, hoping to make of it something larger, more significant. Meanwhile, he kept track of every cent he spent, writing it all down including everything that went into those parcels, neatly wrapped and tied with stout twine, exactly as he had done it when clerking in Groton, except that he sent no bills with them. They were a gift—bread cast on the waters.

A gossamer thin web of idealistic visions, to be sure—"Air castles," Mark Hopkins fondly called them—and something very like that was probably how Amos Lawrence's brother, Abbott, thought of them, though without Hopkins's gentleness of touch.[26] For in all things Abbott Lawrence confined himself to the substantive realities of life. Within that realm much might be changed, but to his mind hoping to build a new and different world would have seemed as foolish as it was naïve. When Harvard was raising money to establish a theological school his name was absent from the list of donors, though it regularly appeared on lists for other projects at Harvard.

In time, too, Abbott Lawrence developed a broad range of serious philanthropic interests of his own, but until midlife he concentrated primarily on business. After his brother retired he took over the management of A. & A. Lawrence and spearheaded the firm's growing involvement in the textile industry, first selling the goods, then acting as an incorporator of the Tremont mill at Lowell, and finally as the developer—through the Essex Company—of the city of Lawrence. And as trade had once made Amos Lawrence the richest businessman in Boston, textiles later did the same for Abbott.

And eventually he expanded his activities to include politics. For four years he held a seat in Congress, and in 1848 he narrowly missed winning the Whig Party's vice-presidential nomination (and hence the opportunity to become president on Zachary Taylor's death in 1850). In 1849, as a consolation prize for having received neither the vice-presidential nomination nor a seat in Taylor's cabinet, he was made American Minister to Great Britain, a post he kept until 1852. After that he held no other office but remained actively involved in politics. Meanwhile, his inborn competitiveness and political ambitions drew mixed reactions from those who knew him. "He still grasps at money though has more than a million and is the richest man of his age here," commented Amos A. Lawrence—Amos Lawrence's son—in 1842, adding: "He loves power too and office. He does not grow better nor happier as he gets older."[27] Even Amos himself at times felt compelled to fire off a blast or two in Abbott's direction. "If my vote would make my brother Vice President, I would not give it," he wrote in 1848, "as I think it lowering his good name to accept office of any sort, by employing such means as are now needful to get votes."[28]

Yet there came a time when Abbott did something that so delighted Amos he could barely contain himself: "Dear Brother Abbott," he wrote, "I hardly dare trust myself to speak what. . . . I thank God I am spared this day. . . . This magnificent plan . . . is a better investment than any you have ever made," to which an "affectionate" brother could not help adding, "more honorable and more to be coveted than the highest political station in our country."[29] What won this dazzling praise was Abbott's donation of $50,000 to Harvard—the largest single gift it had ever received from a living donor—to establish a special school for those students who intended, as he said, "to devote themselves to the practical application of science."[30]

Despite Amos Lawrence's enthusiasm about what his brother had done, nothing could have made plainer how differently the two men approached philanthropy. Grand where most of Amos's benefactions were small and intimate; solidly centered in reality where Amos was forever hoping to accomplish things like training the young "to do their duty"; focused on New England's foremost academic institution, where Amos gave to struggling rural academies and country colleges: Abbott Lawrence's philanthropy operated with all the efficiency of the giant turbines that powered his mills in the city of Lawrence. As a philanthropist, he also looked unblinkingly to the future. His gifts to Harvard were meant to change it, to improve it. "Let theory be proved by practice," he declared, requesting too that it be done with "as much expedition as may be consistant with economy."[31]

Similarly, Abbott's other major philanthropy—building model lodging houses for the poor (a pet project of Queen Victoria's husband, Prince Albert)—laid down a plan for change, and change one could see and touch. If poverty was becoming a serious problem in Boston, why not begin by attacking its physical manifestations, which might just lead to other, more sweeping improvements? (A hundred years later thousands of "urban renewal" projects in the United States would embrace exactly the same rationale.)

Amos Lawrence, meanwhile, believed that the key to helping the poor was to raise them up. "If we do not educate and elevate this class of our people," he cautioned, "they will change our government within fifty years."[32] Elevating the needy may also have been something Abbott wanted to do, but his model housing seemed primarily aimed at ministering to them as they were—"the poor." There was nothing in the plan about building character or ending peoples' isolation by removing the labels that stigmatized them. The fact was, Abbott had little quarrel to pick with the world he surveyed as Boston hurried toward the middle of the nineteenth century. What he sought was mastery of that world.

During his lifetime Amos Lawrence spent "for charitable purposes"—by his son's estimate—at least $700,000. His brother Abbott gave less, but his individual donations were larger, more public; they were reported in the newspapers, while most of Amos's gifts remained anonymous. Amos's son also noted that few people had, as he said, "done as much in proportion to the means which they had to bestow" as his father.[33] Yet however one totaled up the two brothers' giving, there were also changes occurring around them that turned out to fit neither of their visions very comfortably.

In business this was clear in what had become of the Waltham-Lowell system in the textile industry. In financial terms its success continued through most of the 1840s, but during those same years it lost much of its unique character. With more and more textile mills being built across the northern United States, the pressure to hold down costs rose steadily. As a result the mill girls found themselves tending a larger number of machines for the same wage year after year, and when they showed signs of uniting to protest such changes, the owners faced them down. From the mid-1840s on, the owners also had a ready alternative to dealing with the irate demands of Yankee farm girls: hiring Irish immigrants, which the mills began doing with increasing frequency, especially as profit margins shrank even further in the 1850s.

Meanwhile, the stockholders wanted their dividends, and since the treasurers of companies (in effect their CEOs) invariably owned large blocks of stock, the stockholders got what they wanted, as the workers did not. One consequence was that dividends increasingly absorbed available profits, so corners of all kinds were cut, which came to a head in what turned out to be one of the worst industrial disasters of the nineteenth century. On January 10, 1860, all five floors of the Pemberton Mill in Lawrence—which at the time was in full operation—suddenly collapsed to the ground, trapping hundreds of workers. Then, with frantic efforts to rescue them under way, fire broke out in the heaps of rubble covering them. All told, 88 people lost their lives, and another 116 were seriously injured. In the aftermath an investigation revealed that a group of defective columns on the top floor of the mill had caused its collapse. The problem was first detected in 1854, but nothing was done about it.

By the time the Pemberton Mill disaster occurred both Amos and Abbott Lawrence were dead, so they were spared having to confront it. But they did witness the steady deterioration of working conditions in the mills. They also had to deal with two direct assaults related to their involvement in the textile industry, both political in nature and both, in the end, quite damaging.

The first stemmed from the fact that the raw cotton used in the mills at Lowell and Lawrence, as well as everywhere else textile manufacturing took hold, was grown in the American South, much of it with slave labor. At the same time, the mill owners were energetically seeking Southern support in raising tariff rates to meet foreign competition, and as a result they systematically refrained from attacking not only slavery itself but also pro-Southern measures like the annexation of Texas and the Mexican War.

Or so ran the charges against the owners, which eventually led to an open split between contending "Conscience" and "Cotton" factions within the Massachusetts Whig Party—the political home of virtually all the state's cotton manufacturers. The conflict finally reached full boil in 1848 at the annual state Whig convention. With charges flying back and forth in front of five thousand delegates, Charles Sumner, a leader of the Conscience forces, angrily declared that the party's preference for Zachary Taylor (a slaveholder and victorious general in the Mexican War) as its presidential candidate was the product of a vast conspiracy between, as he put it, "the cotton-planters and flesh-mongers of Louisiana and Mississippi and the cotton-spinners and traffickers of New England—between the lords of the lash and the lords of the loom."[34] It turned out that the convention endorsed Taylor's candidacy despite Sumner's dazzling rhetoric, but what remained most memorable in the minds of many was his impassioned assault on "the lords of the loom."

While the Massachusetts Whig Party was being challenged from within by its younger, antislavery members, it was also facing increasingly stiff opposition from its traditional foes, the state's Democrats, and over issues that directly involved the financial interests of the Lawrences and much of the rest of Boston's business elite. As it happened, the issues were old ones, rooted in practices long established in Massachusetts. In time past, when the Commonwealth's government wished to do more than its meager resources allowed, it turned to private individuals, awarding them special privileges—which often included monopoly rights—in exchange for bearing the costs and risks of whatever was to be done. Though useful at the outset, sooner or later such arrangements tended to produce contention. Other people wanted the same privileges, which the original grantees invariably opposed (as in the famous Charles River Bridge Supreme Court case, which the stockholders lost). Or the grantees took advantage of their position to fleece the community at large. Or the state changed its mind and withdrew the privileges, as better, cheaper ways of accomplishing the same objective materialized. Increasingly, too, there arose a broader challenge to the system, namely charges that the whole idea of special privileges was wrong: that they were unfair, that they were corrupt, that they unduly constrained everyone involved, including the public. And as time went on, this became the view most Massachusetts Democrats embraced.

The textile mills in which the Lawrences and others like them invested neither asked for nor received monopoly privileges from the state. Still, to support the mills, as well as to maintain an economic environment favorable to them, an entire network of related businesses had grown up—banks, insurance companies, railroads—all of them controlled by individuals with close ties to the textile industry, and all of them, too, incorporated by the state. Ultimately, it was this concentration of economic power that the Massachusetts Democrats most objected to, and to combat it they brought their guns to bear on the process of incorporation itself, claiming it was purposely designed to favor "the few instead of the many."[35] In the existing system the legislature had to pass a special act to bring a corporation into being. To end that arrangement the Democrats proposed a system of "general incorporation" in which groups interested in corporate status had only to meet certain standard requirements and apply to the state, which would then automatically grant them charters, removing all traces of "privilege" from the process.

Thanks to the Democrats' efforts, general incorporation became law in 1851, yet it made only a modest dent in the power of Boston's business elite. For at bottom, that power had always depended on the elites' access to large amounts of liquid capital and their penchant for working together in ways that benefited them all. Nevertheless the new system had a significance that transcended its substantive impact, because it demonstrated just how strong opposition to the power held by men like the Lawrence brothers had become. Confronted with the deteriorating working conditions in the mills, stigmatized as "monopolists" and "lords of the loom," their political power on the wane, they had unquestionably suffered a serious blow to their moral authority. Accustomed to thinking of themselves and being thought of by others as good men and staunch supporters of what was good for their fellow citizens, good for Boston, and good for Massachusetts, they now found every point in that litany called into question and, by some people, rejected altogether. Open class warfare was hardly about to break out in the streets of Boston, but lines had been drawn that would not soon fade away.

Yet amid the mounting disappointments of those years there remained philanthropy. Along with others in the elite, the Lawrences had been generous before and would continue to be. The question was how philanthropy could best be conducted in the transformed setting of those years. And one answer was to launch a fresh effort to raise money for the Massachusetts General Hospital, though it turned out to be completely unlike the original campaign to fund the institution. In those days the goal had been to involve as broad a cross section of the community as possible, even to the extent of going door to door to solicit contributions. The goal of the new campaign, held in 1844 to enlarge the institution, was $50,000, but this time there was no door-to-door campaign. Instead the whole affair began and ended at a single meeting, with Abbott Lawrence presiding and others making appropriate resolutions. The pattern of contributions was also distinctly different. There were many fewer gifts, but the size of the average gift was much higher, with donations of $500 or more accounting for 29 percent of the total as opposed to only 4 percent of the total thirty years earlier.

In short, supporting the hospital had become the responsibility of the rich. And since the institution primarily benefited the poor rather than the wealthy (who could afford to pay for medical treatment at home) the gulf between the two groups could not have been clearer. A similar division occurred in the case of Boston's major libraries. The oldest of them, the Boston Athenaeum, had been established early in the nineteenth century as a private institution, but many hoped it would one day welcome the public into its elegantly appointed rooms. That day never came. In 1853 the Athenaeum's members voted emphatically to keep it private or, as one of them said, "a memorial to those who had erected and endowed it."[36] At the same time, however, men like Abbott Lawrence were also contributing large sums to another library, established in 1852, to be named—as it would remain—the Boston Public Library.

What was sacrificed in all this, obviously, was the sense of the entire community working together toward a shared goal—of divisions tran- scended, of scattered fragments joined and society made whole. That was also Amos Lawrence's principal objective as a philanthropist, and nothing about the relentless march of change that filled his final years altered, by one whit, his thoughts on the subject. As Mark Hopkins said of him, he retained to the end the kind of "sympathy" that alone, Hopkins believed, could "establish the right relation between the rich and the poor."[37]

But if that sympathy was one of the hallmarks of Amos Lawrence's giv- ing, it seemed to play, at most, a limited role in his brother Abbott's phi- lanthropy. Yet who could dispute the value of either Harvard University or model lodging houses for the poor? If a great distance appeared to stretch between the two, that simply mirrored the social reality in Boston. Nor did Abbott Lawrence's generosity go unpraised. Speaking in Faneuil Hall on his death, Robert Winthrop described him as "the most important per- son" in the community, adding the words from Edmund Burke's eulogy of Sir George Saville: "When an act of great humanity was to be done, and done with all the weight and authority that belonged to it, this community could cast its eyes on none but him."[38]

For his part, Amos Lawrence tried to persuade some of his friends to adopt rural colleges of their own, but only a few of them did. Yet on the other side of the balance, Williams, the struggling place he had taken under his wing, would a century and a half later be considered—in some quarters at least—the finest liberal arts college in America. Also, Abbott's great gift to Harvard failed to accomplish what he hoped it would. Instead of funding the "practical" studies he favored, the money was used in the end to support pure science, thereby paving the way for MIT—a new institution entirely devoted to what he had hoped to achieve. Still, in the contest between the brothers, Abbott at the time clearly came out on top in the eyes of the world.

Taking the two men together, however, the most important contribution they made may well have been the intensity and conviction they brought to the tradition Robert Keayne had established two centuries earlier in Boston. For whatever else was true, the Lawrences did indeed devote both serious thought and a significant portion of their wealth to good works, believing, just as Keayne and George Washington had, that nothing less was expected of them.

Their generosity also established a family tradition that lasted for generations. Amos's son, Amos A. Lawrence, was both a highly successful businessman and a dedicated philanthropist. In turn his son, William, became an Episcopal priest, whose first parish was Grace Church in the city of Lawrence. From there he rose to become the Episcopal Bishop of Massachusetts, and, among his many nonclerical achievements, he helped raise a great deal of money for the Harvard Business School—a task he took on, as he said, out of "loyalty to the business traditions of my family and a conviction that this was a real missionary enterprise for the welfare of the country."[39] The man who gave him that assignment was Abbott Lawrence Lowell, a grandson of Abbott Lawrence's and the president of Harvard University.

Meanwhile, as a clerk just starting out in business in Cleveland, Ohio, John D. Rockefeller was given by his employer a copy of *The Life of Amos Lawrence* [sic], a book which, though he titled it incorrectly, he would later describe as "a great inspiration to me."[40]

5

RICH AS ROCKEFELLER

*In the decades following the Civil War other industries replaced cotton tex-
tiles as the driving force behind American economic change. Using the railroads
and the nation's natural resources on a scale never before dreamed of, those
industries also marked a new era in the creation of wealth. From steel, meat-
packing, and oil arose a class of multimillionaires who proved to be the van-
guard in an ever-expanding legion of entrepreneurs whose ventures produced
profits as rapidly as they did new products.*

*And while the rich were getting richer there appeared for the first time in
America a distinct class of industrial workers. Patterns of family and community life changed as well, and adding to all this were the changes in American
attitudes and values that the new economic order seemed to mandate. Often
torn between celebrating the wonders of industrialization and deploring its
grimmer consequences—the cruel conditions of factory labor, the growing gulf
between the rich and the poor, the damage to the environment, and the general
loss of autonomy throughout society—Americans struggled to find a way to preserve the spirit of fair play and community-mindedness that had characterized
the early industrial world.*

*So too—in the shadow of his oil refineries—did the man who more than any
other individual embodied both the expansive spirit of the age and its darker
side: John D. Rockefeller. The ruthless architect of an empire that won him an
unimaginably large fortune, or the philanthropist whose unparalleled generosity would lead him to spend hundreds of millions of dollars to benefit others: one
could recognize him in either of those descriptions. In fact he was both.*

During a span of years that lasted for just short of a century, John Davison Rockefeller led several different lives, each in a different place, a pattern that began in his youth, much of which was odd and unsettling. A handsome, philandering patent medicine salesman joined in matrimony to a pious, upright woman given to thinking in relentlessly moral terms, his parents—William Avery and Eliza Davison Rockefeller—were unlikely to have provided their children with a placid upbringing, and indeed they did not. Plagued by scandals over William's relations with serving girls in his own home and driven by the irregular nature of his business, the family moved from town to town in upstate New York, then on to Ohio where, after several more stops, they ended up in Cleveland. By then "Doc" Bill had secretly entered into a bigamous second marriage, while Eliza, with singular will and fortitude, had devoted herself to raising their children within the stern bonds of her Baptist faith.

As a product of that strange union, young John D. Rockefeller would be simultaneously scarred and uplifted by it. Though he never completely broke with his father, his feelings toward him grew increasingly negative. His mother, on the other hand, became a figure of veneration, her intense religious convictions matched by his own throughout his life. His upbringing also left him with a penchant for secrecy and a deep need to control everything that touched his existence. Somewhere along the way, too, he acquired a fiercely passionate desire to become rich. If the secrecy represented his father's influence and the need for control his mother's, his longing for wealth—especially when it was taken as a sign of God's favor, as she would have—may have offered a means of uniting the two legacies. Or perhaps it was simply a way of escaping from the entire muddle.

What is certain is that all the basic elements of Rockefeller's personality were evident from the moment he began his business career. He was sixteen and had been lucky enough to receive an excellent education at Cleveland's Central High School, where he did well, but then surprised his teachers and classmates by leaving just two months before graduation. His mother had hoped he would go on to a proper, four-year college, yet instead he took a three-month course at E. G. Folsom's Commercial College, which ended his formal education. While there, he mastered double entry bookkeeping and learned a bit about commercial banking—enough to begin looking for a job, which he did within weeks of finishing at Folsom's. For the next two months he went to every business concern in Cleveland that seemed at all likely to hire him. Finally, on September 26, 1855 (which he celebrated for years afterward as "Job Day"), he landed a position as an assistant bookkeeper at Hewitt and Tuttle, a firm of commission merchants.

During the five years he worked at Hewitt and Tuttle—his "business apprenticeship," he called it later—it became the center of his life.[1] Commission merchants functioned as middlemen, accepting consignments of goods of all kinds from producers and selling them wherever an opportunity to do so arose, generally with the proceeds going to the producers only after the goods were sold, minus a percentage for the commission merchant. In effect, the system facilitated sales by spreading the risks as well as the profits among several different individuals. Goods tended to come in large lots, and often commission merchants arranged for their transportation, sometimes without ever laying eyes on them. Both the profits and the losses could be high, and in every case three things were essential for success: sufficient capital to support the business, good information, and meticulous records.

Inclined at first to focus on bookkeeping, which he did with extraordinary intensity, Rockefeller went on to become adept at seeking out new suppliers as well as new customers. He also had a talent for raising capital—"begging," as he called it later—thanks to a strikingly serious, if not downright somber, manner. "Mr. Rockefeller," as he became known early on, would pay back every cent he borrowed; you could tell that by talking with him, looking at him. Tall and broad shouldered, with razor thin lips and narrow, piercing eyes, he was always immaculately groomed and dressed.

By the time Rockefeller had mastered the art of persuading bankers to lend him ever larger amounts of money, he had left Hewitt and Tuttle to go into business for himself, along with half a dozen different partners at various times, whom one by one he shed, because sooner or later he found them less single-mindedly intent on getting ahead than he was. He was on his third such partnership when he began trading in oil, which changed everything.

For as long as anyone could remember, dark, slimy petroleum had been oozing out of the ground in western Pennsylvania, and for almost as long it seemed that it ought to have commercial value, but figuring out how to both collect it in sufficient quantities and turn it into something people might buy were problems by no means easily solved. Nor did John D.

Rockefeller have anything to do with solving them. It was Professor Benjamin Silliman of Yale University who concluded that an excellent illuminating oil could be distilled from petroleum, and "Colonel" Edwin Drake who, in 1859, successfully drilled for oil in Titusville, Pennsylvania.

After that the rush was on, both to draw the raw petroleum out of the ground and to refine it into what became known as kerosene. Initially Rockefeller was involved in neither activity. He simply handled, in his usual way as a commission merchant, sales of crude oil and kerosene, using Cleveland as his base. Situated at the junction of Lake Erie, the Cuyahoga River, and the Ohio Canal, and served by an ever-expanding railway network, the city was ideally located for commercial activities of all kinds, including the oil business. Though Pittsburgh lay closer to the source of the new "black gold," Cleveland's range of transportation choices gave it an even greater edge as a refining center, which added significantly to Rockefeller's trading profits. In 1863 he also did what many people in Cleveland—as well as Pittsburgh and elsewhere—were doing during the huge oil boom of those years: he built his own refinery. Within two years it had become the largest refinery in Cleveland, and, eager as always for control, he had bought out his two remaining partners, who lacked his enthusiasm for pushing the oil business as far as it would go.

A prudent person might well have shared the caution of those banished partners, for prices in the oil industry seemed trapped on a mad, utterly unpredictable roller coaster. In 1864 alone, the price of kerosene gyrated between $4 and $12 a barrel, and the price of crude oil fluctuated just as wildly. Under those conditions, any investment in the industry could only be seen as enormously risky, but Rockefeller was willing to live with the risks. Kerosene had in fact turned out to be an excellent illuminant and far cheaper than any of the available alternatives like wax candles and whale oil, which only the rich could afford. For a few pennies a day millions of people around the world for the first time could hope to stretch out the day, hold back the relentless onset of night. The market was virtually limitless. The trick was how to develop it, and Rockefeller's great triumph in the oil industry would be to solve that puzzle.

In part it turned out to be a matter of lowering costs. For lower costs meant cheaper prices—prices that not only beat the competition but also brought new consumers into the market who at higher prices would have held on to their money. In economists' terms, the demand for kerosene was elastic: lower prices actually increased demand and thus grew the market.

On the production side, Rockefeller was tireless in monitoring costs and taking initiatives like making his own barrels to avoid paying a profit to outside suppliers. In addition, he constantly expanded his production facilities to capture cost-cutting economies of scale. In what would become a major characteristic of his business he also started buying out rival producers. "We needed volume," he declared.[2] The other defining tactic of Rockefeller's operations was slashing transportation costs, chiefly by winning special treatment from the railroads in the form of reduced charges of all kinds, as well as kickbacks and rebates. Yet those benefits came at a cost, for they increasingly alienated the American public, which saw such tactics as not only grossly unfair but also the true source of Rockefeller's great success.

In reality the issues were more complex. At no point did Rockefeller's deals with the railroads—while often secret and certainly collusive—violate the law as it stood then. As often as he and his lawyers made that point, however, they skated past what the public saw as the real issue: Rockefeller paid less than rival shippers for transportation, and at times the railroads even turned over to him a portion of what his competitors paid to ship their goods. As the competitors and the public saw it, this arrangement gave him an unconscionable advantage, one that poisoned completely any claim that might be made for the justness of his success.

On the other hand, all kinds of goods were and are routinely sold, as the phrase goes, "cheaper by the dozen." And in the 1860s and '70s competition among the railroad lines serving Cleveland was getting fiercer all the time, while Rockefeller, for his part, was shipping ever-increasing quantities of oil over those lines. What, then, could have been more logical than for the railroads to try to attract his business by taking his shipments at reduced rates? Also, thanks to the sheer volume of his shipments, he could regularize them, making it possible for the railroads to regularize their own operations, which in turn brought them significant cost savings. As often as not, too, the reduction in rates which Rockefeller received—and which the public found so reprehensible—originated in proposals made *to* him by the railroads.

Even people who understood such arguments, however, were prone to condemning the entire system as deeply wrong and unfair, and they were right. For ultimately Rockefeller used his leverage with railroads both to cut costs *and* to stifle competition by forcing rival refiners lacking such leverage either to go out of business or to sell their firms to him for whatever he chose to pay. This he did time and time again, too.

The most spectacular early example was the infamous "Cleveland Massacre," which occurred in 1872. The prelude to it was the creation of the South Improvement Company (SIC), an enormous conspiratorial effort by the three principal railroads serving Cleveland—the Pennsylvania, the New York Central, and the Erie—plus a small number of refiners led by Rockefeller, to divide up for their own benefit the shipment of oil across the entire northeastern part of the nation. Aimed initially at bringing the petroleum producers in Pennsylvania into line, it failed in that mission because the producers retaliated by stopping the flow of crude oil all but completely. Yet the SIC had other potential uses, as Rockefeller set about teaching his fellow oil refiners in Cleveland.

By then his refinery, in addition to being the city's largest, had morphed from the simple partnerships of its early years into the enterprise more grandly and anonymously named Standard Oil. From the start, too, Standard operated as a joint stock company, with a capitalization that, by 1872, had reached $3.5 million. Most of the shares had been snapped up by a small number of wealthy investors, yet predictably Rockefeller held on to the largest single block of stock himself, and not far behind him was his brother, William, who was one of the company's top executives.

To someone less driven than Rockefeller, all of these initiatives might have seemed poorly timed, coinciding as they did with a severe depression in the oil industry, due primarily to excess refining capacity. Yet he would always believe that bad times offered unique opportunities, which he proceeded to illustrate dramatically when, in 1872, in a single stroke he bought up twenty-two of Cleveland's twenty-six oil refineries. It was a stunning achievement, though in the minds of some people it left an ineradicable stain on Rockefeller's reputation.

The critics, including most of those who sold out to him, would claim that he brutally pressured them through his ties to the SIC: if they did not sell their businesses to him they would be ruined by confiscatory railroad rates. Rockefeller later claimed that he never once mentioned the SIC in his negotiations with the other refiners: instead he offered them a safe haven in times of great peril. "We will take on your burdens," he remembered saying. "We will unite together and build a substantial structure on the basis of cooperation . . . for our mutual protection."[3] To give added weight to such claims, he offered those willing to sell the opportunity to take payment either in cash or in shares of Standard Oil stock and strongly advised them to take stock, which, as it turned out, proved to be an immensely profitable investment.

Still, the sellers hated him—because he had outmaneuvered them, but even more because he invariably paid them less than they believed their businesses were worth. And if the terms were replacement costs plus what accountants refer to as the "goodwill" of a business (its value as a functioning enterprise) beyond a doubt he did underpay them. Yet many of the refineries he bought were ramshackle affairs in poor condition, and few of them, if they were operating at all, were earning a profit. Rockefeller was also planning to close a fair number of the businesses he bought, in order to reduce kerosene production in Cleveland and thus keep prices on an even keel. Nor were there any other potential purchasers in sight, and in addition there was his power, through the SIC, to deliver a death blow to any company that held out.

So in effect the price of the refineries Rockefeller wanted to buy was whatever he said it was and not a penny more, as would so often be true in the years to come. For the events of 1872 in Cleveland inaugurated a sweeping rush of fresh acquisitions by Standard Oil that would end by raising its size and share of the market to stunning proportions. In later battles, however, Rockefeller tended to treat his adversaries more generously than he had in Cleveland, which, after all, better suited his claim that his goals were actually benign—they were meant to help everyone in the oil industry by bringing order to it, thereby rendering secure not only his stake in it but also the investments of those who joined in his efforts.

"The day of individual competition in large affairs is past and gone," he would later declare unabashedly, thereby rejecting completely traditional, devil-take-the-hindmost capitalism in favor of cooperation among businesses.[4] But embracing that novel position publicly was not something he chose to do in 1872. Nor had he yet imagined taking control of the nation's entire refining capacity, or so he would also claim later. "None of us ever dreamed of the magnitude of . . . the later expansion. We did our day's work as we met it, looking forward to what we could see in the distance and keeping well up to our opportunities."[5] True perhaps, but, his stunning victory over his fellow oil refiners in Cleveland, along with his role in organizing the SIC, which his biographer Ron Chernow describes as "an astonishing piece of knavery," did for the first time focus attention on him in the nation's press (including a mention in the *New York Times* misspelling his name). And the terms in which he was described were anything but complimentary.[6] If he had still to become the figure symbolizing everything bad about American business, he was on his way.

His reaction—which for years would remain the same—was to say nothing at all in his own defense. He believed absolutely that he was right and his motives were honorable. That seemed to be enough. Yet his silence only fed the public's deepening belief that he was driven by the darkest of motives, welling up from the hidden recesses of a truly evil mind. And as if to confirm that view, Standard Oil—swelled by its acquisition of refineries in key locations like Pittsburgh, Philadelphia, and New York—would soon control a monopoly of the refining business and transform itself yet again, this time into the Standard Oil "Trust." By then the company had also become the target of a growing number of investigations in the states where it did business, an assault eventually joined by the federal government in Washington.

Yet all the while Rockefeller continued to maintain his outward calm, saying nothing, revealing nothing. A weaker person might have buckled under the strain; he remained steadfast and firm. In part this was the result of his inborn strength. Also buoying him up, however, was the essential goodness he saw revealed in his behavior away from the tensions and pressures of business. If the world condemned the actions it saw as a monument to greed and selfishness, his private life, he believed, was in every way unexceptionable.

As dour and reserved as Rockefeller usually seemed, in the company of those he allowed to penetrate the barrier he constructed around himself he could be warm and charming, even funny. By Gilded Age standards he treated his labor force well, and Standard Oil executives found him a fair if demanding employer, who both delegated responsibility and welcomed suggestions from those who worked for him. In the upper reaches of the company's management, too, he formed a number of lasting friendships, always believing, as he wrote in his autobiography, "that a friendship founded on business . . . was a good deal better than a business founded on friendship."[7]

In personal terms, however, Rockefeller's greatest support came from his family—his mother, but even more his wife, Laura Celestia Spelman, and their four children (a fifth died in infancy). He had met "Cettie" at Central High School, and in every way she was the perfect mate for him—serious, thoughtful, and unusually well educated for the time. But before marriage was even thinkable, he had to establish himself in business. In the meantime, Cettie finished her education and began making her way as a teacher.

The two finally married in 1864, commencing a union both highly sat-isfying and—as important—built around the unshakable religious faith that was so vital to them both. Though raised a Congregationalist, Cettie willingly joined the Erie Street Baptist Mission Church, of which Rocke-feller had been a member since his earliest days in Cleveland, and which together they would make the center not only of their religious devotions but also of their social life. If all this seemed to give their activities a rather narrow focus, there was no sign that either of them minded. "The world is full of *Sham,* Flattery and Deception, and home is a haven of rest and freedom," John wrote Cettie at one point while he was away on business.[8]

The Rockefellers were also dedicated parents. He often took afternoons off to play with his growing brood. He joked with them, balanced plates on his nose to amuse them at dinner, and taught them to ice skate, swim, ride horseback, and bicycle. Three girls and a boy, who was the youngest of them and named after his father but known all his life (though never by his parents) as "Junior," they spent their early years in a house on Eu-clid Avenue, Cleveland's "Millionaire's Row." Locals liked to call it "the most beautiful street in America," but "the Rockefeller place" was rather plain compared with those of most of their neighbors. Certainly there was nothing opulent about it—nothing resembling the ostentatious luxury with which people like the Astors and the Vanderbilts were surrounding themselves—and the same was true of "Forest Hill," the family's summer home. Six miles from the center of the city, it had been built by Rocke-feller and several other investors as a health resort, but when it failed to make money he bought it himself. Ringed by piazzas trimmed with typi-cal, Victorian-style "gingerbread," it was far from lovely, but again it fit the bill by being so thoroughly *un*grand.

Living simply, scorning luxury as both wasteful and immoral (until the age of eight Junior was made to wear his sisters' outgrown dresses), the Rockefellers also led their children in a constant round of religious devotions—daily prayers, church on Sunday followed by hymn singing at home and still more prayers. In addition, they went to great lengths to guard the family's privacy and protect their offspring from danger. For years none of them went to school or played much with other children. Instead, taught by governesses and tutors, they spent most of their days at home. Then, in 1875, the ever-expanding scope of Standard Oil's busi-ness led the family to begin spending winters in New York City. But rather than buying property there they stayed for years in hotels—again a tighter, more controlled environment.

For all its oddities, Rockefeller's family life did help provide him with crucial support in his embattled rise to great wealth. Year by year Standard Oil grew larger, he grew richer, and the public came to like him less, but Cettie continued to stand by him, and for a while at least, the children re-mained blissfully unaware of it all. He had, too, another source of solace—one which would sustain him all his life—and that was giving money away.

The initial recipient of his largesse was the Erie Street Baptist Mission Church. He missed tithing there by a bit during his first year in business but soon went well beyond that mark. By 1881 his charitable giving totaled $61,000, and three years later it reached almost twice that figure. He still strongly favored Baptist churches, missions, and schools, but he also gave a significant amount of money to individuals who simply wrote asking him for help, an activity in which the entire family joined, debating over dinner how to respond to various appeals.

His most interesting philanthropy during those years, however, was what became Spelman Seminary—and later Spelman College—in Atlanta, which was established expressly to educate African-American women. The largest financial commitment Rockefeller had made up to then, it grew out of Cettie's family's passionate commitment to abolition and later to helping the freed slaves remake their lives. Both causes had Rockefeller's full support, though characteristically he refused to attach his name to Spelman. And while he gave generously to it, he insisted that he not be its only backer: others had to be found to add their support to his. He also required that it be soundly managed, yet refused to play any role in its day-to-day operations. All of which would become standard features of his philanthropy in the years to come.

Even with his commitment to Spelman, however, by the 1880s both Rockefeller's wealth and the calls on his generosity continued to grow by leaps and bounds. Swamped with requests for money on all sides—sent now to the man increasingly seen as the richest person alive—he found himself less and less able to cope with such appeals. In the beginning he had truly enjoyed weighing their merits. Now that was out of the question. On one day a single steamer from abroad brought five thousand "begging letters" to his doorstep. The burden on him was immense. "I was up until eleven o'clock last night and the night before on this general character of work, trying to help to devise ways and means" he wrote in 1892.[9]

But he never did find adequate "ways and means" to continue the personal, small-scale charity that had once given him such pleasure. One thinks of Amos Lawrence and his lovingly assembled packages of goods; for John D. Rockefeller the spirit behind such giving, as strongly as he felt it, had to be ignored. Although in some cases he might still lend a hand to a needy soul, beyond that the logistics were simply too complicated.

One obvious solution to the problem was to focus on fewer, larger projects. And since his most ambitious project to date—Spelman College—was in the field of education, it made sense to concentrate new giving there. The result was the University of Chicago, founded under the aegis of the American Baptist Education Society but largely financed—at least at first—by Rockefeller, beginning with a $600,000 gift in 1889.

Over the next three years he contributed an additional $2.16 million to Chicago, and having at first balked at hearing the school described as a "university" (and flatly refusing to have it named after him), he eventually accepted the university label. For that is what Chicago soon became, with its dazzling array of departments, programs, and graduate schools, spreading over the wide swath of land on the south side of the city donated to it by department store tycoon Marshall Field. In letters to Rockefeller, the institution's charismatic president, William Rainey Harper, called it "an educational trust," borrowing a term from the world of business, while proudly boasting: "Already it is talked of in connection with Yale, Harvard, Princeton, Johns Hopkins, the University of Michigan, and Cornell."[10]

Yet Rockefeller had only wanted to create a first-rate Baptist College in the nation's second largest city and grew increasingly annoyed as Harper blithely dashed ahead with his own, much grander vision. Worse still, Harper expected him to continue paying for each new jewel in Chicago's academic crown, claiming "a university that is properly operated always has a deficit."[11] Rockefeller disagreed, and in 1897 he took decisive steps to rein in Harper's extravagance, insisting that he make his plans clear ahead of time and give Rockefeller the opportunity to oppose any new expenditures. For Harper it was a serious blow, but he managed to hang on at Chicago until his death from cancer in 1906. Shortly beforehand Rockefeller had magnanimously written: "I have the greatest satisfaction and pleasure in our united efforts for the university and I am full of hope for its future."[12] Still, there was no gainsaying the fact that he had been burned by his experience as leading benefactor of Chicago. In the future he would be more careful in giving his money away—even to the best of causes.

Meanwhile, in the '90s Rockefeller had also begun having troublesome medical problems—insomnia, depression, and continuing intestinal disorders—apparently as a result of stress. More than once he described himself as approaching "the edge" of a nervous breakdown. As causes he cited both anxiety over philanthropy and, though less often, business worries. Financially Standard Oil was doing well, but the public's anger at it continued to mount, as did the number of governmental investigations targeting it. More than once Rockefeller was obliged to testify at such proceedings, but his answers to the allegations against him—if clear and stated with earnest conviction—persuaded few people, as shown by the enactment of two pieces of legislation directly aimed at the means Standard Oil had used to monopolize the oil industry: the Interstate Commerce Act, which struck at rebates, and, in 1890, the Sherman Anti-Trust Act.

As heavily as these problems weighed on Rockefeller, too, Cettie—who had once taken a keen interest in his business affairs—though still lovingly supportive, was retreating more and more into a private world of religious and family matters. Perhaps it was a reaction to watching her husband become an object of public scorn, even hatred. (Could it be that he was guilty after all?) Or perhaps it was simply advancing age. Rockefeller's daughters were also growing more distant from him, which left Junior as the only member of the family who offered any hope of being able to provide the kind of support he needed. And in time he would do precisely that.

Before then, however, two other people—both outside the family—would have a major impact on Rockefeller's life during these years, though they started from radically different points. One was Frederick T. Gates, who had been trained as a Baptist minister but ended up working for Rockefeller. The other was Ida Tarbell, a talented and intrepid journalist who loathed him.

Blessed with an enormous talent for organization, Gates initially left the Baptist ministry to serve as executive secretary of the American Baptist Educational Society, through which Rockefeller made his early donations to the University of Chicago. Thereafter he guided Rockefeller in his deepening and increasingly rocky commitment to the university, and in the process Rockefeller came to both admire and depend upon him—so much so that he eventually hired Gates to work full-time for him. Though his duties were never strictly defined, his chief area of responsibility was philanthropy. He took over the burden of dealing with the "begging letters," but more important, Rockefeller encouraged him to think broadly about "the difficult business of giving," as he would later call it in his autobiography, and the results proved startling.

In 1905 Gates wrote his employer: "Two courses are open to you. One is that you and your children while living should make final disposition of the great fortune in the form of permanent corporate philanthropies for the good of mankind . . . or at the close of a few lives now in being it must simply pass into the unknown like some other great fortunes, with unmeasured and perhaps sinister possibilities."[13] In short, Gates thought Rockefeller was not giving enough money away, and he was right. In 1902 he had earned $52 million in *income* alone. Such riches were unprecedented, certainly in the United States, and drawing on them he had lavished money on both Spelman College and the University of Chicago. Yet others, with smaller fortunes—like Johns Hopkins and the Lawrences in Boston—had done as much. And before long Rockefeller did start ramping up his giving to the heights Gates urged him to aim at, laying out tens of millions of dollars instead of the occasional gift of several hundred thousand.

Yet in the meantime *McClure's Magazine* had begun publishing Ida Tarbell's devastating series of articles on Standard Oil, and over the next three years she battered without letup on both the company and its founder, adding in 1905—again in *McClure's*—a brilliant two-part analysis entitled "John D. Rockefeller: A Character Study." A year later the complete run of articles came out in book form.

From the start Tarbell was a woman with a mission. Her father had gone down in defeat battling Rockefeller in the Oil Regions of Pennsylvania, and she gave not an inch in her attack on him. Meticulously researched and uniformly well written, her articles also quickly caught the attention of the public in a way that nothing about Rockefeller had done before. To her he was the sum total of all evil, as heartless and cruel as he was ambitious and greedy, which was how many Americans now came to think of him. Even his preference for plain living Tarbell dismissed as nothing more than "parsimony made a virtue," and in the same spirit, Forest Hill, the family's beloved summer home, became "a monument of cheap ugliness."[14]

How much of Tarbell's attack Rockefeller chose to read is anybody's guess. In public he maintained absolute silence about it, consistent with his response to earlier bouts of public criticism. Yet those had been mere pinpricks compared to the gaping wounds Tarbell inflicted on his reputation, and his silence only compounded the problem.

In retrospect, too, exactly how to balance Rockefeller's plummeting public standing with his dramatically increased philanthropic giving is an interesting point to debate. Later he spoke only of "the joys of giving and the duty one owes to one's fellow man."[15] On the other hand, in 1905, just as the final installments in Tarbell's opus were appearing and five months before Gates's cautionary letter to him about making "final disposition" of "the great fortune," the House of Representatives in Washington, D.C., had unanimously passed a resolution calling for an immediate antitrust investigation of Standard Oil. The timing suggests that public opinion and the resulting political considerations were indeed crucial, at least in Gates's mind. Time was running out; Rockefeller had to move quickly. And so he did, as the great outpouring of donations over the next several years made clear.

By then, too—increasingly worn down by illness and anxiety—he had turned what began as a gradual withdrawal from Standard Oil into a full-fledged retirement. In writing of the decision, Gates claimed that business "had ceased to amuse Rockefeller," that "it lacked freshness and variety and had become merely irksome."[16] Regardless of his reasons, thereafter Rockefeller was free to do as he wished, which more than ever meant giving money away.

Or what passed as giving money away, for in truth his philanthropies were more complicated than that simple phrase implies. No matter how good the cause, it had to be conducted according to sound business principles. The very process of giving, too, was organized the same way, with fully spelled out objectives, detailed agreements about how they were to be achieved, and clear-cut lines of authority governing the entire process—all crafted by experts in whatever field the initiative was to take place. There were to be no repeats of what had happened at Chicago. And to help ensure that everything went as it was supposed to, the money was invariably funneled through one of three great philanthropic foundations Rockefeller created: the General Education Board, the Rockefeller Institute for Medical Research, and the largest of them all, the Rockefeller Foundation. "Benevolent Trusts," he called them, and each one functioned much like the central executive committee charged with managing the far-flung corporate enterprises that made up Standard Oil.

Each of them also had its own endowment, consisting for the most part of the tens of thousands of shares of Standard Oil stock that Rockefeller donated to them over the years. In turn, the foundations accepted applications for support, chose which ones to favor, and distributed the funds to the lucky recipients. But those funds came from the *income* earned by the stock. The shares themselves remained with the foundation, and thus under family control, for the trustees of the benevolent trusts consisted almost entirely of family members, with a small admixture of trusted associates, at least in the beginning.

From Rockefeller's standpoint this had obvious importance, since the remainder of his own fortune was also invested in Standard Oil, but the system had other virtues as well. It truly did operate in businesslike ways, and at the same time it lifted from Rockefeller's shoulders the need to be constantly caught up in the details of what was done, though from time to time he did insert his oar, as when, for example, a Baptist group he particularly admired was in danger of having its appeal for funds turned down.

Yet there was one great disappointment associated with the entire arrangement, and that was the failure to win for the Rockefeller Foundation the imprimatur of a federal charter of incorporation. Though its significance would have been largely symbolic, everything possible was done to have the necessary legislation passed by Congress. But it was clear the public wanted no ties linking the nation's government to anything bearing the Rockefeller name, and with most of their representatives likely to vote accordingly, the effort was dropped.

The other notable defeat the Rockefellers had to face in those years was the Supreme Court's decision to accept the government's plan to break Standard Oil into its component parts. There was a chance that had the company's executives cooperated with President Theodore Roosevelt the outcome might have been different, but Standard Oil's usual method of dealing with politicians had long been to bribe them rather than negotiate with them, and in this case there was never a chance that would work. Thus Rockefeller was left to watch the dismantling of what he had spent so many years building. But as painful as the experience was, the results offered at least a measure of consolation. The day of the Supreme Court's decision Rockefeller advised the gentleman he was playing golf with to buy Standard Oil stock, which proved to be good advice. After the breakup of the trust, shares in the individual companies that had composed it rocketed upward in value, as did their dividends, reaching heights well beyond those achieved under Standard's umbrella. Meanwhile, too, even though electric light rapidly was replacing kerosene, the rise of the automobile would soon create an even larger demand for petroleum products, ensuring that Rockefeller would continue to grow richer year by year.

There were other things to be grateful for as well. In the game of golf he found the perfect pastime, and for the rest of his life he remained a passionate golfer, building courses at each of his three homes so he could play throughout the year. He also broke a longtime rule and began talking with members of the press, who were charmed by his wit and wry sense of humor. All the while, too, funds from his foundations were accomplishing extraordinary feats like stamping out hookworm in the American South. And for amusement, as well as further polishing his image, he would soon

begin handing out shiny dimes to everyone in reach—a pastime he credited Amos Lawrence for inspiring.

As part of his campaign to recraft his public image, Rockefeller also let
himself be persuaded to produce an autobiography. Most of what it contained had appeared earlier as a series of articles (like Tarbell's pieces on
Standard Oil) in the *World's Work,* a popular magazine of the time. The
articles, in turn, were based on conversations between Rockefeller and
publisher Frank N. Doubleday, held while the two played golf. The result (generally assumed to have been ghostwritten by Doubleday) had a
beguilingly chatty, relaxed air to it, quite unlike the edgy defensiveness of
Robert Keayne's *Apologia.* Here was the Rockefeller who charmed reporters with his wit and humor, rambling on without a care in the world, by
his own account, "a garrulous old man, [telling] some stories of men and
things which have happened in an active life."[17] Nowhere, of course, in
either the articles or the book was there a word of contrition or regret, let
alone any hint of the all-consuming passion for wealth and power that was
so often assumed to be Rockefeller's chief motivation in life.

Nor did the image of the garrulous old man, happily rambling on and
on, change by one iota Ida Tarbell's mind about Rockefeller. "He is a mastodon of mental machinery. And would you ask a steam plow for pity?
Would you look for scruples in an electric dynamo?" she fumed.[18] And in
one sense, certainly, she was right. Closely read, Rockefeller's book is much
less casual—much more tightly engineered—than it seems at first glance.
In the opening chapter, for example, he combined a story about cutting
down a tree in his family's yard as a young boy (because he thought the
tree spoiled the view) with a description of his love of tree-planting on his
various estates and a discussion of what he saw as the proper relationship
between business and friendship. As disjointed as all this appeared, there
was an overriding point to it. Just as Rockefeller felt that friendships based
on business were to be preferred to businesses based on friendship, in his
landscaping activities he actually made a practice of selling plant material
grown on one of his estates to the other two. In effect, sound business
principles governed everything he did, even his most cherished pleasures.
That was the message of the chapter.

Similarly, if he ran his philanthropies like businesses, he also felt that the best philanthropy of all was a well-run business—one, as he said, "carefully considered with relation to the power of employing people at a remunerative wage, to expand and develop the resources at hand and to give opportunity for progress and healthful labor where it did not exist before."[19] Just as in business, too, competition in philanthropy was to be avoided at all costs. Facilities got unnecessarily duplicated, wealth was needlessly dispersed, and the entire economy suffered as a result. As he said, "It may be urged that the daily vocation of life is one thing and the work of philanthropy quite another. I have no sympathy with this notion."[20]

His autobiography also touched obliquely on one of the most tantalizing issues raised by his life, and that was how he compared with Andrew Carnegie. As the public saw it, for decades the business world had been dominated by those two colossal figures. Both were men of enormous will and energy, both became hugely rich, and both could claim prodigious accomplishments as philanthropists. At one point they clashed over the Mesabi iron ore mines, which Rockefeller owned for a while, but otherwise their relations remained cordial if distant. Their private thoughts were another matter. Among his cronies Carnegie was known to refer to Rockefeller as "Wreckafeller."[21] Rockefeller was more circumspect, yet that did nothing to allay the public perception that the two of them competed constantly. For years Carnegie was known as the world's richest man, but in that respect Rockefeller eventually outpaced him. By 1919, the year Carnegie died, both men had given roughly $300 million away, yet Rockefeller's total continued to grow, netting more than another $200 million before his death. So in the long run Rockefeller won the philanthropic competition in a walk, though in 1907, when *Random Reminiscences* was put together, the full story had yet to emerge. What was clear, however, was that Rockefeller and Carnegie had very different opinions about many things—including both the businesses in which they loomed so large and philanthropy.

While Rockefeller proudly highlighted his respect for his fellow executives as well as the labor force at Standard Oil, Carnegie's record in both regards was abysmal. To keep control of Carnegie Steel he compelled his partners to sign an "iron-clad" agreement, permitting them to sell their shares only back to the company itself and at book value, a price many times lower than the stock's actual worth. And though he wrote articles vigorously supporting workers' rights to a fair share of the wealth they created, when labor troubles broke out at his steel mill in Homestead, Pennsylvania, he hurried off to his castle in Scotland, leaving one of his partners, Henry Clay Frick, to deal with the situation, knowing full well that Frick would treat the strikers mercilessly, as indeed he did, halting the spread of unionism in the steel industry for forty years.

Unlike Rockefeller, too, Carnegie postponed his generosity until late in life, leading skeptics to argue that he turned to philanthropy chiefly as a way of atoning for his company's actions during the Homestead Strike. But before he could begin his atonement—if that is what it was—he had to have the money to give away, which happened only after he managed to sell Carnegie Steel to J. P. Morgan, as the centerpiece of U.S. Steel for $300 million, insisting that he be paid in cash. He then proceeded to give virtually all of it away, and again, unlike Rockefeller, he earmarked most of it for projects he himself chose, the largest number—3,600—being public libraries built in cities and towns across the United States.

There was, too, an even more basic difference between Rockefeller and Carnegie as philanthropists. Carnegie quite literally gave almost his entire fortune away, which Rockefeller never came close to doing, at least in any literal sense. The millions of dollars in stock with which he endowed his foundations remained invested in the businesses from which the money had come—chief among them Standard Oil—and thus continued to be productively employed in the nation's economy. In contrast, Carnegie's libraries, paid for in cash as they were built, took capital out of the business of making steel, ultimately constituting a kind of tax on society at large.

Toward the end of *Random Reminiscences,* writing about philanthropy, Rockefeller referred scornfully to "the man who plans to do all his giving on Sunday."[22] While he nowhere compared that creature to Andrew Carnegie, the similarities are not hard to find. Put off for most of his life and conducted in parochial, highly personal ways, Carnegie's generosity—if dazzling in scale—came at too high a cost to society, or so Rockefeller seemed to feel. Yes, the nation needed both steel mills *and* libraries. The point was to build the libraries with the *income* from the steel business, not the capital that was its lifeblood. As Rockefeller said of the man who planned to do all his giving on Sunday, he was "a poor prop for the institutions of the country."[23]

Yet whatever Rockefeller thought, Carnegie's standing with the public rose steadily during those years. People liked the libraries. They touched lives in direct and palpable ways, particularly the lives of children. Indeed, with his stocky build, white beard, and rosy cheeks, Carnegie made a perfect Santa Claus, opening his pack full of surprises for thousands of communities and their citizens. And as the libraries actually began to appear, bit by bit memories of Homestead faded, until by the time Carnegie died, his image as a great and generous public benefactor was all but set in stone. Rockefeller's reputation would undergo a similar change, but it took longer and was more complex.

Less fortunate in his appearance than Carnegie, late in life he suffered from alopecia, a condition that caused the complete loss of hair over his entire body. As a result, he acquired an eerie, almost spectral look, which persisted even after he started wearing wigs, for by then a mass of wrinkles covered the parchment-thin skin of his face. And that was how, all too often, pictures showed him: a weird, wizened old man, his lips clamped shut in a look of grim determination.

Yet in reality, his final years were less dark than those pictures suggested. Cettie was gone, but he dearly loved golf, as he did giving all those dimes away. And he absolutely doted on Junior, who in every way had lived up to his father's hopes for him. "I just felt like crying like a baby after you went away," Rockefeller wrote, following one of Junior's visits to Florida.[24] There was also, of course, his philanthropy, plus the children and grandchildren he saw at lunch every Sunday when he was in residence at Kykuit, the house overlooking the Hudson River that Junior had persuaded him to build. And the children would grow up to be interesting characters, one of whom, Nelson Rockefeller, even became a serious contender for the presidency of the United States and did eventually become vice president. But the time Rockefeller spent at Kykuit—enmeshed as it was in the rigidly formal routines Junior had devised for the place—never seemed quite to his liking. In later years he stopped traveling north altogether and remained in the simpler, more relaxed surroundings at his house in Ormond Beach, Florida.

Though Rockefeller had always hoped he would live to be a hundred, it was not to be. He died in Florida in 1937, three years short of his goal.

Despite the fact, too, that the place at Ormond Beach had been his favorite home, he was not to be buried there. Instead his body traveled by train to Kykuit, where, within its high stone walls, as hymns played softly on the organ in the music room, family members welcomed a small circle of friends to a simple memorial service. Yet for all the solemnity of occasion, Kykuit would be only a temporary stopping place. The next day the casket was again loaded on a private railroad car and sent to Cleveland, where in Lake View Cemetery, between the graves of his wife and mother, John Davison Rockefeller was finally laid to rest in a bombproof enclosure, covered with thick slabs of granite to prevent vandalism.

Predictably, after his death oceans of ink chronicled his life in dozens of different versions, some complimentary, some not. Whether it was Tarbell's "mastodon of mental machinery" you saw, or the stunningly generous philanthropist, there was more than enough evidence to support either view, yet in truth no single story line could ever do justice to Rockefeller's life. In building his fortune he had pushed to the limit, and then some, the accepted business practices of his day. As a philanthropist he had chosen bold new strategies for giving away wealth while simultaneously preserving his hold on it—and, it should be noted, the power that went with it. Hated by some, extravagantly admired by others, he went to his grave the enigma he had always been.

Like the Lawrence brothers, he had both faced and mastered—though far more spectacularly—the challenges of blending economic change with a palpably demonstrated concern for other human beings. And if the two brothers had come to see that challenge in quite different ways, Rockefeller transcended the gulf that separated them. He liked risk no better than Amos Lawrence, but unlike Lawrence he learned to live with it. Nor did he ever seek, as Abbott Lawrence did, power in the political arena to add to his wealth. He was content to rest his reputation on what he accomplished in business and philanthropy. He also felt none of Robert Keayne's need to credit God for his success. As he said, "The only thing which is of lasting benefit to a man is that which he does for himself."[25]

As if to mark that belief, beside his grave in Lake View Cemetery would eventually be erected a great stone obelisk—a single shaft thrusting upward seventy feet—the tallest structure in the cemetery. Though it was designed by sculptor Joseph Carabelli, its proportions and profile against the sky appear to match exactly those of the Washington Monument in Washington, D.C. Presumably this was no accident, yet the message the similarity was meant to convey was left to the viewer to decide. Certainly in most obvious respects there was nothing especially Washingtonian about John D. Rockefeller. Yet both men played dominant roles in the events of their day; both were commanding figures who lived in the full glare of public notice, and saw their lives become the stuff of legend long before they died. Behind the shared palimpsest of fame, too, lay another similarity. For just as Washington had ended by transforming himself into the person his fellow Americans most wanted him to be, so ultimately did Rockefeller.

Was he in fact a good and generous man? Even if the answer remained unclear, certainly by the end of his life he had come to act like one, as all the hundreds upon hundreds of worthy projects supported by his fortune testified. And while his motives may have remained suspect, on the face of it the results could at least be taken as convincing proof of the power of American public opinion to tame even the worst demons of high capitalism. From those who had unfairly seized great riches an irate populace looked for much in return, and Rockefeller's response was nothing if not lavish.

Thus had he managed to satisfy—as before him Robert Keayne, George Washington, and the Lawrence brothers also had—the earnest hope of so many of his fellow citizens: that wealth and democracy could in fact be fused. Rich as Rockefeller, or rich as We the People? Was there a difference? To this day visitors still bring shiny dimes to lay on the steps leading to that tall stone obelisk in Lake View Cemetery in Cleveland.

LEGACIES

6

HEIRS

At its height, John D. Rockefeller senior's fortune is sometimes said to have reached $300 billion in modern dollars, but a more reliable figure (adjusted for the growth of domestic product) is $192 billion, which in 1918 represented 1.6 percent of the value of the nation's entire economy and makes him—still—the richest American of all time. In a nutshell this is the challenge Rockefeller would forever pose to any notion of the easy compatibility between great wealth and democracy. Yet by the time he died much of his money had been given away. Or so it appeared. The reality was that, thanks to the way he had structured his generosity, his fortune would survive largely intact for another generation, as did the power that went with it. For family members continued to exercise significant, if diminishing, control over his philanthropic foundations, and the chief items in their endowments remained the shares of oil corporation stocks he had given them, along with the voting rights belonging to those shares.

Meanwhile, too, just as Rockefeller himself had done, his son managed to donate over half a billion dollars to philanthropic projects during his lifetime, using for the most part the income from the various stocks and bonds Rockefeller had given him—an income which in 1928 alone reached $50 million. In addition, "Junior" managed to transfer $102 million to his wife and children, with the expectation that they would perpetuate the family tradition of meeting "the responsibilities inherent in the possession of wealth." And so they did, though inevitably after his lifetime the great fortune—as a consolidation of wealth in individual hands—did begin to shrink, as did the generosity associated with it.

But even allowing for its diminishing scale, tracing the Rockefellers' giving through the years offers an unusually revealing view of how the philanthropy of the very rich has changed and developed over time. And one fact which emerges as a result is that it could and did remain very much a work in progress, reaching out constantly in new directions. At times, too, it generated more than a little controversy within the Rockefeller family, besides echoing in a variety of ways the ambiguity of Rockefeller senior's own achievements in life, including his complex relationship with his often very anxious son and namesake.

Philanthropy as Autobiography

John D. Rockefeller, Jr., would always idolize his father, who was in fact a loving and supportive parent. Yet the man who could play happily with his children for hours on end also—in attempting to shield them from whatever influences outside the family he could—created problems for them that would last a lifetime. Growing up without schoolmates or friends could not have been easy. Nor could spending the winter months shut up in hotel rooms have been much fun. Added to those problems, too, the Rockefeller children had to contend with their parents' strict Baptist moral code, which permitted no compromises, no departures for the one true way.

As a consequence of all this—plus, no doubt, the fact that he was both the youngest child and the only son in the family—"Junior" was painfully shy and ill at ease as a boy. Twice before the age of eighteen he suffered from severe "nervous" attacks, and in both cases the cure turned out to be spending the winter at "dear old Forest Hill" with only his mother for company. But happily, the clouds of gloom and isolation did begin to lift once he went off to Brown University, from which he graduated in 1896. He was elected to Phi Beta Kappa, held several class offices, and, more important, encountered a totally different social world from the one he knew at home. He made friends, flirted with girls, regularly attended dances, and even gave one himself, much to the dismay of his parents, whose religious views held dancing to be thoroughly sinful.

Then after graduation came a summer abroad, following which he took a job in his father's office at 26 Broadway, which must have seemed like a fine opportunity. But he soon discovered that success in college did not translate all that easily into success in the real world—or at least in his father's version of it. For he was given no specific job to do, had no clear-cut duties. And with too much time on his hands he began speculating in the stock market and eventually lost more than $1 million—funds that he did not have, but which his father graciously offered to give him.

In a more useful development, his presence in the office brought him in contact with Frederick Gates, who became his mentor in family matters in general and in philanthropy in particular. In turn, Gates could count on Junior's support when he needed it. "Mr. Gates's letter to you seems to me a powerful and unanswerable argument," he wrote his father after Gates's dramatic warning about the consequences of failing to disperse Rockefeller's immense fortune. "I very much hope it may seem wise to carry out this plan."[1]

By then, too, Junior had acquired a second mentor—whose influence would be even greater than Gates's—in the person of Abby Aldrich, one of the belles he had flirted with at Brown, who became his wife in 1902. The daughter of Senator Nelson Aldrich, a leading figure in the Republican Party, she had led a much less sheltered life than Junior, and had sophisticated tastes as well as a warm, outgoing manner. She also had a mind of her own. When Junior asked her soon after their marriage to start keeping a daily record of her expenditures as he had been made to do by his father, she answered flatly, "I won't!"[2] And that was that. From the start, too, Abby had firm ideas about the kinds of philanthropic activities her husband—as the principal heir of his spectacularly rich father—should pursue.

Up to then Junior's principal charity had been teaching a Bible study class at the Fifth Avenue Baptist Church, an activity not universally applauded. "With his hereditary grip on the nation's pocketbook, his talks on spiritual matters are a tax on piety," scoffed the *Pittsburgh Press*.[3] Abby's views were gentler but just as emphatic. Writing her husband ("Instead of speaking of it because I am afraid it may cause you some pain"), she urged him to give up the Bible class, arguing that his time and energy could be, as she said, "better spent on philanthropic work along broader lines"—on what she called "really big things."[4]

Yet just as Abby was beginning to give Junior the self-confidence he so badly needed, Ida Tarbell's assault on Standard Oil brought it all to a grinding halt. For Junior, her articles proved utterly devastating, and by 1904 he had reached the point where a trip abroad seemed essential to preserving whatever remained of his emotional balance. He returned in less than a year yet was still unable to handle even his personal correspondence.

But his spirits did receive one heartening boost when his father put him in charge of building a house on land he owned overlooking the Hudson River. The project had been Abby and Junior's idea in the first place and was, after all, a way of occupying his time. Coincidentally, too, as a young man, Rockefeller himself had supervised the building of a house in Cleveland for his parents. With typical efficiency he got the job done on time and on budget—a feat that was not to be repeated at Kykuit (Dutch for "lookout"), as the new house on the Hudson would be called. On the contrary, by the time the place was finished it was years behind schedule and vastly more expensive than anyone had anticipated. All of which could have been a disaster for Junior, but in fact it turned out otherwise.

On one level the problems plaguing Kykuit's building amounted to a classic case of too many cooks. Having decided to build, Rockefeller worked with the architectural firm of Delano and Aldrich—already on its way to becoming the premier creator of lavish American country houses—to produce a design the key component of which was a floor plan he himself had devised. But once Junior was put in charge he hired two new architects, Ogden Codman to do the interiors and William Welles Bosworth to design the gardens. For the fact was that, without forewarning or fanfare, he had decided to do everything in his power to alter the house his father had planned. And unlike Delano and Aldrich, Codman and Bosworth would be reporting directly to him.

All Rockefeller had wanted was a simple country place to use as an escape from the pressures of city life. Junior and Abby, on the other hand, had set their hearts on a decidedly grander house, done in classical style—the sort of place rich Americans were increasingly building during those years to display both their wealth and the freshly minted social status it brought. To be sure, there were limits to how far Junior would go down that road. He had no intention of imitating the Vanderbilts' glitteringly opulent "palaces" at Newport. But he did want something a good deal more imposing than his father had in mind. In the end, too, he won.

Four stories high, clad in stone, with elegant classical details everywhere—columns, vaulted ceilings, a music room with mirrored doors, a pediment over the main entrance filled with statues of ancient deities—the new house signaled unmistakably the Rockefellers' wealth, along with an appreciation of cultural traditions stretching back in time for centuries.

Every bit of it, too, had been accomplished by Junior in the face of endless complaints from his father.

The gardens were a particular bone of contention. Rockefeller's original budget for them had been $30,000. Their final cost was forty-five times that amount—a mind-boggling $1,300,000. Yet the elaborate terraces stepping down from the hilltop where the house stood, the artful landscaping that both made the most of the view of the river and hid the village of North Tarrytown next to it, the rose garden, the Japanese garden, the orangerie for overwintering tender citrus trees, and the graceful stone teahouse with its Pompeian style furniture all came at a price and took quantities of time to create.

But despite Rockefeller's constant complaints, he continued to pay the bills and never did what he might have done—simply call a halt to work on the gardens. Nor did he blame Junior for what was happening. It was all Welles Bosworth's fault. "His manner is pleasant; his method is luxurious," and, "I should pity the man of moderate means who fell into his hands."[5] Still, there were no fits of towering rage, just a running litany of sarcastic remarks. In fact, with his jaunty banter unaccompanied by anything harsher, Rockefeller almost seemed to be making a game of the whole affair. And in a sense he may well have been doing just that, though with a serious purpose in mind.

Because the more he pushed his son, the more Junior pushed back, in a demonstration of unflinching will that would have done credit to his father in the heyday of his domination of the oil industry. Here was a performance Rockefeller could both understand and admire. Even if the result was a house he would never quite like or be comfortable in, Junior had succeeded in creating something of his own—not just another piece of the vast universe controlled by his father—and in the process had become, truly and completely, John D. Rockefeller's heir.

During those years, too, he was showing his independence in other ways. In 1910, in what he later described as "one of the most important decisions of my life," he resigned as both a vice president and a board member of Standard Oil, chiefly in response to the corporation's under-the-table efforts to influence politicians. Rockefeller's only remark on hearing the news was, "John, I want you to do what you think is right."[6] And more notable still was Junior's response to the notorious Ludlow Massacre, involving a strike at a Colorado coal mining company in which the Rockefellers held a controlling interest.

At issue was the right of the miners to organize and bargain collectively with management, which had led to a relentlessly escalating conflict resulting finally in the deaths of several strikers as well as two women and eleven children. In the aftermath Junior decided, despite his father's strong objections, to go to Colorado to meet with the miners. And once he did, an agreement was reached—which Rockefeller senior liked even less— meeting the miners' demands for unionization and collective bargaining (albeit in a company union). When she heard the news Abby wrote Junior, "It all makes me very happy and hopeful. I told the children this afternoon what a fine, brave thing their father was doing."[7] She did not spell out what she meant by bravery in this case, but she did not need to.

Junior's decision to sever his ties to Standard Oil and his actions in Colorado made it abundantly clear that he had no intention of pursuing a career in business. Instead, with his father's full blessing, he proposed to devote his energies entirely to philanthropy. A solid foundation already existed there, and the work promised to be both interesting and important, as in fact it turned out to be. Broadly speaking, he divided his efforts between overseeing the philanthropic organizations his father's wealth had created and developing new projects of his own.

Thus he became the first president of the largest of all the "benevolent trusts," the Rockefeller Foundation, and after being elected chair of its board of trustees in 1917 served for twenty-three years in that capacity, thereby definitively underlining the closeness of the ties between the Foundation and the Rockefellers. But the arrangement was also not without problems, for it had the potential to raise anew the suspicions of manipulative self-interest on the Rockefellers' part that had fueled Congress's refusal to grant the Foundation a national charter of incorporation—as did a number of other decisions made by the Rockefellers. In conveying his final grant of funds to it, Rockefeller senior had stipulated that up to $2 million of the Foundation's annual income should be set aside for, as he put it, "such specific objects as I may from time to time direct."[8]

To thus impose his will on the Foundation's trustees and staff may not have violated the law, but it was certainly a public relations mistake. And the same was true of a decision Junior made to set up within the Foundation a program in industrial relations, headed by Mackenzie King, who had coached him in handling the Ludlow Massacre (and who later became prime minister of Canada). With the Massacre still fresh in people's minds it was easy to assume that the plan was aimed primarily at whitewashing the Rockefellers' connection with the tragedy. In truth the evidence suggests otherwise, though critical comments made at the time about the initiative did teach Junior how important it was for the Foundation to refrain from involving itself in anything that touched too closely on family concerns.

Soon afterward, too, he persuaded his father to give up all control over the use of any part of the Foundation's funds. And at the same time he was making a concerted effort to bring new talent to the board of trustees, leavening what up to then had been a carefully blended mix of family members, longtime friends, and trusted advisers. For the Foundation truly to work "for the general good," it had to reflect that fact in every way possible, as did the other three family foundations—the Rockefeller Institute for Medical Research, the General Education Board, and, a new addition to the list, the Laura Spelman Rockefeller Memorial, named for Rockefeller senior's wife—in all of which Junior would be actively involved.

There was, too, an urgent need to find talented, qualified people capable of managing the work of the foundations on a day-to-day basis. And as his father had done at Standard Oil, Junior worked to bring together groups of individuals whose judgment he trusted and gave them the authority to decide what needed doing and to get it done. While this pertained to every organizational level, the crucial decisions, obviously, were those involving the positions at the top. And the single most important choice Junior made in that regard was selecting Raymond Fosdick to replace Gates as his chief adviser in all matters relating to philanthropy.

Not only was Gates aging, but he had parted company with Junior over the Ludlow strike. Junior also hoped to move forward in the new century with a fresh vision, which Fosdick provided. Gates had risen through the Baptist ministry; Fosdick was a lawyer by training and had held a number of public service posts at home, as well as abroad, where he became a staunch advocate of the League of Nations. On several occasions Junior offered him a full-time position on his staff, but while he took part in the management of all the major Rockefeller philanthropies, Fosdick preferred to maintain his own law practice. A practical idealist, he had a great capacity for hard work, plus notable skills as an institution builder.

During his many years of service Fosdick would prove especially valuable in giving greater global reach to the activities of the family foundations, and one area where that proved especially important was public health. Thirty years earlier the Rockefellers had launched a campaign to radically alter American medical practice by focusing on disease and the treatment of it, based on systematic research. One early result of that effort was the discovery of a way to prevent the spread of hookworm disease in the American South. Subsequently the center of such work shifted to the Rockefeller Institute for Medical Research—later renamed Rockefeller University—but its broader geographical dimensions were overseen by the International Health Division of the Rockefeller Foundation, which scored its greatest single victory in a twenty-five-year struggle to develop a vaccine against yellow fever, ultimately saving millions of lives around the world.

Often the men and women who worked on such projects—including Fosdick—held views more liberal than Junior's, but his primary goal was to get the job done. "The only way you can help me," he said in his first interview with Fosdick, "is to tell me at all times exactly what you think."[9] If the result involved ideas new and unfamiliar to him, then so be it as long as they seemed to have a chance of succeeding. He also continued to loosen his control over the foundations, as evidenced by the growing number of times he found himself outvoted by his fellow trustees, with no great concern on his part.

Yet ultimately it was not from the foundations but from finding on his own new ways of giving that Junior derived his greatest satisfaction. Nor were his objectives always as neatly framed as his father had implied they should be when he equated well run philanthropies and successfully managed business enterprises. As a result of what he learned while serving as foreman of a grand jury convened to investigate the "white slave traffic" in New York City, for example, he established the Bureau of Social Hygiene to continue to combat prostitution—as well as venereal disease and later juvenile delinquency and drug addiction—which became a model for similar efforts in many other cities. An earnest desire to break down barriers among existing Protestant faiths—despite his parents' unwavering attachment to the Baptist Church—led him to support organizations like the Interchurch World Movement, the Institute of Social and Religious Research, the World Council of Churches, plus Christian missionary work in Asia and elsewhere, and also the building of Riverside Church in New York City as a nondenominational place of worship. A similar flexibility was evident in his support of and later outspoken opposition to the Eighteenth Amendment banning the sale of alcoholic beverages in the United States.

In a different vein altogether was his passion for preserving sites of natural beauty, which resulted in the donation of millions of dollars toward the creation of places like Acadia National Park on Maine's Mount Desert Island, Grand Teton National Park, the Jackson Hole National Monument, the Redwood Forest in California, the Great Smoky Mountain National Park, plus the Palisades Interstate Park and Fort Tryon Park, both along the Hudson River.

And in stark contrast to his father's interests—but doubtless with a strong push from Abby—Junior avidly acquired works of art, most of which eventually ended up in museums. His initial effort in that regard was collecting Ch'ing Dynasty Chinese porcelains, the largest single addition to which came in 1915 when he purchased a good part of a collection that had previously belonged to J. P. Morgan. The cost was high, and lacking the necessary funds he asked his father for a loan, only to have his request refused. "I feel afraid of it," was the parental response, to which Junior replied: "I have never squandered money on horses, yachts, automobiles or other foolish extravagances. A fondness for these porcelains is my only hobby . . . [which] while a costly one, is quiet and unostentatious and not sensational."[10] Moved, if still not entirely convinced, Rockefeller went ahead and provided his son with the money he asked for—and as a gift, not a loan.

Eventually Rockefeller's collection of Chinese porcelain became one of the finest in the world. But his greatest triumph as a collector came in the field of medieval art, where a long-standing interest in works of the period led him to underwrite the creation of the Cloisters Museum in Manhattan's Fort Tryon Park. To it he donated a wealth of paintings, sculptures, and architectural fragments, including parts of five separate cloisters that were incorporated in the fabric of the building itself. Of the museum's many treasures, however, none was more appealing than the bewitchingly beautiful unicorn tapestries, which Junior originally acquired for his own house but then reluctantly sent on to grace a room especially built for them at the Cloisters.

In asking his father for funds to acquire the Morgan porcelains Junior had used the word "educative."[11] In sharing his medieval treasures with visitors to the Cloisters he demonstrated how his private pleasures could be used for broader public purposes. There were to be other such projects too, though unlike the Cloisters most of them would involve neither collecting art, nor building structures for its display, but rather the restoration of existing sites and buildings. And among all the hundreds of philanthropic endeavors Junior supported these would become his favorites. The temples of ancient Egypt, the Agora in Athens, the Forbidden City in Peking, Chartres Cathedral, the Palace of Versailles, Reims Cathedral, and Philipse Manor and Washington Irving's Sunnyside in the Hudson River Valley: one by one they attracted his intense—indeed his passionate—attention. In general, too, the work was based on detailed archeological research, which he also supported through contributions aimed at expanding knowledge in the field.

But the project of this sort closest of all to his heart was Williamsburg, the colonial capital of Virginia. Thanks to his efforts, the entire center of Williamsburg was completely remade, and with a clear goal in mind. "I wasn't trying to recreate a lovely city nor was I interested in a collection of old houses. I was trying to recreate Williamsburg as it stood in the eighteenth century," Junior remarked at one point.[12] Yet if it took only a handful of words to state that goal, actually bringing it to life proved to be a task of Herculean proportions. In his biography of Junior, Raymond Fosdick stated that, by 1956, 720 buildings in Williamsburg's center had been moved or torn down; 82 eighteenth-century buildings had been restored; 404 buildings had been reconstructed on their original sites, and 83 acres of gardens and green spaces had been re-created, at a cost, with everything else involved, of over $60 million. Through the years the family foundations would give away far more than that, but to this day Colonial Williamsburg—as it came to be called—remains the costliest single philanthropic project ever funded by Rockefeller money.

Junior did not come to the work in Williamsburg in a single great rush, however. It happened in a series of stages, beginning with the deft and tireless salesmanship of Dr. William A. R. Goodwin, who in 1903 had been appointed rector of Burton Parish Church, the town's oldest surviving place of worship. Though he left soon afterward, in 1923 Goodwin returned as a member of the faculty of William and Mary College. And having earlier worked to restore Burton Church, he took on a number of similar projects, which in time played midwife to a gradually evolving notion of restoring large parts of the town to the glory of its eighteenth-century past. The great problem was money. Unable even to pay for proper plans of what he hoped to accomplish, Goodwin was forced to go, hat in hand, to everyone he could think of who might be willing to help, including John D. Rockefeller, Jr., who at first turned him down flat.

But Goodwin persisted, dangling the bait in ever changing guises, which in time did bring Junior down for a visit, and then another, and finally produced a commitment to underwrite a preliminary set of drawings and plans showing what a restored Duke of Gloucester Street—Williamsburg's impressively wide main thoroughfare—might look like. It was those drawings that clinched the deal; the moment he saw them Rockefeller was hooked.

Here was an entire world, a storied, documented, verifiable piece of history that could be brought to life in three dimensions and historically appropriate colors. Today we might call it a theme park, implicitly acknowledging the large role that modern choices inevitably play in such cases. But for Junior what he achieved at Williamsburg was purely and simply the truth. In embracing it, too, he did what he generally refused on principle to do when giving money away: he acted alone, without others joining him. In time he even chose to live in Williamsburg for two months every year—one in the spring and the other in autumn—at Bassett Hall, a carefully restored, if also judiciously enlarged, eighteenth-century house, which in addition to period furniture contained works of American folk art, which Abby had begun collecting and which eventually included enough pieces to fill an entire museum of their own in Williamsburg.

From Bassett Hall Junior and Abby would walk to the movies at night, peeking in the windows of the houses as they went along to see how the residents were faring in this extraordinary return to another age. Then there were the crowds of tourists to watch as they sampled the wonders of the place: the Governor's Palace, with its period antiques, and the handsome Capitol building, where America's first legislative assembly met—both rebuilt from the ground up on their original sites. From there one could go on to Raleigh Tavern, heavily restored to convey a sense of how politics and socializing mingled in the government of colonial Virginia. For children, too, there was the fun of being shown through those places by gracious guides in period dress, plus seeing red-coated soldiers drilling in front of the Powder Magazine and the jail. In the evening families could share meals in buildings looking much like Raleigh Tavern, also with servers in period dress. And for those who wished, there was a large, tastefully arranged store, with reproductions of the furniture, fabrics, and wallpaper on view in the buildings they had seen, thanks to all that Rockefeller money.

Behind it all, too, lay a lot of carefully done research—countless property deeds and estate inventories pored over; plus newspapers and files of private correspondence read and reread. The earth was also painstakingly explored for evidence of early building activity as well as artifacts illustrating people's daily lives—how they supported themselves, what they ate, what they wore. Yet along with all that research there was also some significant editing that gave a definite character to the final result. As the public saw them, the Duke of Gloucester Street and the lanes leading off it were all pristinely swept and the lawns next to them neatly trimmed. There was no mess anywhere, no piles of rubbish, no pigs or chickens wandering about, no dung heaps with their attendant flies and stink, just pretty houses with well-kept gardens, interspersed with grand public buildings, each made of row upon row of rose-colored brick flawlessly laid in Flemish bond. And more striking still, there seemed to be no evidence of slavery at all, no black "interpreters" (as the guides were called), no buildings identified as slave quarters. Yet with all such items airbrushed out of the picture, the world Rockefeller re-created at Colonial Williamsburg was at best a flawed rendering of reality.

In time critics would note with increasing frequency the omissions at Williamsburg—the artful attempt to sanitize the past, to clean it up for public consumption. And efforts were made to address the problem. As for why it had occurred in the first place, the obvious and no doubt largely correct explanation was that Williamsburg's planners, to augment the educational aspects of the enterprise, had hoped to create a pleasant experience for those who came and incidentally paid a not-insignificant amount of money to sample the delights prepared for them. And things like bad smells, evidence of fairly low levels of public and private sanitation and cleanliness, and, yes, being confronted with the vital role slavery played in life in colonial Virginia probably would have made for some less than appealing moments.

Ultimately, too, Junior was less interested in portraying everyday life in Williamsburg than he was in showcasing the political system centered there—including iconic figures like George Washington, Patrick Henry, Thomas Jefferson, and George Mason and how they came to occupy the positions of power they did. And in general the research showed that those iconic figures, as well as most other members of Virginia's political establishment, came overwhelmingly from the colony's upper class. They were independent gentlemen of means, and the way they exercised power directly reflected that fact. Simply put, at the heart of it all was rule by a highly self-conscious elite.

And interestingly enough, comparable groups can be found at every one of the sites Junior became involved in restoring: in the Athenian Agora, the city's prosperous civic-minded merchants; in France's cathedrals and monasteries, the educated priests and monks who preserved the knowledge of the past that flowered anew during the Renaissance; at Versailles, the courtiers who gave shape to the early modern era's greatest nation-state; and even in the scenes of Ming Dynasty court life depicted on the Chinese porcelains Junior so treasured. In every case the pattern was the same: individuals of established position who stepped forward responsibly and unselfishly to serve, to improve, to benefit not only themselves but the greater good as they saw it. Also, in addition to their public spiritedness, many of them took an active interest in art and architecture, the results of which became yet another legacy they passed on.

Considered together, Junior's campaigns to reconstruct the material settings of bygone historic eras are indeed impressive. And his choice of the particular points he wanted to emphasize in the process do not necessarily lessen the worth of what he achieved. But it is hard not to notice how selective the entire effort was, as well as how much his own life was mirrored in the blending of privilege and power at the heart of his restorations. To make that particular leap himself would have struck him as inexcusably vain, yet who can say where his inner thoughts wandered?

There were other elements of his life that could not be parsed so easily, however. For one thing, his taste in art and architecture was not, in the end, shared by the person he cared most about. For in her aesthetic interests Abby came to move in directions that to him seemed the very antithesis of everything he most valued. She was profoundly moved by modern art and would become one of the founders and leading supporters of the Museum of Modern Art in New York City. Her personal collection remained much smaller than she would have liked, chiefly because Junior had no interest in owning the art she found so exciting, considering it both brutal and ugly. "I am interested in beauty," he commented at one point. Yet all he found in modern art was "a desire for self-expression, as if the artist were saying, 'I'm free, bound by no forms, and art is what flows out of me.'"[13] Here, in fact, was the very antithesis of all Rockefeller admired about the lives he memorialized at places like Williamsburg. But ironically, as little as he liked modern art, he would become the driving force behind the creation of one of the great monuments of architectural modernism in America, which—irony upon irony—would even bear the family name: Rockefeller Center.

Unlike most of Junior's carefully planned ventures, Rockefeller Center came into being almost by accident. As an act of civic duty he had underwritten an agreement enabling the Metropolitan Opera to lease from Columbia University a large tract of land fronting on Fifth Avenue in New York, which was to be developed around a new home for the Opera. Then almost immediately afterward came the Great Crash of 1929, which negated the Opera's plans and left Junior facing $3.3-million annual rent payments to Columbia backed by only $300,000 in current rental income from the property. The choice he faced was either, as he wrote later, "to abandon the entire development" or to persist with it in "the definite knowledge that I myself would have to build and finance it alone."[14] He chose the latter course, which took almost an entire decade to complete.

Architecturally the results—a group of six towers, each of a different height, thrusting upward with no ornament above the ground floor except the exterior expression of their inner structure in windows and taut masonry surfaces—were at first roundly criticized. "Utility sans beauty," and "revolting, dull and dreary," declared the *Herald Tribune*.[15] But in time opinions changed. As *Fortune* magazine put it in 1936, "Sophisticates who had cried out with the esthetes against the Center suddenly found themselves developing an affection for . . . [its] odd mixture of massiveness and knife-blade thinness."[16]

Thus was born a great New York City landmark and what eventually became one of the key components of the Rockefeller family fortune. For if it began with an act of philanthropy, the assumption always was that the development would make money, as indeed it did by leasing to others office space in those same soaring towers. And in addition to what it did for the city—and the Rockefellers—it brought jobs to an estimated 225,000 people during the depths of the Depression.

But there were also darker moments in Rockefeller Center's creation. One of the best-known artists to be employed on the project was Mexico's Diego Rivera, who was commissioned to create a mural for the lobby of the RCA building. The result—celebrating labor in a pictorial representation of Rivera's Marxist beliefs—led to a protracted argument in which the major sticking point became the inclusion of a representation of Lenin's head in the mural. When asked to remove it, Rivera refused. On the contrary, he said, he would rather see the mural destroyed than "defaced" in this way—and so it was, predictably producing a storm of outraged protest that did the Rockefellers scant good.

Yet in retrospect a more interesting topic is the larger notion that lay behind "Rock Center," as family came to call it. In early versions of the plan the principal tenant of the building where Rivera's mural made its all too brief appearance was Radio Corporation of America. But like the Opera, RCA ran into financial difficulties, and while it did not withdraw from the project it did drastically cut back on the space it planned to occupy. That circumstance in turn led to a reevaluation of the name of the project, which was to have been "Radio City." At first, when "Rockefeller Center" was proposed as an alternative, Junior objected strenuously because he did not want "the family name plastered on a real estate development."[17] Eventually he was persuaded to change his mind, however, which took care of the "Rockefeller" part of the name. But equally interesting is the other half of it—the "Center" idea as a concept, and what it was meant to convey.

The issue seems doubly significant because in the years ahead the Rockefellers would be leading players in the creation of several other "centers" in New York City. At the suggestion of his son Nelson, Junior purchased and donated to the United Nations the site on the East River where its headquarters were built. In the 1950s and '60s, another son, John D. Rockefeller III, became one of the principal movers behind the building of Lincoln Center. And later yet another Rockefeller son, David, would play a similar role in establishing the World Trade Center. In the end, too, all this centering would change not only the physical layout of New York, but also, in crucial ways, the lines of purpose and power that determined both how things were done in the city and the ways in which it was perceived by the world at large.

For the Rockefellers, moreover, one suspects that family history also played a vital role. When they moved to New York in the 1870s it was a rough-and-tumble place driven chiefly by the same force that had brought them there: greed. To continue to grow, Standard Oil needed enormous infusions of capital that could only come from Wall Street. At the same time the Rockefellers came, too, the rich were carving out an exclusive social preserve for themselves in the upper reaches of the grid adjacent to Central Park. But was that all New York was to be—a place to grab gobs of money and spend it on vulgar displays of unbridled ostentation? More than most people, the Rockefellers had reason to hope not. For if New York was to remain the capital of all greed, where did that leave its wealthiest family?

What was needed was a sweeping remapping—both literally and figuratively—of the city's character and energies, a remapping that both softened and counterbalanced the enormous sway of Wall Street and the Fifth Avenue mansions of the Astors and the Vanderbilts. No one could do it alone, but no one had a greater need or more resources to bring to the effort than the Rockefellers. Hence the centers, each of which offered a fresh and appealing way of conceiving of the city: at Rockefeller Center, as the hub of modern communications and popular entertainment; at the UN, as the center of international diplomacy and the pursuit of world peace; at Lincoln Center, as the home of some of America's premier institutions in the performing arts; at the World Trade Center, as the crossroads of global commerce and economic expansion. And to list these is, in fact, to encompass a significant part of what continues to give New York its uniqueness. It also speaks powerfully of the depth and restless drive of the city's protean ambitions during "the American Century"—or as the family's historians have labeled it in a book of the same name, "The Rockefeller Century," which is clearly an overstatement, but then again not totally off the mark.[18]

By the end of 1933 Junior had moved the family office from 26 Broadway to Rockefeller Center and, on November 1, 1939, he personally drove home the final spike in the huge project. Meanwhile, the previous decade had been a period of high anxiety for him. Among other things he had had to loan the Center $75 million of his private funds. In later years that loan would play an important role in the family's philanthropic giving, but at the time it served to underline just how large a portion of the Rockefeller fortune had been risked in developing the Center, which explained not a little of his anxiety about it.

Yet these were the years, too, when the bulk of the work at Williamsburg (as well as the Cloisters) was under way, offering Junior a ready source of solace for his worries. The Center and Williamsburg also functioned in tandem in other interesting ways—both were building projects, both were hugely expensive, yet they looked in totally different directions: Rockefeller Center to the future, Williamsburg to the past, where Junior was always most comfortable. Indeed, given their size and scope along with their similarities and differences, they seem to provide a handy pair of bookends for much of Junior's adult life, shaped as they were by a combination of happenstance and measured responses to it: the great wealth that almost literally dropped in his lap; his determination to be a good and faithful steward of it; and the extraordinary amount of painstaking thought he invested in that effort.

The question of consequences is harder to assess. Rockefeller Center remains a triumph and has become what the great majority of Americans think of first—and perhaps only, now—when they encounter the name Rockefeller. Colonial Williamsburg, meanwhile, struggles to attract visitors in a world where people seem to care less and less about the long-ago times it seeks to re-create, and where it also must compete with hundreds of other "historical" sites offering educational and uplifting experiences to touring families. Yet to a significant degree those same sites follow—whether knowingly or not—the model Junior pioneered at Williamsburg.

Then there were all the projects he took on or continued with during the 1940s and '50s. If none of them reached the scale of Williamsburg or the Center, their range alone is something to marvel at: a continuing interest in the Frick Museum, on whose board he served for many years and to which he planned to leave eight works from his personal collection; large donations to the United Negro College Fund, plus ongoing gifts to individual black colleges the family had long been associated with—Spelman College, Tuskegee, and the Hampton Institute; regular support of the Palestine Archaeological Museum, to which he had earlier contributed $2 million; money for building the United Nations Library in Geneva; $5 million to the Harvard Business School; major donations to his alma mater, Brown University, as well as to other schools including Dartmouth, Princeton, Mount Holyoke, Bryn Mawr, Wellesley, Smith, Harvard Law School, American University in Cairo, Lingnan University in China, and the University of Genoa, and also to the Near East College Association; support for the American Birth Control League and Planned Parenthood; funds for the completion of the Jackson Hole Wildlife Foundation project; $20 million to the Sealantic Fund "to strengthen and develop Protestant theological education"; and donations to the completion of new quarters on First Avenue in New York for the Memorial Sloan-Kettering Center for Cancer and Cellular Diseases, to which he had contributed land acquired at a cost of $3 million, plus a personal grant to Mme. Curie for her work with radium.

Altogether Junior's charitable giving included $192 million to the family foundations, $71.7 million to churches and religious institutions, $63 million to American historical restorations, $58 million to American colleges and universities, $44 million to parks and conservation, $35 million to libraries and institutes, $12 million to cultural organizations, $11 million to hospitals, $9.5 million to relief agencies, $2.5 million to French restorations, and $22.8 million to "miscellaneous" benefactions, for a grand total of over $520 million—all in 1950 dollars. All of it, too, on top of the millions of dollars given away during his lifetime by the family foundations.

What did it all add up to beyond the numbers? One thing it did was create an example of personal philanthropy on a scale never before or since duplicated by any other American. It also balanced remarkably closely institutional giving through the foundations with acts of individual generosity. It could have become more tightly focused and organized; it could also have been more broadly and variously scattered. That it was neither seems to have been a matter of calculation on Junior's part. It reflected both who he was and how he saw the opportunities given him in life. He meant to do great things that left a lasting mark, but that did not mean erecting any single, monolithic monument to himself or to his family. Indeed—as has been said before—there was something Medici-like about the whole effort, for within the soul of that great Renaissance family there lay an urge to combine what many might have thought uncombinable—vast wealth and dedicated public service, deep religious conviction as well as a love of art that upon occasion appeared all too pagan in form and spirit. Junior in the end could claim to have attempted a similar set of reconciliations and made them work at least as often as might have seemed possible.

Breaking Apart

Such was the character of "the Rockefeller Century." But to label it such is also to imply that by the end of the millennium the towering role the family had played in national life was ending, as in truth it was. Nor would any subsequent Rockefeller come close to achieving what Junior had done as a philanthropist. Yet there had been a third act to the drama, for Junior and Abby had six children—a daughter and five sons—all of whom led lives much patterned, if not always comfortably so, on the heritage the previous two generations of Rockefellers had constructed for them.

Warm, supportive, and loving, at least with her sons, Abby won and held their hearts from the beginning. Junior, on the other hand, was a strict disciplinarian, described by David, the youngest—and the only one of them to have published an autobiography—as cold, distant, and demanding. David also pointed to, as others have, Junior's extreme dependence on Abby and what, as a result, was a tendency to begrudge the time and attention she gave their children.

In the case of the oldest two of those children, the stresses in their upbringing became plain as they matured. Named for her mother, Abby—or Babs, as she was called—was a rebellious teenager and a difficult young woman, bent on flouting the conventions her parents lived by. She smoked, she drank, she drove too fast, and she partied with a will. John D. III, on the other hand, grew up much as his father had, tormented by self-doubt and anxiety. Still, in time both Babs and young John learned to keep themselves on something approaching even keel, and in Babs's case that turned out to mean establishing a significant measure of distance between herself and the rest of the family.

Perhaps because their parents fussed less over them, the four younger boys—Nelson, Laurance, Winthrop, and David—grew up to be more relaxed and self-confident than their older siblings. Still, they had to confront the sundry rigors imposed on each of them by their father—including keeping track of every last nickel they spent. And then there were all the odd contradictions that went with being Rockefellers, like having to learn to cook so they would not be overly dependent on servants, while spending most of their time in one or another of the family's huge houses, including the largest private residence in New York City, which Junior had commissioned Welles Bosworth to design, as well as the hundred-plus-room "cottage" in Seal Harbor, Maine, where they summered, not to mention Sunday dinners at Kykuit with their grandfather, who by the time they knew him devoted most of his time to playing golf and Numerica, a parlor game involving cards printed with numbers. He was also, they all knew (because they were told constantly), a *Great and Good Man.*

Financially, as they grew older, the members of the third generation were kept on a short leash by having to ask for money to meet a significant part of their living expenses. Their grandfather too had waited a long time before settling on his son the tens of millions of dollars of stocks and bonds he eventually did. But there had been no strings attached when he did so, and the money came without his asking for it. Junior, on the other hand, moved to create the so-called 1934 Trusts—which finally gave his children financial independence—only after several years of not-always-polite pressure from them, as well as changes in the federal tax code that threatened to take a very large bite of the family fortune unless something were done to prevent that from happening, which the new trusts accomplished. They also made it possible to dole out the money over time, as income from principal, not the principal itself, except in extraordinary cases.

In spite of those constraints, the Rockefeller brothers did manage to achieve notable success in their chosen fields. As Junior had done, John D.

III involved himself in dozens of worthy causes. Both Nelson and Winthrop were elected state governors, and Nelson ended his political career as vice president of the United States. Laurance became a prominent environmentalist and venture capitalist, while David rose to become CEO of Chase Manhattan Bank. Yet surely what most pleased Junior was the fact that they were all dedicated philanthropists.

In part it was a joint effort that took the form of yet another family foundation, the Rockefeller Brothers' Fund, which was established in 1940. Initially the money to operate it came from annual contributions of $50,000 from each of the brothers, an amount that increased over the years as their wealth grew. Then, as a way of showing his approval of what his sons were doing, Junior transferred to the Fund the remainder of the repayments due him on his $75-million personal loan to Rockefeller Center. And later, in his will, he stipulated that the residual portion of his estate—eventually valued at $72 million—should also go to the Fund, turning it into one of the nation's leading philanthropic foundations, with some $6 to $9 million to give away every year.

As the Fund's assets grew so did the reach and variety of its grants. Initially they went largely as "citizenship" donations to the kinds of organizations all wealthy families tended to support—things like the Boy Scouts and the Red Cross. Later, larger grants were added to institutions that had particular ties to the family, as well as to projects in which one or another of the brothers had a special interest. Thus up to the late 1960s a total of $6.6 million went to the Museum of Modern Art (MoMA) and $2.3 to the Jackson Hole Preserve, plus $2.5 million to Lincoln Center and $2.2 million to the Population Council, both projects in which John D. III was playing a leading role. At first, too, all of this was amicably arranged. But by the early 1970s cracks were beginning to appear in the brothers' unity. Long before then, too, they had embarked on philanthropic projects of their own, leading in quite different directions.

Of all the brothers the one who most closely followed the pattern established by their father was John D. III. He devoted his life to philanthropy, and—in addition to chairing the Rockefeller Foundation's board for many years—he supported a strikingly broad range of causes, including population control, improving relations between the United States and Asia, Colonial Williamsburg, and the American Bicentennial. Along the way, too, he left some imposing monuments, among them Lincoln Center, the Asia Society headquarters in New York City, International House in Tokyo, and two first-rate art collections, one in Asian art that eventually found a home in the Asia Society, and the other in American painting, which near the end of his life he arranged to donate to the Fine Arts Museums of San Francisco.

Like his father, too, John D. III assembled a cadre of experts to advise him in his philanthropic work. He also established a foundation of his own and at every turn labored to bring to his philanthropic efforts a thoughtful adjustment of means to ends, for example, dividing his fine arts giving between the East and West Coast. And still another thing he shared with Junior was an intense dislike of modern art. Yet he permitted his wife (assuming he had any choice in the matter), Blanchette, to become actively involved at MoMA and ultimately chair of its board.

Unlike his older brother, Nelson focused his philanthropic energies chiefly on a single area—art—exactly as his mother, Abby, had hoped he would. Already during his junior year at Dartmouth she was writing him about MoMA's founding: "A new Museum of Modern Art, wouldn't it be splendid! It will be ready for you to be interested in when you get back to N.Y. to live."[19] And so it was. Before long he was serving as a member of the museum's board, and in 1934 he pledged $100,000 to it. He also tried to persuade Abby to chair the board, which she refused to do. Nor was Nelson's interest in art confined to a single area. He collected Mexican art plus primitive art from around the world, much of which eventually came to the Metropolitan Museum in New York to appear in a new set of galleries built largely with funds he provided. And there were other collections as well—Chinese ceramics of the Han and Tang Dynasties (far heavier and bolder than the pieces his father collected), as well as eighteenth-century European porcelains, and notable examples of large-scale modern sculpture, which he deftly placed in the gardens around Kykuit. In addition, he built a Japanese-style house there and employed a full-time curator to keep track of his collections and the loans from them that he constantly made to museums around the world.

Nelson and Laurance shared the closest relationship among the brothers. (The unusual spelling of "Laurance" was in honor of John D. Rockefeller Sr.'s wife, Laura.) And like Nelson, Laurance tended to concentrate

his philanthropic efforts more narrowly than John D. III did. He also had
an active career as a venture capitalist, chiefly in aviation and resort development. As a philanthropist his primary concern was preserving and
protecting the natural environment. In addition to serving on the boards
of a dozen or more organizations dedicated to that cause and contributing generously to them, he advised four different presidents—Eisenhower,
Kennedy, Johnson, and Nixon—on environmental issues, and in 1969 he
was awarded a National Medal of Freedom for his work in the field. He
was also a longtime supporter of the Memorial Sloan-Kettering Cancer
Center and for many years chaired the board of the Rockefeller Brothers'
Fund.

The fourth of the brothers, Winthrop, played a less prominent role than
the others as a philanthropist. Sometimes referred to as the black sheep of
the family, he entered into a much publicized and disastrous marriage to
Barbara "Bobo" Sears, the daughter of a coal miner, who previously had
been married to Richard Sears, Jr., heir to the Sears retail fortune. After the
marriage ended, in a drawn out, messy divorce, he decided to leave New
York and settle in Arkansas, where his main interest became politics. Yet
he too established a foundation, plus an institute, and an arts council—all
devoted to improving the economic, educational, and cultural life of his
adopted state.

Next to Nelson, Winthrop's younger brother, David, became the best
known of the five brothers, chiefly due to his globe-trotting years as CEO
of Chase Manhattan Bank. It was not a position that came to him as part
of his birthright; as he makes clear in his autobiography, he had to fight for
it, and thanks to all his frenetic traveling he seemed to succeed handily in
it. Yet the picture was not totally rosy. During his time as its head, Chase
was edged out of its position as New York's largest financial institution by
City Bank—perhaps, some argued, because City spent more time tending
to its knitting at home.

Whatever that fact meant to David, over his lifetime he would prove to
be the most generous of all the Rockefeller brothers. Active in every one of
the family's principal philanthropies and a generous contributor to each,
he took three of them in particular under his wing: Rockefeller University
(originally the Rockefeller Institute for Medical Research), MoMA, and
the Rockefeller Brothers' Fund. On top of many earlier gifts, he set aside

$100 million for each of the three in the opening years of the twenty-first century.

Despite all that the brothers accomplished as philanthropists, there remained a large gap in that regard between them and their parents. And the same would be true of the next two generations of Rockefellers, for by then the great family fortune had been divided into far too many separate pieces to even imagine erecting the mighty philanthropic edifices that had once been both the norm and the hallmark of the family's giving. Temperamentally, too, the younger Rockefellers were inclined to favor smaller, more personal acts of generosity, as well as ones that could be kept from the glare of public attention. They were, after all, children of the 1960s who tended to be suspicious, on principle, of large, highly publicized undertakings of all kinds.

In a much-read and sharply critical book about the Rockefellers written during the 1970s, Peter Collier and David Horowitz depicted the children of the brothers' generation—whom they interviewed and quoted at length—as being actively opposed to the pace and scale of their parents' lives, not to mention to the preoccupation with power that seemed to shape so much of what they did. Said daughters Marion and Laura of their father, Laurance, "I feel sad for him in a way. He missed the boat! Daddy could have been creative." And: "He's always getting off one jet and on to another; hasn't got time for anything especially for understanding himself."[20] Or from Mary, Nelson's daughter: "My father, well I love him for his warmth. But he stands for power, and I think it's very important how one relates to power. It stands as a warning."[21]

And indeed power—getting it, using it, hanging on to it—had been at the center of the Rockefellers' lives ever since John D. senior's earliest days in business. If that was no longer to be the case, the end of an era had definitely been reached. There were other signs of the change as well, including the shifting relationships among the brothers themselves, which up to a point was inevitable given the different paths they followed in life. Yet in time those differences turned into disagreements, some minor, others more serious. In that respect the end of Nelson's time as vice president and his return from Washington proved to be a watershed of sorts. When the brothers were young, it was Nelson who had planned their games and later galvanized them into action on a variety of fronts, including dealing with their father on financial issues. But as politics claimed more and more of Nelson's time, the leading role fell to John III, who, if diffident at first about his new position, had come to quite enjoy it, and was not a little annoyed at having Nelson sweep back into the scene expecting to regain his place as commander in chief.

Referring in his diary to Nelson's "power grab," John III finally brought matters to a head in a no-holds-barred letter accusing his brother of playing "power politics [which] just are not appropriate on the home front," and informing Nelson that he simply had to change his ways "for the good of the whole" and "what the family stands for." This had to be done, too, as quickly as possible, because, as he said, "time is running out."[22] In reply Nelson furiously demanded that John III "withdraw" his letter at once, which eventually he did, though by then the breach was beyond repair.[23]

Bubbling in this rancorous stew were three issues: the management of the family office, the Rockefeller Brothers' Fund, and Kykuit, which Nelson had taken over following Junior's death in 1960. His program for the family office included clarifying, streamlining, and rendering more efficient its operation, all of which was done in time. With regard to the Fund, the particular point at issue was whether it should contribute to establishing a school of osteopathy planned by Dr. Kenneth Riland, who had long been treating Nelson for back pain. By then the Fund's trustees had firmly committed themselves to broadening the scope of its activities, just as the Rockefeller Foundation had done half a century earlier, and that included moving beyond family-related philanthropic concerns—all of which Nelson called into question, with no apparent willingness to compromise.

Yet oddly enough the toughest nut facing the brothers was what to do with Kykuit. After his father's death in 1937, Junior and Abby had moved into the house, and for the next twenty-three years it was kept as nearly as possible exactly as it was on the day the patriarch breathed his last. When Abby suggested changing an overly "fussy" arrangement of vases and lights in front of the house, Junior consulted Welles Bosworth, and on his recommendation nothing was moved by so much as an inch.[24] On all such issues, in fact, Junior treated Kykuit exactly as he did his many restorations—as a living memorial to times past, another great historical site, illustrating in its tasteful restraint the social and cultural values of the family who had built it and made it their home, though unlike those earlier projects this one would be verifiably accurate in every detail.

Meanwhile, Junior had sold the place (as he did Rockefeller Center) to his sons in order to get it out of his estate for tax purposes, with the proviso that his second wife (Abby had died of a massive heart attack in 1948) could live out her life there if she wished, which she had no desire to do. So with her permission, Nelson—having earlier, amid great scandal, divorced his first wife—moved in with his second wife, Happy Murphy, and their two young children. And with typical gusto Nelson set about changing Junior's meticulously tended museum in dozens of ways—installing pieces of his enormous collection of modern art throughout the house, as well as in a set of galleries especially constructed for that purpose in its basement, building a pair of swimming pools next to the house in what had been a sunken garden, installing a soda fountain in the stone teahouse, and dotting the surrounding landscape with more than fifty massive examples of modern sculpture.

From the beginning, Happy Rockefeller remembers, he talked of eventually opening the place to the public, and in his will he left his share of the estate to the National Trust for Historic Preservation, stating it was his hope that the Trust would conduct public tours of the house and gardens. Yet the road to that point turned out to be full of complications. Between 1962 and 1985 no fewer than twenty-two studies of the possible uses of the property and its future were made. All the while, too, the brothers—with mounting acrimony—were addressing the same issues. Initially, the strongest disagreements were between Nelson and John III, who resisted Nelson's plans for Kykuit yet neglected to propose any clear-cut alternative of his own. Then in 1978 he was killed in an automobile accident, and the following year Nelson died of an apparent heart attack under circumstances that may forever remain awash in unanswered questions.

In any case, with the two older brothers gone, and Winthrop having earlier sold his share of the estate to his four male siblings, it fell to Laurance and David to settle Kykuit's future, and they too disagreed both with one another and with Nelson's plans for the place. Feeling that the last thing the Rockefellers needed to memorialize the family was a mansion stuffed with precious objects and surrounded by gardens that took a staff of two hundred to maintain, Laurance hoped to see the house torn down and the land around it turned into a public park. David, on the other hand, wanted the place left intact and perhaps opened to the public, but only after his lifetime.

More years went by, during which the stalemate was further muddled by the fact that David also wanted the property owned and managed by an organization closer to the family than the National Trust. Among the various candidates, he eventually chose the Rockefeller Brothers' Fund, and plans were made to have it purchase the place from the Trust. But at the eleventh hour those plans had to be scuttled because the Trust's new board chair, Robert Bass—a Texas billionaire who ironically enough owed his freshly minted fortune to the oil business—insisted that Kykuit be turned over to the Trust and, as Nelson's will had stipulated, opened to the public as soon as possible. Months of negotiations plus a fresh spate of planning documents followed, but in the end Bass had his way, and groups of tourists—carefully shepherded—began passing through "the Rockefeller Family Home" in the spring of 1994, fully a decade and a half after Nelson's death.

In addition to providing an intriguing chapter in the age-old battle between new and old money, the opening of Kykuit to the public could be seen as yet another example of the Rockefeller family's public-spirited generosity. The value of the house and the collections of art in and around it made it the largest single philanthropic gift of Nelson's life. And on top of that there were the payments David and Laurance had made to keep up the place while its future was being debated, plus the several millions of dollars David contributed to readying the house for public tours. If Robert Bass had won his battle with David, it was David, in the end, who wrote the checks that made it all happen, however reluctantly.

But to what end? The house finally was made available to the public, most of whom were probably drawn there chiefly by curiosity about how people with so much money lived. But obviously for the Rockefellers themselves, far more than that was at stake. However odd it was to see the brothers quarreling over a property only one of them had any interest in living in, the place, they all seemed to believe, said something important about them as a family—but they also proved utterly incapable of agreeing about what that might be.

Yet there was one clear significance to Kykuit's opening as a public attraction. For as it stood, it abundantly represented what had become a major characteristic of the Rockefellers' philanthropy. John D. senior hadn't cared a hoot about art. It was Nelson and Abby who added that dimension to the family's experience and, in time, to its giving, and much of what the two of them, plus Junior, cared about could be seen at Kykuit: their interest in architecture and Junior's passion for Chinese porcelains, plus Abby's for modern works, through the tutelage she had given Nelson. And the same deep attachment to art was evident in the lives of at least two of the other brothers—David, who collected, as his mother and Nelson had, primarily modern art, and John III, with his devotion to Asian art and secondarily to American painting. Like the others, too, John III worked to ensure that his collections found permanent homes in the museums he chose. For the public dimension of collecting was vital not only to him but to all of the Rockefellers. The magnificent works of art they acquired were meant to be like stones dropped in pools of water, sending outward ever-broadening ripples of education and uplift to the untold thousands of people who would see them, which in turn is what gave it all its larger philanthropic meaning.

As always, however, there was another side—less public, less outward-looking—to the effort. When Junior began collecting Chinese porcelains he delighted in spending hours on the floor rolling the pieces around to be sure they exhibited the rounded perfection he longed for. Similarly for Nelson the challenge of finding the perfect spot for every one of his sculptures could take weeks of having them moved from place to place—by helicopter if necessary—until he was sure he would never have to move them again. As his brother Laurance said: "There was great therapy . . . great joy to it."[25] In the same spirit Junior had written: "In a well-rounded life, beauty plays a real part."[26] To which Abby, who did so much to nurture a love of art in the family, added, "I believe [art] not only enriches the spiritual life, but that it makes one more sane and sympathetic, more observant and understanding, regardless of whatever age it springs from, whatever subject it represents."[27]

Therapy, joy, sanity, sympathy, and understanding: these are concepts that relate to the inner self, to a world of individual thought and feeling that is quintessentially personal and private. Art, then, could have two meanings—one public, the other private. And so the Rockefellers seemed to think of it, which made it a very different proposition from the large, precisely targeted, rationally organized projects that took shape under the auspices of the family foundations in the early years of the twentieth century. Art, with all its personal, emotional content, came later. Yet once it entered the mix it became an ever more important part of it. The question is why.

First it should be said that the change was in no sense a matter of eliminating one thing and replacing it with another. The Rockefeller family foundations continue to this day to function as energetically and usefully as ever. And if proof is needed of just how earnestly the family remains committed to such efforts, among the many organizations that have proliferated under its auspices is the Rockefeller Philanthropy Advisors (RPA), which helps wealthy individuals find their way along the road that led to the creation of entities like the Rockefeller Foundation. Currently RPA employs a staff of forty, in four different locations in the United States, who work to provide—as its website states—"research and council on charitable giving." At the top of its list of services, too, is "establishing a foundation, Charitable Giving Fund, or other giving vehicle." Currently RPA works with "more than 160 donors," and has "overseen more than $3 billion to date in grantmaking across the globe."

But if RPA is largely about what has become traditional philanthropic giving, in allocating their own resources the Rockefellers have tended to let such efforts operate in tandem with other, individual choices. And in particular those choices have focused on art. During his lifetime Junior donated $192 million to the foundations, which was $10 million more than his father had given. Yet he also gave $113 million to historic restorations, museums, and other cultural organizations—categories totally absent from his father's giving. And in the next generation the trend continued to the point where by far the largest portion of Nelson's giving was similarly directed, though his brothers were inclined to spread their generosity in more balanced ways.

There was, then, no hard and fast fault line running through the Rockefellers' philanthropy, but there was a clearly discernible shift over time, for which a number of plausible explanations might be given. Among other things, art—especially the kinds of art the Rockefellers collected—turned out to be a spectacularly profitable investment. Within a decade or two of the time Nelson bought canvases by artists like Matisse and Picasso for a few thousand dollars, prices for comparable works rose to tens of thousand of dollars and then to a million or more. Today they sell for many times that amount. A single sculpture by Alberto Giacometti, roughly the size of the one Nelson placed next to Kykuit's front door, has recently sold for as much as $100 million at auction. Such enormous increases in value, too, could occur while one continued to enjoy the works in private—as Junior did with the unicorn tapestries and many of his other treasures. Then, when the time finally came to turn them over to museums, there were the enormous tax deductions earned as a result.

It should also be noted, however, that when the Rockefellers began collecting art in a serious way, and for thirty or forty years afterward, no one could have predicted the astronomical increases in prices that have subsequently occurred in the art market. So it is difficult to make financial considerations the principal agency driving the family's collecting, which brings us to less tangible considerations—and again the world of private pleasures and solace art represented. For people constantly compelled to live, whether they liked it or not, in the glare of public attention here was a way of escaping, of constructing—for and by oneself—a sense of who you were and what your life meant. For John D. senior, it had been road-building and golf, plus giving away shiny dimes and bantering, off the record, with reporters. His descendants wanted something different.

They also seem to have felt the need to surround themselves—in private as well as in public—with palpable emblems both of their own worth as human beings and of personal control. They chose the works they lived with, they arranged them around themselves as they wished, and they decided the time and manner of their transfer to the public realm. In a curious way, too, these benefits paralleled John D. Rockefeller's achievement in building Standard Oil. There, too, impulses and actions, both private and public, personal and impersonal, came together to produce a truly wondrous result—one, too, that could be thought of as forever floating above simple calculations of morality. John D. senior had said that a productive, well-run business enterprise was the best form of philanthropy: greed and public welfare inextricably bound up with one another. Yet just in case it turned out the balance had been struck at the wrong point, he gave half a billion dollars to more conventional philanthropies, which among other things freed his descendants to look for new forms of generosity, other pleasures.

Still, one is tempted to ask, could the very large sums paid by the Rockefellers to acquire what has to be one of the greatest collections of works of art ever assembled by a single family have been, from a social standpoint, more usefully employed in other ways? And whatever the answer may be, one can also wonder whether we as a people should continue to reward those activities with the very generous tax benefits they currently enjoy. Such, at any rate, are the thorny conundrums that have come to compose the lives of the latter-day Rockefellers, no less than—for better or worse— our lives with them.

7

SUCCESSORS

Current estimates of the Rockefeller family's total wealth put it, still, as high as $110 billion. The ties uniting family members have also remained surprisingly durable, at least in formal ways, despite sharp disagreements that came to divide the brothers' generation. One reason for this is the family office, once at 26 Broadway, but now housed on three floors of the GE Building in Rockefeller Center. Affectionately known as "Room 5600," it oversees everything from the day-to-day management of family members' personal expenses to making airline, even dinner, reservations for them.

Added to these activities are regular family meetings, organized by generation, as well as the ongoing involvement by various Rockefellers in the family foundations, which continue to grow in number. Yet the present position of those same foundations also reflects the decline in the magnitude of the Rockefellers' giving compared to that of other very wealthy families and individuals. To take only a single example, the centerpiece of the family's generosity has always been the Rockefeller Foundation itself, which by any standard remains a formidable engine of American philanthropy. But where once it reigned supreme, today among the hundred largest philanthropic foundations in the United States it ranks only sixteenth in total assets ($3.3 billion) and thirty-fourth in annual giving ($145.1 million as of July 18, 2011).

Ahead of the Rockefeller Foundation on both lists appear names long familiar in the annals of American wealth—Ford, Johnson, Kellogg, Kresge, Mellon, and Reynolds; yet there are many more names that speak unmistakably of new money—Gates, Buffett, Paul Getty, Packard, Simons, Annenberg, Helmsley, and the Waltons. Such additions to the list, too, are emblematic of still broader changes in the shape and character of wealth in American society. And one way to understand those changes is to look closely at the richest of today's rich—who they are, where their money comes from, and where it goes. Happily there is a convenient source to use for this purpose.

The List

Since 1982 *Forbes* magazine has been compiling and publishing annually a list of the 400 richest people in the United States. Conceived, fittingly enough, in the glow of Ronald Reagan's first term as president, it quickly became the blue plate special on the menu of items feeding the nation's hunger for information about the very rich.

The format is simple. Every year the 400 are listed in order of the size of their net worth (and alphabetically on a second list), accompanied by brief notes indicating the amount and source of every listee's wealth, whether it has risen or fallen during the preceding year, their age and place of residence, as well as icons indicating what the editors call their "Passions and Pursuits," which include things like yachting, horses, planes, the environment, and supporting improvement in education. In addition there are articles discussing distinctive features of that year's list and some of the people on it. In short, what we are offered is a bundle of facts that can be the subject of either serious study or engaging parlor games—take your pick.

As for where the facts come from, there is no specific formula used in compiling the list, and consequently no hard and fast way of judging its accuracy, though the magazine's editors do describe a process that is both energetic and impressively wide-ranging in the variables it seeks to cover. "Throughout the year our reporters meet with the list candidates and their handlers and interview employees, rivals, attorneys, ex-spouses and securities analysts. We keep track of their moves: the deals they negotiate, the land they're selling, the paintings they're buying, the causes they give to, Securities & Exchange Commission documents, court records, probate records, tax records, federal financial disclosures and Web and print stories—we dig through them all. In calculating wealth we put a price on all assets, including stakes in public and privately held companies, real estate, art, yachts and planes."[1] And on top of all this, information is "system-atically" gathered on listees' debts and given "a hard look."[2] For the 2011 list the editors state that they started with 570 "prospects" and interviewed 88 billionaires personally.

Much of the evidence used in compiling the list thus rests on hearsay and is at bottom impressionistic in other ways. Who is to say what Face-book founder Mark Zuckerberg is worth? In 2011 while the company was still privately held, *Forbes* put his wealth at $17.5 billion, a very large jump from the year before—making Zuckerberg seventeenth on the list. In such cases *Forbes* claims to base its evaluations on the worth of similar publicly traded companies. But in this instance there were none. Also, the mag-azine's use of consultations with "list candidates themselves" and "their handlers" involves testimony by people who presumably might find it in their interest to reckon overexpansively—to inflate assets and minimize debts. For most of those who "make the list," doing so is, after all, a source of pride, and for some surely, a much-sought-after badge of achievement—less an accounting than an anointment.

But for all the quarrels one might pick with *Forbes's* list, there is noth-ing else like it, or to measure it against. Nor has it been much criticized, at least publicly, perhaps because in the end it gives people information they find useful, or at any rate are happy to have. For *Forbes* as well it has been a satisfying undertaking, selling, as it does year in and year out, more copies than any other issue of the magazine.

The list also has led to the publication of a lively and eminently readable book—*All the Money in the World: How the Forbes 400 Make—and Spend—Their Fortunes,* co-authored by Peter W. Bernstein and Annalyn Swan. In it the material presented by *Forbes* over more than two decades is ana-lyzed and supplemented by insights and anecdotes gathered by the authors themselves. "Inspired, insightful and lots of fun" is how *Publishers Weekly* described the book.[3]

The tidbits of information in it run the gamut from minibiographies of some of the more colorful individuals on various 400 lists to a discussion of the forty-one items that make up the *Forbes* "Cost of Living Extremely Well Index," including a Hermes Kelly Bag ($6,250), an ounce of Joy per-fume ($400), a Patek Philippe gold watch ($17,000), and a Sikorsky he-licopter ($11 million). On a more serious level, Bernstein and Swan also highlight a number of key trends that emerge from following changes in the 400 list across time. Thus they note that the initial 1982 list contained a gaggle of du Ponts, none of whom are currently listed. Inherited fortunes still loom large, but the amounts involved are much higher. Overall, in fact, the average net worth of the 400 has risen steadily. So has the number of Californians in the group while, as Bernstein and Swan observe, the number of New York City residents has fallen. There has been, as well, a definite rise in the proportion of people in finance and a corresponding drop in the number who owe their wealth to manufacturing. Also, entertainers and media personalities, once absent, now make regular appearances on the list.

Almost all of these trends have been noted in one or another of the annual *Forbes* 400 issues. Rather, the most interesting parts of *All the Money in the World* are those discussing the qualities of mind and character the 400 have exhibited along the way. Frequently luck has played a significant role—even sometimes poker winnings—but more often the lucky break is happening to be in the right place at the right time. Crucial, too, is seeing possibilities other people miss—in new ways of thinking about business, in new technologies, and in new systems for greasing the skids to move things ahead more quickly and efficiently, to cut corners and slash costs, to do better, bigger, smarter deals. And always there is the implacable will to succeed, to bend the world to make it conform to your vision, to risk all in a single bold stroke, to leave no stone unturned and take no prisoners, no matter what others might think: in short, to believe that—as Bernstein and Swan put it in one of their chapter titles—"Winning Is Everything."[4] Winners also tend to be much less encumbered by old ideas and old traditions. Hence, the authors observe, the relatively more successful careers of those in the 400 who qualify as "Blue Collar Billionaires," referring to their origins, as well as those without college degrees as opposed to those with them.

But laying aside issues of background and education, the personal characteristics Bernstein and Swan ascribe to the 400, if not unexpected, seem unlikely to strike the average reader as uniformly appealing. Even if one chooses—as *All the Money in the World* decidedly does—to stop well short of seeing the individuals in question as monuments of arrogance and greed, it would be difficult to summon up warm feelings toward many of them. Nor does how they appear to see themselves help much on that score, or so the authors suggest, remarking with elegant understatement: "as a rule the *Forbes* 400 is not for the faint hearted."[5] Yet in general Bernstein and Swan work hard at keeping their approach as balanced as possible—neither overly critical nor too forgiving. And to a substantial extent they succeed, though they leave until very near the end the vital subject of philanthropy, thereby giving it special (even redeeming?) significance.

A profile of the 2011 *Forbes* list (the most recent one as of this writing)—using the magazine's own calculations and categories—could be sketched as follows: listees' average age, 65; average net worth, $3.8 billion; total net worth of the group as a whole, $1.5 trillion; number of women, 42; number of those whose net worth grew over the preceding year, 262; number whose net worth shrank, 72; number of newcomers to the list, 18; number of dropouts, 24; states with the highest number of listees, California (88), New York (64), Texas (47), Florida (29), and Illinois (18); city with the highest number of listees, New York (63, with Dallas as a distant second at 17); percentage of those who made their money themselves, 68.8; percentage of those who inherited all or part of it, 29.8; sources of wealth by numbers—investments (for which finance might be a better designation) (96), technology (48), energy (37), media (37), food and beverage (30), service (28), real estate (27), fashion and retail (24), manufacturing (17), sports (16).

The oldest member of the group is David Rockefeller at ninety-six; its youngest member is twenty-seven-year-old Dustin Moskovitz, who made his money in Facebook. The range in net worth runs from $59 billion (Bill Gates) to $1.05 billion. The editors also consider it significant that thirty-two of that year's 400 had received advanced degrees from Harvard. And when those who rank in the top twenty of the 400 are broken out as a separate group, the area that dominates the list is technology, with seven entries, as opposed to finance, with four.

The list of twenty also contains one surprising feature: nine of those who appear belong to only three families—four Waltons, heirs of Wal-Mart's founder Sam Walton; three members of the Mars family, who owe their fortune to the candy business (M&Ms in particular); and Charles and David Koch, whose wealth comes from a variety of sources clustered around the largest privately owned business in the United States, which had its beginnings in the oil refining industry. The combined assets of these individuals total $178.4 billion, all of it, it should be noted, founded on inherited wealth. And elsewhere in the magazine, the editors list seven other families with two or more members on the larger 400 list, including three Coxes (media), eleven Pritzkers (hotels), seven Cargills (agribusiness), four Duncans (energy), three Ziffs (publishing), two Newhouses (publishing), and five Johnsons (household products).

What all this consanguinity among the 400 listees suggests is how concentrated—even within a highly select group—great wealth can and has become. Nor does it end there. For scanning the 400 list reveals thirty-five other people—unnoted by the editors—who are related to one another, including, among others, a third Koch, four members of the Hearst newspaper publishing family, two Lauders (cosmetics empire), two Newhouses (publishing again), two Ross Perots (senior and junior), and two Tischs (Loews theaters and hotels).

That *Forbes* should have failed to comment on the fact that combining all the available information, just under 20 percent of its richest Americans are related to at least one other person on the list seems curious. But it could, after all, darken a bit—with its intimations of strikingly high levels of wealth concentration—the generally upbeat message the editors seem eager to convey about their subject. Noting as well that a high proportion of the family fortunes in these cases began with inherited money could have a similar effect. And by the same token, the editors have nothing to say on the growing inequality of wealth in the United States. The closest they come to the issue is presenting data showing that while President Barack Obama's mention of millionaires and billionaires rises during elections and budget fights, "he drops the subject quickly once those are over." In other words, there is no substantive issue at stake here; it's simply a matter of campaign rhetoric.

Avoiding the wealth distribution issue in this case is, of course, but a small part of the much larger question posed by *Forbes*'s decision to identify and chronicle the activities of the richest of the American rich. For the whole point of its 400 list is to highlight the existing *inequality* of America's social and economic order—and if not simply to celebrate it, certainly not to challenge it. Nowhere in the entire enterprise is there even the tiniest whiff of populist angst.

Apart from the list itself, the 2011 issue of the magazine includes, as usual, a frothy mix of articles aimed at getting us inside the world of the very rich. But what the editors most want us to notice—as they claim in a brief preface (written in answer to what they describe as "the tax-the-rich schemes circulating in Washington")—is that the 400 list is "becoming more meritocratic each year" and that, in the sentence they choose to end with: "This is a working elite."[6] The list of articles, too, does seem to be tailored to fit those conclusions. At least fourteen of them, a higher number than for any other category, relate directly to the world of work—getting money, keeping it, and keeping it growing. Appropriately, too, in a period of substantial economic turmoil, the emphasis generally is on handling risk and finding ways of investing that are both moderately safe and innovative enough to pay significant returns, a game the 400 appear to be playing with more than a little success, assuming the editors are correct in asserting that the combined net worth of the group in 2011 was 12 percent higher than in the preceding year.

But there are almost as many articles on non-work-related subjects, including several on politics and what the editors describe as "charity," as well as on the kinds of glamorous and exciting pastimes usually associated with the lives of the very rich—living in expensive houses in exclusive communities, vacationing in exotic places, collecting artworks, owning racehorses, yachts, and airplanes as well as sports teams and posh restaurants, plus immersing oneself in an endless stream of luxurious consumer goods. In this connection the editors note that their "price list" for eight such items (sable coats, thoroughbred racehorses, face lifts, helicopters, etc.) rose 4.5 percent during the year as opposed to the 3.6 percent for inflation generally.

And, of course, an added pleasure of being rich enough "to make the list" is the company you join, which includes more than a few bona fide celebrities—figures like (to pick only a dozen) Bill Gates, Warren Buffett, Jeff Bezos, Michael Bloomberg, Mark Zuckerberg, Rupert Murdoch, Ralph Lauren, Ross Perot, Donald Trump, Oprah Winfrey, Steven Spielberg, and Ted Turner. Also one could include the owners of the New England Patriots, Detroit Red Wings, Boston Bruins, Cleveland Cavaliers, Boston Red Sox, Baltimore Ravens, and Philadelphia Eagles—all of whom are on the 400 list. Or, in historical terms, there are the surviving heirs to two of the greatest American fortunes ever made: David Rockefeller and William Ford, Sr. And of course Steve Jobs is on the list—for the last time.

To be sure, balancing work and pleasure is what most of us try to do in life, and the facts presented for the 400 listees give a picture of impressive success in that regard. They also tell us what we seem to want to believe: that being rich—if more than just a carefree romp in the sun—is indeed fun. Again, however, in the current climate *Forbes*'s editors seem eager to stress the serious side of the equation. And to that end they devote a considerable amount of space to philanthropy.

The front of the 2011 *Forbes* 400 issue is literally made up of four separate covers—one after another—each featuring a different person. And two of the four, Ted Turner and George Kaiser, have had notable careers both in business and as philanthropists. In both cases (as well as the other two) *Forbes* had what its "chief product officer" describes as unique access to the men in question, and both are presented as highly complex individuals.

To anyone who knows anything at all about Ted Turner—and most people do—this description will come as no surprise; Kaiser is much less well known. In other ways, too, they are very different from one another: Turner, the headline-grabbing star of dozens of dramas, most of which he composed and staged himself; Kaiser, a very private person who had to be coaxed for months before agreeing to meet with *Forbes*'s reporters. And where the reach of Turner's philanthropic efforts is nothing if not global, Kaiser has targeted much of his generosity on his native Tulsa, Oklahoma, though in the hope, he has said, of using Tulsa as a laboratory for testing ways of approaching problems that could have a much broader application.

In business Turner's signal achievement was the creation of CNN, the world's first twenty-four-hour, all-news broadcasting network. As a philanthropist he has supported scores of causes, "starting with," as he is quoted in *Forbes,* a "promise to care for the planet Earth," which has included supporting nuclear disarmament, environmental programs of all sorts—among them alternative energy development—women's rights (with a special focus on ending female genital mutilation), protecting endangered species, population control, ending poverty, and, oddly enough, painting parking lots white instead of black.[7] As a philanthropist he feels that "voluntary initiatives" are more acceptable than governmental efforts "because people don't want to be commanded anymore today."[8] Unquestionably the most dramatic example of this belief is his 1997 personal pledge to donate $1 billion to the UN. Thus far he has paid off $866 million of that amount and has hopes of getting other billionaires, Warren Buffett included, to help with the rest.

George Kaiser—the son of a Jewish father who led his family out of Nazi Germany and eventually settled in Tulsa, where he joined his uncle in an oil-drilling company—went to Harvard and dreamed of finding a place in the foreign service. But when his father had a heart attack he joined the family business, which under his management became one of the largest oil and gas producers in the state. From there he expanded into banking and private equity ownership. On the 2011 *Forbes* list he ranks thirty-first, with an estimated net worth of $10 billion, and has created a family foundation with $4 billion in assets, putting it on a par with the Rockefeller Foundation.

In his giving Kaiser follows an investment-oriented philosophy focused on dealing with poverty by providing better educational opportunities. Beginning at the preschool level with a program entitled Educare, he has developed centers in Tulsa and across the country, working closely with other wealthy local families as well as with Bill Gates and Warren Buffett's daughter Susan. From early education, he has branched out into supporting programs in teacher education and donating $62 million to the University of Oklahoma to create a School of Community Medicine to provide better primary medical care for poor families. The rationale behind all of this reaches deep into traditional American democratic values. "From the days of our founders the social contract of the United States has been equal opportunity," Kaiser has said. "A newborn child bears no responsibility for the circumstances of her birth and yet is often destined to a life of advantage or disadvantage based on those circumstances. The American commitment to equal opportunity is not being fulfilled. . . . With what we know, it is morally offensive not to act."[9] In a sidebar next to its article on Kaiser, *Forbes* presents a list of the ten largest philanthropic gifts made by 400 listees over the preceding year. Kaiser is on the list, as are Warren Buffett, Larry Ellison, and Mark Zuckerberg. Of the ten gifts, seven, like Kaiser's, are designed to support education.

Yet another article on philanthropy in the 2011 *Forbes* 400 issue "re-counts" a conversation between Bill Gates, American's richest man, and Dustin Moskovitz, the young Facebook billionaire, who ranks ninety-first on the list. Entitled "A Course on Giving," it is an odd piece—less an exchange between the two men than their individual responses to questions asked them by a *Forbes*'s interviewer. Gates repeats what he has said many times before about the foundation he and his wife, Melinda, established, noting that after his retirement from Microsoft it became, as he said, "my full-time thing."[10] Moskovitz, who by contrast is only just beginning to be interested in philanthropy and has yet to do any serious giving, remarks: "If you're talking about ramping up to giving hundreds of millions of dollars a year, you need to invest upfront time"—at least ten years of "study," he goes on to estimate.[11] Supportively, Gates remarks, "Well, I was 45 when I really made the substantial donations to the foundation."[12]

There are also issues on which Moskovitz and Gates disagree: Moskovitz likes the idea of proceeding alone in his giving: Gates has learned that it is often highly useful to partner with others. Both men are drawn to large projects like ending malaria, but Gates is inclined to lower his sights just a bit. Both state that their parents played a significant role in their choice to "give back," yet Gates also credits "some really exemplary people" as role models in this regard.[13] "If Rockefeller, Carnegie and Ford hadn't done what they've done it just would have been that much less likely for any of us to think foundations can have these audacious goals."[14]

Two men, earnestly determined to do good with their wealth: one quite young, the other middle-aged. Yet both Moskovitz and Gates are conscious that there exists a tradition of giving in the United States which they hope to carry on—one in new and innovative ways, the other by following some of its best-known past practitioners. And whatever else may be true, by publishing such articles with its annual 400 list *Forbes* does seem to be eager to highlight the subject of philanthropy and do it in a compelling way.

As for why that should be so, one answer could be to combat the growing concern about inequality in America. Yet there is another explanation, and that is an intriguing campaign launched by the two richest men on the 400 list—Gates and Warren Buffett—to bring philanthropy to the fore whenever wealth in America is discussed. They have named it the "Giving Pledge," and what it does is encourage the nation's richest individuals to commit themselves publicly to devoting half or more of their fortunes to philanthropy.

Pledging

Partnering together was not new to Buffett and Bill and Melinda Gates. In a spectacular move in 2006 Buffett announced that he would be turning over a major part of his wealth to the couple's philanthropic foundation, convinced that they would do as good a job of spending it as he could and also, in the bargain, prevent an inefficient duplication of labor. Accordingly, in the year prior to the publication of the 2011 *Forbes* list, he contributed $3.27 billion in Berkshire Hathaway stock to that effort, with much more to come in the future.

As Buffett described it, the Giving Pledge was "about asking wealthy families to have important conversations about their wealth."[15] It was also "a moral commitment to give—not a legal contract."[16] The means of gathering signers, he said, was similarly informal: "The way I got the message out was to get a copy of *Forbes,* and look down that 400 list and start making calls! Bill and Melinda did the same thing."[17] Most of the calls were to people whom the trio already knew were interested in philanthropy. And out of the group they called, roughly half of them agreed both to sign the Pledge and to tell their personal stories, which would be posted on the Giving Pledge website.

Topping the group of forty signers listed by *Forbes* in 2010—the year the Pledge made its debut—were Gates and Buffett themselves. Other well-known individuals were Michael Bloomberg, Barry Diller, Diane von Furstenberg, T. Boone Pickens, Ted Turner, and David Rockefeller. All told, the Pledge signers committed themselves to donating an impressive $120 billion, at a minimum, to philanthropy. Yet the results may not have been quite as promising as the numbers suggested. Included among the Giving Pledge's forty signers in 2010 were twelve wives adding their signatures to those of their husbands, who appeared alone on the *Forbes* 400 list. Omitting them reduces the signers to only thirty-eight of the 400. And even at the level of forty, they equaled no more than 10 percent of the list, which could well have seemed disappointing, unless one wanted to rejoice that the glass was at least a tenth full.

Over the next year the number of Pledge signers on the 400 list grew to forty-four (again eliminating spouses), as one could tell by the icon now routinely shown next to their names on the list, along with those indicating the ownership of art collections, racehorses, yachts, and airplanes. Among the newcomers were Carl Icahn, Mark Zuckerberg, Michael Milken, and Steve Case. And at the level of forty-four, the Giving Pledge signers rose to 11 percent of the *Forbes* 400, which, if still quite small, could in time become large enough to be seen as more significant, if similar increases continued to occur.

Interestingly enough, the evidence also shows that on several key points the Giving Pledge signers differed sharply from the *Forbes* 400 group as a whole. Their average net worth was much higher: almost double that of the larger group ($7.64 versus $3.8 billion). More of them came from California or New York and fewer from Texas, Florida, and Illinois. The fields in which they made their fortunes were also different, with finance and technology getting a combined total of 65 percent, versus 36 percent for Giving Pledge signers as a whole. Pledge signers were more likely, too, to have gained money over the preceding year (82 percent versus 66 percent). And, as one might predict, more of them made their money themselves, as opposed to inheriting all or part of it (86 percent versus 68.8 percent).

Their wealth rising decisively, and in those fields at the cutting edge of personal wealth creation in the United States—all, as well, due largely to their own efforts—such is the portrait that emerges from an analysis of the Giving Pledge signers appearing among *Forbes*'s 400 richest Americans. In that exclusive band of the richest of the rich, here was a yet richer and more enterprising phalanx of high achievers, marching out ahead of their fellow billionaires. Also, though it is not as easy to document qualitatively, the Pledge signers shared other characteristics. Almost all were better known than the majority of the *Forbes* 400. Even if the exact details of their lives remained murky to the public at large, their names cut a wider swath through American life and claimed more space in the national imagination—and not always for reasons that were uniformly endearing, which in turn might help explain why they chose to sign the Giving Pledge in the first place.

To take only a single example, the rise of Mark Zuckerberg—the founder of Facebook—on the *Forbes* 400 list has been nothing if not spectacular. Between 2010 and 2011 alone he shot up from thirty-fifth to fourteenth on the list, putting him, at the age of twenty-seven, ahead of Larry Page, Steve Ballmer, Michael Dell, Paul Allen, and Steve Jobs—all major players in technology, a field some of them entered before Zuckerberg was even born. Adding a dash of cold water to these facts, Zuckerberg, on the subject of the 400 list, says: "If I could, I wouldn't even be on the list."[18] And in fact, along with all the fame and admiration Facebook has brought him, it has been at times a bumpy ride—chiefly due to continuing criticism of his handling of the breaches in users' privacy.

Then too, there was *The Social Network,* a movie that *Forbes* described as a "dark mythologizing of the Facebook creation story."[19] In it Zuckerberg appears as alternately oblivious and ruthless, "a haunted mogul, à la Citizen Kane, who chooses his company over his friends,"[20] according to *Forbes.* Yet as its editors also noted: "Despite the hand-wringing more than 1 million people a day continue to join the network [which] may soon become the internet's prime marketplace, eclipsing Google." Meanwhile, in conversation with talk-show host Charlie Rose on late-night TV, Zuckerberg seemed pleasant enough and not at all interested in moving beyond connecting people to selling them anything. Of course, businesses do not always grow as their founders imagine they will, though whatever the future might hold for Zuckerberg, his name did appear as a Giving Pledge signer in 2011—as it had not in 2010—which was, after all, something he could do to underline the basic goodness of his intentions. And whatever the future might hold for Facebook and Zuckerberg, his name did appear as a Giving Pledge signer in 2011, as it had not in 2010, which was, after all, something he could do to underline the basic goodness of his intentions.

Forbes also chose to close its article on Zuckerberg by noting that when a group of "activists" opposing some of the company's practices staged a "Quit Facebook" day in the spring of 2011, "only 37,000 people said they would leave."[21] Admittedly that number is tiny compared to the hundreds of millions of Facebook users around the world; still, it is not exactly insignificant.

Reasons

When asked—as all Giving Pledge signers are—to make personal statements about themselves, they have come up with a fascinating array of thoughts. And on the subject of what led them to consider scaling the imposing heights of generosity required of signers, their answers were especially diverse—far too diverse, certainly, to permit easy generalizations. Some of the explanations given more often than just a few times included (in descending order of frequency): wonder at the good fortune that produced the wealth needed to engage in serious philanthropy and the feeling that there was a corresponding responsibility to do so; parental or family influence; the opportunity to "make a difference" and see it happen during one's own lifetime; a feeling of indebtedness to one's community, to the nation, and to the world at large; the chance to be associated with the Gateses and Warren Buffett; concerns about poverty and the need to find solutions to it; and the belief that having too much money would be harmful to one's children, coupled with a desire to teach them the importance of "giving back." As a coda, it is worth noting that only two people wrote at any length about religion, and only one mentioned "guilt" as a reason for giving.[22]

The notion that they were "blessed" with great good luck was often expressed by Giving Pledge signers quite poignantly. "We look upon our financial position with a mix of disbelief and humility, never having dreamed that we would be in this position," wrote Laura and John Arnold (hedge funds).[23] eBay founders Pierre and Pam Omidyar put it this way: "When eBay went public in 1998, Pam and I suddenly found ourselves in a position of great wealth. In a matter of days we went from making a modest living to landing a spot on *Forbes* list of richest Americans. It was a surreal experience."[24] And from David Rubenstein (leveraged buyouts): "I never expected, in my wildest dreams as a youth or as a young professional, to be in a position where anyone (other than my immediate family) would care what I would do with my money."[25]

Two other items often mentioned—parental guidance and the opportunity to be associated with the Gateses—also produced a fair number of emotional musings. "My thinking is rather simple: I learned as a young boy that sharing with others is the right thing to do, a lesson I observed from my father's willingness to share even our meager means with those less fortunate," commented Sidney Kimmel (retail).[26] From Lynn Schusterman (the only woman among the Giving Pledge signers, who also wrote movingly of her Jewish faith in relation to her philanthropic activity): "I was raised in a household in which giving back was a core value. One of my fondest childhood memories is holding my father's hand as he visited less fortunate elderly people who had no one else to care for them."[27]

On the Gates-Buffett connection, wrote Michael Bloomberg: "I am thrilled that my friends Bill Gates and Warren Buffett are bringing together this group, which could have an unprecedented impact on what philanthropy can achieve."[28] And George Kaiser felt the same: "I am entranced by Warren's and Bill's visionary appeal to those who have accumulated unconscionable resources, to dedicate at least half of them back to purposes more useful than dynasty perpetuation."[29]

Yet if Kaiser was right about the purpose of the Giving Pledge, it is less obvious that among the other signers it worked quite as he—and Gates and Buffett, if they agreed with him—hoped it would. Did it in fact encourage the signers to dig deeper, to give more "back"? On the bases of what they themselves said, it would be hard to argue that it did. Time and again they mentioned they had already established philanthropic foundations or other systems of planned giving, and usually had done so long before. More than a handful also seemed to want it clearly understood that it was *not* the Giving Pledge, but rather long-standing beliefs and feelings of their own, that motivated their generosity.

That included Michael Bloomberg: "For decades I've been committed to giving away the vast majority of my wealth."[30] And while Ray and Barbara Dalio (hedge funds) also admired what the Gateses were doing and were happy to sign the Pledge, they stressed that, as they said, "We had planned to give most of our money to those it will help anyway."[31] So had Larry Ellison: "Many years ago I put virtually all of my assets into a trust with the intent of giving away at least 95% of my wealth to charitable causes. I have already given hundreds of millions of dollars to medical research and education. I will give billions more over time."[32] And, wrote Michael and Lori Milken: "From the time we began formal philanthropic programs in the 1970s we've made contributions at a rate that will assure distribution of the overwhelming majority of assets during our lifetimes."[33]

Nor could anyone top David Rockefeller on such matters: "For five generations my family has experienced the real satisfaction and pleasure of philanthropy."[34] Yet in his own way David Rubenstein (leveraged buyouts) was equally emphatic: "In signing the Pledge, I did not honestly do anything more than I had already intended to do, as I said to Bill Gates when he talked to me about the Pledge. I actually had already made arrangements to ensure that a good deal more than half my resources would have gone to philanthropic purposes."[35] The same was true of Walter Scott (construction, Telecom): "While I'm pleased to respond to the appeal you are making with Bill and Melinda Gates to promote 'Giving Pledges' among our peers, I made that commitment long ago."[36]

And the coda here is even more noteworthy. Addressing his remarks to Warren Buffett, one of the Giving Pledge signers—Bernard Marcus (Home Depot)—wrote: "Thank you for calling to discuss my participation with you and Bill Gates regarding your philanthropic philosophy. It brought back memories of our conversation 15 years ago when I tried to convince you to do the very same thing."[37] *The very same thing?* Was Marcus talking about the act of giving itself or simply about publicizing it? It is impossible to tell.

There is, however, some related evidence that may be relevant here. In explaining why they signed the Pledge several members of the group explicitly distinguished between how it would affect their own behavior and the larger impact it might have. After mentioning that "for many years" he had been "quietly doing my own version of the Giving Pledge," Ted Forstmann (buyout specialist) described how Michael Bloomberg had convinced him to sign the Gates-Buffett pledge by arguing that "it would help encourage others to participate and would result in helping many needy causes."[38] Carl Icahn (leveraged buyouts) said much the same thing: "Until Bill, Melinda, and Warren started this project, I never considered going public with my intentions . . . I hope that by adding my voice with those who are supporting this project, we will all encourage others to participate."[39]

Among those who expressed similar thoughts were Harold and Sue Ann Hamm (oil and natural gas), Sidney Kimmel, Bernard and Billi Marcus, David Rubenstein, and of course Gates and Buffett themselves, who, according to a number of accounts, stressed this theme heavily in their conversations with potential Giving Pledge signers. Lynn Schusterman's remarks were particularly revealing in this respect: "As you know, my initial reaction to your kind invitation to sign the Giving Pledge was one of reticence and concern. Would my stepping forward make a difference? Could doing so be misconstrued as an act of self-aggrandizement rather than one motivated by a deep appreciation for the transformation power of philanthropy?"[40]

In the end Schusterman decided to sign the Pledge, thanks largely—as she explained—to the teachings of her Jewish faith. But the conflict she saw between signing for the purpose of self-aggrandizement and signing to further a worthy cause was not unusual. Neither was the highly individualistic way Schusterman approached the whole subject of philanthropy. Certainly there was no suggestion of unanimity in the Giving Pledge signers' remarks, either on what led them to give as generously as they did or on why they decided to sign the Pledge—no overarching pattern or unifying party line—just a handful of similarities here and there. As Edythe and Eli Broad (investments) explained, for them philanthropy was "intensely personal. No two people have identical views on what causes to champion and what approaches will fix social ills."[41]

Chaos, then? Not quite, for there remained one point among the Pledge signers where substantial agreement did occur, and that was on what philanthropic causes they found most appealing. Two in particular were mentioned time after time: one was medical research, and the other, education. And while medical research was a fairly straightforward matter, education raised a bundle of issues that offer a useful way into the minds and concerns of those who chose it as the object of their generosity.

Pledge signers targeted all levels of education but most preferred to concentrate on early schooling, an area they saw as consistently failing to meet the nation's needs, and by a wide margin. Especially eloquent on this score were Walter Scott (construction and telecom), the Broads, Ray and Barbara Dalio, Harold and Sue Ann Hamm, Carl Icahn, George Lucas, and Michael and Lori Milken. "It's scary to think of our educational system as little better than an assembly line with producing diplomas as our only goal," wrote Lucas. "We need to focus on building an education system that promotes different types of learning." Education, he continued, was "the key to the survival of the human race."[42]

The Broads' concern with education, as they explained it, fell closer to home. "We are dismayed by the state of America's K-12 public education, and wanted to work to restore it to greatness."[43] Also concerned with the state of American education, the Dalios described themselves as believing "deeply in equal opportunity, so much so that we feel that not contributing to it is tantamount to helping to perpetuate an injustice." And to their minds, "providing equal opportunity" meant, above all, "delivering quality education . . . to help all people capable of helping themselves."[44] Harold Hamm made much the same point: "Education helped me to end the cycle of poverty in my family. We are grateful for the educational opportunities that we had, and we are passionate about helping to provide better educational opportunities for people in need."[45]

Others who felt similarly about the nation's educational system included Carl Icahn, who declared: "I want to maintain America's position as the world economic leader by improving the competitiveness of our educational system. America's children, especially those from underprivileged backgrounds are in a sense undervalued assets. . . . I believe, without significantly changing the method we use to educate our young students in this country, we will lose our hegemony."[46] Michael and Lori Milken agreed, though if anything their sense of urgency was even stronger than Icahn's. The goal, they believed, should be "seeking out . . . and rewarding exceptional teachers and developing programs that can help America regain the educational leadership it once enjoyed."[47] In a characteristically thoughtful way Lynn Schusterman made the same point but with greater optimism. "While the times are difficult and our standing in the world is under attack, we remain an unparalleled driver of innovation as well as a beacon of freedom, democracy and justice for much of humanity—a status we will maintain only by pursuing and achieving in every corner of our educational system."[48]

In addition to the Pledge signers who preferred directing their philanthropy to education, the 2011 *Forbes* 400 list contains twenty-one other people with a strong enough interest in the field to have earned the icon symbolizing it next to their names on the 400 list. This tends to occur further down in the net worth ranking, nonetheless it serves to further emphasize the importance of education in the philanthropic planning of the very rich.

In the remarks the Pledge signers made about education, too, along with a distinct sense of urgency, there was also what may have mattered even more, a feeling that here was an area where they might be able to see during their own lives meaningful results. As Michael Bloomberg put it: "Making a difference in people's lives—and seeing it with your own eyes—

is perhaps the most satisfying thing you will ever do," and in this case, the difference could be both enticingly broad and pivotal—not just providing better schools for the nation's young, but also altering society in fundamental ways.[49] As George Kaiser wrote: "America's social contract is equal opportunity." And in achieving that goal, he felt, "we have lost ground in recent years."[50] That had to be changed.

Eli and Edythe Broad, in their sweeping vision, took a page from the same book: "We are convinced the future of the middle class, our standard of living, our economy and our very democracy rests on the strength of our public schools," to which they added, "and we have a long way to go."[51] The unfulfilled social contract, the lack of equality of opportunity, the plight of the middle class and, indeed, of American democracy itself: everything stood precariously poised, and there lay the risk as well as the opportunity, both of which seemed to be calling for truly transformative solutions with education presented time and again as the key to change.

Several Pledge signers who supported educational reform also related it directly to their personal histories. For them education had been a vital point of entry, an indispensable launching pad from which to propel themselves upward in life. The same people, too, tended to see what they took to be a grave crisis in the mounting failure of the American educational system to give those most in need what they themselves had received from it. Yet despite their sense of urgency, a majority of their fellow Pledge signers found other causes to support. Here as elsewhere diversity was the rule.

What then, should we think about the Giving Pledge and its signers? And did the results match the hopes that had led Buffett and the Gateses to initiate it? On both points it is necessary to backtrack a bit in time. By the spring of 2009 the worst of the financial crash of the year before was over—at least in the United States and at least for the time being. Still, the damage to the nation's economy had been immense, and the conviction that it had been caused by the self-seeking, irresponsible actions of a small group of very rich people was becoming increasingly widespread. Such was the setting in which the idea of the Giving Pledge began to take shape. Its genesis was a secret meeting on May 4 of a small circle of billionaires, led by Gates and Buffett and held—at the invitation of David

Rockefeller—at the President's House of Rockefeller University. Present among others, in addition to Gates, Buffett, and Rockefeller, were Ted Turner, Michael Bloomberg, and Oprah Winfrey. Within two weeks news of the event had leaked to the press.

If anything was said at that first dinner meeting about a Giving Pledge, there is no record of it. Rather, the idea gradually took shape at a series of similar occasions, held both in the United States and abroad, always within what Gates described as "a cone of secrecy."[52] The mix of people present changed from meeting to meeting, both to bring in new ideas and to enlarge the core group. (So much for Buffett's description of casually making phone calls to win support for the project.) Among the suggestions that surfaced in the beginning were a movie on the subject of philanthropy, a conference of the rich, and national recognition of large givers through awarding them presidential medals.

But increasingly the idea of a pledge took hold, though some people worried about its highly public nature. And Gates felt that giving away only 50 percent of one's wealth was a "low bar" to set for signers: they should have been asked to pledge more.[53] But the others stressed the need to get as many signatures as possible, as soon as they could, so the bar remained at 50 percent. And by the spring of 2010 the organizers were ready to go public (and hence make that year's *Forbes* 400 issue).

Obviously time was of the essence. Would that have been so, or indeed would the Giving Pledge have materialized at all absent the financial and economic turmoil of those years? It is of course impossible to say, but it seems unlikely. Angry "populist" (as they got labeled) attitudes toward the rich were on the rise. Perhaps the Giving Pledge could help stem that tide by bringing into public view an identifiable group of very rich, very generous people—thus raising their profile and creating a space for them in the popular imagination, which made it, in turn, an essentially defensive move.

This was a plausible interpretation certainly, and other pieces of evidence fit such a view, especially in Gates's case. He had already had one protracted and devastatingly unpleasant tug–of–war with American public opinion, caused by the monopoly charges leveled at Microsoft by the federal government. From that point, too, dated his first large philanthropic donations. It is harder, on the other hand, to construct a similar analysis of Buffett's motives. He had been saying for years that he planned to give most of his money away during his lifetime, but he did not begin doing so until 2006, when he climbed on board the Gateses' philanthropic bandwagon.

Yet in fairness it should be noted that once Gates began giving his money away in large chunks he seemed to quite enjoy himself. Buffett was another matter. It is unclear how much pleasure he got from philanthropy. The main thing was to do it as quickly and efficiently as possible, which partnering with the Gateses accomplished. But most of the other Pledge signers seemed to genuinely relish acting on their generous impulses. Many thought of it as a second career, and sometimes one far more rewarding than making money. Nor do their remarks seem shot through with noticeable undertones of fear. They may have been afraid for the nation's future but not evidently for their own.

Palpably present in the signers' remarks, however, are two other things: the pronounced diversity of their reasons for giving and the edginess of their desire to emphasize the fact that they were longtime givers; that their generosity was not a matter of suddenly taking action in response to recent events, including changing public attitudes toward the very rich. As they eagerly pointed out over and over again, they had been engaged in serious philanthropy for decades, and most had long since established family foundations for that purpose.

Why did they make such an issue of the point? It is impossible to say for sure, of course. But if one were to look at the matter from their perspective, it cannot have been all that easy to have the two richest men in America come bustling along, urging you to commit to something you had been doing for years, especially when they themselves were—relatively speaking—novices at the game of philanthropy. Yet if such thoughts did occur to anyone, only Bernard Marcus went so far as to even hint at them. Perhaps the others thought it would be impolite to do so. And again, more than a few signers mentioned how pleased they were to be associated with Buffett and Gates in backing the Pledge.

Was that enough? That depends on what Buffett and the Gateses hoped to achieve. A larger increase in the number of signers the second year would have been nice. So, too, no doubt, would have been greater unanimity among the signers about why they gave as generously as they did.

Helpful, too, might have been less insistence on how much longer, as individuals, without having to pledge, those same people had been engaged in major giving. For all of these points tended to diminish the impression of a widespread, broad-gauged welling up of generosity—a *movement*. They also, of course, challenged the familiar American narrative justifying great wealth through faith in the universality of the impulse driving the rich to give and give.

In short, the story line was skewed. As generous as these individuals were, they proved steadfastly resistant to the hoped-for interpretation of their actions. What they wanted the world to see and understand was how unique they were as individuals, how impossible it was to generalize about them. Their narratives were their own and nobody else's, and while they would sign the Giving Pledge it did not—could not—change who they were or their role in supporting the scores of worthy causes they did.

Renegades: Steve Jobs and Oprah Winfrey

Although arguing that a fair number of the Giving Pledge signers were knowingly working at cross-purposes with the Gates-Buffett team might stretch the point too far, candidates for that distinction can readily enough be found. And one obvious place to look for them was among all those people on the *Forbes* 400 list who chose not to sign the Pledge. In 2011 there were over 350 of them. But of all the holdouts two in particular stand out, both because of the controversy surrounding their refusal to sign and because of the place they occupied in the hearts of large numbers of Americans. One was Steve Jobs, and the other was Oprah Winfrey.

In the history of modern information technology others may loom larger than Steve Jobs as architects of its ongoing, increasing spread around the globe, but no one deserves more credit than Jobs for anchoring it in peoples' affections. This in fact is what he did best, and in later years, even as his body increasingly fell victim to the cancer that eventually killed him, his most memorable performances were introducing Apple's new products—iTunes, the iPhone, the iPad—to the world. The master of the rollout, he obviously loved the role, and people loved him in it: the darkened auditorium, the single spotlight on him as he walked onstage with his company's latest triumph in his hand, to sweep the audience off its feet with awe at seeing something that many of them may have fantasized about without the least idea of how to summon it into existence. Then he explained the thing, which proved to be even more magically wonderful than anyone could have imagined—except him. It was pure drama, inimitable and unforgettable.

So, too, was his entire life, if you wanted to see it that way: the driven kid working in his family's garage with his geeky best friend to invent the prototype of the personal computer; the founder of Apple who in his twenties had already piled up a $100-million fortune; the sometime-hippy who arranged to have himself schooled in Zen Buddhism; the entrepreneur forced out of his own company who went off to oversee the development of a radical new way of making animated films, which turned out to be hugely successful; the prodigal who returned to Apple to rescue it from almost certain collapse; the man capable of great charm who was also subject to cataclysmic rages that appalled his friends and co-workers and drove more than a few of them away. Steve Jobs was all of these, and woven together they do add up to a riveting story that people delighted in, as he himself seemed to do.

Of course, any number of items were left out of that version of the story, one of the most interesting being that Jobs seemed to have little if any interest in personal philanthropy. That circumstance had been— Andrew Sorkin wrote in the *New York Times* shortly before Jobs died— "long whispered about but rarely said aloud."[54] For the truth was, Jobs was not a prominent philanthropist. Far from it. And on that subject, Walter Isaacson—in the biography raced into print as Jobs was dying—added some not so subtle shadows describing Jobs as "generally dismissive of philanthropic endeavors," and "contemptuous of people who made a display of philanthropy or thinking that they could reinvent it."[55]

Presumably Isaacson's remarks were based on interviews, but the facts also speak for themselves. Along with refusing to sign the Giving Pledge, Jobs is nowhere to be found on the list of those making gifts of $1 million or more maintained by Indiana University's Center on Philanthropy. And, as Sorkin observes, "there is no public record of Mr. Jobs giving money to charity. . . . Nor is there a hospital wing or an academic building with his name on it."[56] In 1986, soon after being forced out of Apple, he did set up the Steven P. Jobs Foundation, but within fifteen months he shut it down, pleading lack of time. As for Apple, the company he founded, in 2007 the *Stanford Social Innovation Review,* which reports on nonprofit organizations, described it as one of "America's least philanthropic companies."[57] And indeed, when Jobs returned to it in 1997, he closed the company's philanthropic programs in order, he claimed, to restore it to profitability. Only in September 2011, after years of record-breaking profits, did Apple finally announce its decision to begin matching its employees' philanthropic donations.

There were, to be sure, any number of explanations offered by friends and admirers of Jobs for his lack of generosity. He was too busy building Apple and keeping it at the cutting edge of change to do anything else. Others argued that the vast changes he presided over in the field of technology were in themselves gifts of enormous value to the world. "He does not owe anything else to anyone. If I was in his position I would not allow a rent seeking parasite like Warren Buffet [*sic*] through my door, let alone tolerate him lecturing me on what I should do with my money," commented one person on Sorkin's blog. And in the same vein another reader remarked: "Steve Jobs' giving is what he has given: unrelenting commitment to creativity. Personally, I have received an enormous gift from his vision—as we all have who believe in Apple—a rugged belief not to settle but to reach and reach until you're there."[58]

To reach and reach until you are there: it was a fair description of what seemed to drive Jobs in life. But there were also some points about his attitude toward philanthropy in general and the Giving Pledge in particular that neither his critics nor his supporters mentioned. An important factor in his work life was his long and often strained relationship with Bill Gates. In the beginning their paths were quite similar: tinkering with computers in garages, going on from there without ever graduating from college, and ultimately creating rival companies that came to dominate the field of personal computers. Gates's company, however, became much larger and eventually big enough to be perceived as a profiteering monopoly. And it was in the face of that development that Gates embarked on large-scale philanthropy. Apple, on the other hand, developed a very different identity: a quirky enterprise with brilliantly designed products that many people adored. And for them Jobs could do no wrong. He was David, battling Gates's cruel and rapacious giant, Microsoft.

It was not, of course, quite that simple. Gates and Jobs were rivals but also friends in an odd way, that saw them both borrowing (or stealing?) ideas from one another, while saying, in private, generally unkind things about each other. Yet when Jobs returned to Apple, Gates put up $150 million to help get the company back on its feet. From time to time they even appeared in public together in sessions full of gentle joshing.

But always the question remained: which one of the two, in the end, would come out on top? Nor ultimately was it a matter of profits and losses or company size, let alone how much money you had. What mattered was how you were seen by the American people. Gates for a fact had more money and proposed—with much fanfare—to give most of it away. He even worked at trying to adopt the folksy, humorous style his partner Warren Buffett cultivated with such success. But Jobs was admired, loved, and treasured in ways that Gates never would be. And from those heights he could look down and—as rumor had it—scorn Gates's generosity. Certainly he had no reason to sign the Giving Pledge. What others saw as philanthropy was not part of his story. He had no desire to follow its imperative; he did not need it.

Neither did Oprah Winfrey. And as was true of Jobs, her life can be read as a constant struggle to be herself, to do what others said could not be done, to resist being neatly pigeonholed by anyone or anything. Nor have those challenges diminished as she currently struggles with her decision to end her daily talk show and concentrate on running her new cable TV network, OWN.

The major details of Oprah's life are well known: her deeply abusive childhood (one of her earliest memories was of being whipped daily by her grandmother; later there were repeated sexual assaults by other relatives and "friends" of the family), her teenage pregnancy, followed by her growing determination to make something of herself, her bouts of drug use and sexual promiscuity, her constant weight problem, her early years in broadcasting, her sense that what she wanted more than anything else in that arena was a daily TV talk show of her own, the realization of that ambition, and the stunning success that has made her, if not the richest woman in the United States, then certainly the richest woman to have earned her fortune herself.

The biography on her website notes that after moving to Chicago in 1984 she started a daily, half-hour TV show of her own, which in less than a year expanded to a full hour. In 1986 it entered national syndication and quickly became the country's highest-ranked talk show until she finally ended it in the spring of 2011. At its height it was broadcast in over 140 countries and had an estimated 42 million viewers a week. The hundreds of honors showered upon her include: selection for all six of *Time* magazine's 100 Most Influential People in the World lists (the only person to have made every one of them); the Elie Wiesel Foundation's Humanitarian Award; induction into the NAACP's Hall of Fame; the Association of American Publishers' AAP Honors Award; the United Nations Association of the United States of America's Global Humanitarian Action Award; and, in addition to multiple Emmy Awards, the National Academy of Television Arts & Sciences Lifetime Achievement Award (when she was only forty-four years old). Year after year she has also appeared on *Forbes* magazine's 400 list.

Point by point all of this is recounted in a plethora of books about Oprah, ranging from conventional biographies to scholarly monographs like Janice Peck's intriguing *The Age of Oprah: Cultural Icon for the Neoliberal Era,* as well as in publications like *The Uncommon Wisdom of Oprah Winfrey: A Portrait in Her Own Words,* which, though "unauthorized," is essentially autobiographical in character. There are also countless magazine and newspaper articles about her, plus her own magazine, *O.* Like other highly successful individuals, though, she is not universally admired. Self-promoting, shallow in conception and outlook, or worse, a misguided, ultimately dangerous concoction of feel-good pap that systematically misrepresents the realities of American life: these are some of the criticisms leveled at her "message." Reduced to their essentials, they present her efforts as a form of exploitation—a means of enriching herself at the expense of her naïve and gullible viewers. Fumed author and activist Barbara Grizzuti Harrison after publishing a piece in the *New York Times Magazine* entitled "The Importance of Being Oprah": "Her show . . . I just can't watch it. You will forgive me, but it is white trailer trash. It debases language, it debases emotion. It provides everyone with glib psychological formulas. These people go around talking like a fortune cookie."[59]

Still, Oprah's viewers seemed to remain perpetually enthralled and uplifted by her determination to encourage those who appeared on her show each day to—as her website once proclaimed—"Dare. Dream. Do." And unlike Steve Jobs she has chosen to give back her wealth on an impressive scale. Her largest philanthropic project to date has been establishing, at a cost of tens of millions of dollars, a school for young girls in South Africa, which for a time went badly due to various sexual scandals involving its students. But when people spoke critically of the place, her reaction, according to one of her biographers, Kitty Kelley, was bold and to the point; "To hell with your criticism. I don't care what you have to say about what I did. I did it."[60]

She has also been generous on many other, less-controversial fronts, which on at least one occasion extended to buying a young boy an alarm clock so he could get to school on time. What she did not do, however, was sign the Giving Pledge, which in turn might seem all the more surprising since, in effect, she was present at its creation. When the press finally got wind of that first meeting hosted by Buffett, Gates, and Rockefeller, her name was prominently featured among those who attended. Indeed it was part of what gave the meeting its interest and mystery. Why would Oprah be at such a gathering? What could it mean?

And if her presence that evening did not go unnoticed, neither did her absence from the list of those who committed themselves to the Giving Pledge list. Commented Kelley, "The name of Oprah Winfrey, the world's first black female billionaire, was conspicuously absent from the Midas list of do-gooders released this week by Warren Buffett and Bill Gates."[61] According to Kelley, rumor had it that Buffett was going to call Oprah to see if she would change her mind, and Kelley predicted he would fail—"I'll wager that the lady in question, whose net worth is $2.4 billion, will be unresponsive."[62]

In Kelley's opinion Winfrey did not want the kind of attention that would go with signing the Pledge focused on her personal finances. Such scrutiny would be, Kelley wrote, "loathsome to someone as controlling as Oprah."[63] Perhaps. Possibly, too, she did not want to appear to be caving in to the fat cats. But chances are, her motives were more complex than either of those explanations suggests. Rather, two other things were likely to be uppermost in her mind. Like Jobs she did not need the Pledge to improve her image. And like Jobs she had already given the greatest gifts she had to the American people. For him it was the ability to guide them through cyberspace to the things they valued most; for her it was the constant and unstinting gift of herself—her attention, her sympathy, her encouragement—lavished on those she interviewed daily on her TV show as well as on her audience. She meant to persuade them to forge better lives on their own. Their encounter with her was designed to begin that process, and the amount of energy, conviction, and feeling she poured into the effort day after day was truly a wonder to behold. This had been particularly so after the 1990s, when her show underwent something of a change in direction, which she summed up by declaring, "I have had enough of people's dysfunction. . . . What are you willing to do about it?"[64] That was the question she asked again and again.

Oprah's generosity also remained distinctly apolitical. "I think I could have a great influence in politics," she has said, "and I think I could get elected." But she also thinks what she does "every day has far more impact."[65] And if she is not interested in running for office, she also supports no political party (though she did endorse Barack Obama in the 2008 presidential campaign), has no consistently stated political agenda or, apparently, any overarching political worldview.

Meanwhile, she goes forward with her extraordinary life. After twenty-five years she did indeed leave her daily TV show (an event that was heralded for months beforehand by weekly televised peeks at the preparations for "The Final Show"). What lies beyond that milestone is impossible to tell. For the time being she proposes to concentrate on running her TV network, though the road ahead looks rocky, given the current low viewer numbers and falling advertising revenues. But it is difficult to imagine her changing in any fundamental way either her principles or her goals. She will remain the person who has both entertained and inspired tens of millions of devoted fans, presumably to the benefit of many of them and not incidentally to her very substantial enrichment, with its accompanying generosity. She will remain, in short, what she has become: one of America's good rich, like Steve Jobs, with a story all her own to tell, in which the Giving Pledge could have no role. Though being Oprah she might just turn around tomorrow and sign it. Yet if she does, it will be for reasons uniquely hers.

8

WEALTH AND AMERICAN DEMOCRACY

On September 17, 2011, a group of about a thousand protesters gathered in lower Manhattan to register their feelings on various loosely connected issues, including the unequal distribution of wealth and power in the United States. More specifically their goal was—as the name they operated under indicated—to "Occupy Wall Street." What they ended up occupying was Zuccotti Park, a small grassy common two blocks away, which they renamed Liberty Square and where they began camping out in tents. On September 24 a clash between the New York City police and the protesters over their wearing of masks resulted in eighty arrests, but for the time being they were allowed to remain in the park. On October 1, more than five thousand protesters marched on the Brooklyn Bridge, seven hundred of whom were arrested. On October 5, a group estimated at between five thousand and fifteen thousand marched less than a mile from Foley Square to Zuccotti Park, with only a few arrests made. By then as many as thirty-nine organizations, including the New York Transport Workers' Union Local 100, were supporting Occupy Wall Street. Within a few days similar demonstrations had spread to Houston, Austin, Tampa, San Francisco, Los Angeles, and Portland, Oregon. By October 15 over a thousand American cities were involved as well as eighty-two foreign countries.

Studying this sequence of events, one almost hears the tumbrels approaching, but Occupy Wall Street was—emphatically—not that kind of event. In late November the city ordered the tents and other accoutrements of outdoor living removed from Zuccotti Park, which occurred largely without incident, though the breakup of encampment left a host of questions in its wake. What would the protesters do next? What were the movement's plans, if in fact it could be described as a movement at all? What goals would it pursue? What form would its organization, post-Zuccotti, take? What impact, if any, would it have on the 2012 national elections? What kinds of alliances would its leaders seek to forge with existing political groups? Indeed, who were its leaders? As 2011 moved to a close all of these questions floated in the ether, shot through, moment by moment with thousands upon thousands of messages generated by millions of electronic devices around the globe—a concatenation that produced not the slightest consensus on any of the points at issue.

But there are some questions to which answers are possible—chiefly because they focus on the past, rather than on the present or the future. And one of those questions is, what led to Occupy Wall Street in the first place? Or, to put the query in a somewhat different light: why had it been so long in coming? On that version of the question, too, the preceding chapters of this book can offer some useful insights.

In point of fact, Occupy Wall Street had its beginning in a call issued by Kalle Lasn and Micah White, the editors of *Adbusters,* a Canadian-based, anticonsumerist magazine. Sent to *Adbusters'* sixty thousand "friends" in June of 2011, proclaiming that "America needs its own Tahrir"—referring to the massive Egyptian protests of a few months earlier—it proposed that on September 17 a phalanx of twenty thousand people should flood into lower Manhattan, remain there, and incessantly repeat one simple demand, in a plurality of voices.[1]

The demand Lasn and White had in mind was for "Barack Obama to ordain a Presidential Commission tasked with ending the influence money has over our representatives in Washington."[2] Already by the time the protesters had settled in Zuccotti Park countless other demands had sprung up like summer wildflowers. Yet what became and remained the quasi-official rallying cry of the phenomenon seemed to focus squarely on the issue of inequality. "We are the 99 percent," chanted the protesters, delivering a message short and catchy enough to be picked up instantly by the media. The point was to draw attention as dramatically as possible to what the protesters saw as the enormous gap separating—in economic and political terms—a minuscule number of hugely rich individuals from the remainder of the population. Hence the 99 percent and the 1 percent.

In sum, a massive failure in equality, in fairness, indeed in democracy it-self: that was Occupy's indictment, and it received support from a number of other quarters—if not at first from many politicians, then at least from a wide range of persistent voices in the media. Even more influential was a report published in October of 2011 by the Congressional Budget Office documenting the rising disparity of incomes in the United States during the years from 1979 to 2007 (the period for which the relevant data were readily available). The most striking features of the CBO's findings were that:

- During the years in question the average real after-tax income of the top 1 percent of the population grew by 275 percent.
- The corresponding growth in income for the middle three-fifths of the population was less than 40 percent, and for the bottom one-fifth only 18 percent.
- As a result of those changes the distribution of after-tax income in the country had become, as the authors stated in their summary: "sub-stantially more unequal in 2007 than in 1979."
- By the end of the period the total income of the most affluent 20 percent of the population had grown to be larger than the combined incomes of the remaining 80 percent.
- Meanwhile, the top 1 percent had more than doubled its share of the nation's income.

Translated into graphs and pie charts, these numbers made a major splash, especially when accompanied by other data, including the results of several reports providing the opportunity to compare levels of inequality around the world. "Inequality in America is worse than in Egypt, Tunisia or Yemen," blared one headline—which was true, and to that list could have been added every one of the other so-called rich nations (Germany, Japan, France, Italy, etc.) as well as Saudi Arabia, Jordan, Syria, Israel, India, Pakistan, and most of the nations of Africa.[3]

Presumably all this came as news to a great many Americans. Yet even those who already understood that significant inequality was a fact of national life had at best a sketchy sense of just how large it loomed. In another study, Dan Ariely of Duke University and Michael I. Norton of the Harvard Business School found that when asked to estimate the percentage of wealth owned by different groups, moving from the poorest to the wealthiest, those who responded (including Harvard Business School alumni) underestimated, and by a significant margin, the amount of inequality such an exercise revealed. For example, they judged that the richest 20 percent of the nation's population controlled 59 percent of its wealth, while the correct figure was close to 84 percent. The same people believed that the level of American inequality—even though they underestimated it—was too high and ought to be lowered.

If Americans are not as equal as they think they are, or as they want to be, the evidence also clearly shows that inequality has been on the rise for decades in the United States, which a few thoughtful observers had been pointing out for a while. In 2005, for example, Janet Yellen, speaking as president and CEO of the Federal Reserve Bank of San Francisco—one of several key positions she has held in the field of economic policy planning—addressed the issue head-on. Noting that with the economy performing well (as it still seemed to be at that point), she observed that much of the resulting gain had, as she said, "gone to just a small segment of the population—those already in the upper part of the income distribution," adding that, as a result, "economic inequality has grown," which she believed "could, ultimately, undermine American democracy."[4]

For all Yellen's trenchant analysis, however, the subject of inequality failed to arouse much public interest for another four years, by which time the economy lay in tatters, by which time, too, the wealth gap—or "the Great Divergence," as *New York Times* columnist Paul Krugman liked to call it—had grown apace.[5] In discussing the causes of inequality Yellen concentrated on factors like changes in technology, globalization, and CEO compensation, as one would expect an economist to do. Krugman, on the other hand, leveled a good part of the blame at "a reliable set of defenders" who have systematically put, as he said, "a more benign face on the phenomenon" than it deserved.[6] In short, we had been hoodwinked into believing what was not true. Again and again we were told inequality did not exist, or that it did not matter. Both were wrong according to Krugman.

Together Yellen and Krugman painted an arresting picture—cool economic determinism combined with a passionate hunt for evil-doing villains—to explain what is by no means easy to explain: how relentlessly inequality had risen over the last four decades, and why until very recently we had paid so little attention to it. What the two of them left out, however, was the extent to which we ourselves have been deeply complicit in our own undoing, which goes to the heart of the thesis that this book, in its scattershot way, has endeavored to present.

If the stories sketched in the preceding chapters show anything, it is that they are just that: *stories,* not one story. Together they have three salient features in common—namely that they are about people with a lot of money, that more than a few of those people angered their fellow Americans in the process of becoming rich, and that in the end they redeemed themselves, chiefly by giving away a good portion of their wealth to help others. Yet the details surrounding those points of similarity are so diverse as to make it impossible to construct a single narrative that does more than scratch the surface. Not only did the people in question come by their money in quite different ways, but their generosity also took different forms and stemmed from different motivations. Rockefeller's giving spanned his entire adulthood and was much influenced by his religious beliefs. In other instances the crucial decisions seemed to grow from an epiphany occurring relatively late in life. Both Robert Keayne and Abbott Lawrence belong to this category. Yet while Keayne, like Rockefeller, was moved by religious convictions, Abbott Lawrence was not. Neither was George Washington. Arguably, too, in some cases generosity was fused with unmistakable elements of defensive strategizing, but not in all, as Amos Lawrence's giving demonstrates.

So there is nothing systemic at work here: no broad pattern repeating itself time after time, whatever the circumstances. And nowhere is this more evident than in the objects on which these individuals chose to lavish their generosity. Between Robert Keayne's "Market House," George Washington's freed slaves, Amos Lawrence's packages of miscellaneous dry goods sent to perfect strangers, his brother Abbott's model lodging houses for the poor, and John D. Rockefeller's "philanthropic trusts" lie enormous variations in purpose, vision, and achievement. These were islands in the ocean, separate and distinct from one another, not stops along a highway leading inexorably from Puritan Boston to present-day Manhattan and Silicon Valley. And the same diversity characterizes the good works of both the Rockefeller heirs and the Giving Pledge signers. Even with the full weight of the Rockefeller legend and Buffett and Gates's challenge to corral them into line, they remained implacably independent, inseparably wedded to their own individual agendas, which in the case of the Giving Pledgers meant distancing themselves from not only the great majority of the *Forbes* 400, who chose not to sign the pledge, but also, in the end, its promoters, Gates and Buffett. And then there were the unredeemable renegades—Jobs and Winfrey—islands utterly unto themselves.

Philosophically there is in all of this a highly complicated logic at work. While we hold fast to our faith in democracy—in equality—we do recognize that reality rarely if ever conforms to that faith. So we modify it by asserting that what we really care about is equality of opportunity, and when that faith too fails, as it often does, to manifest itself in sufficiently wide-ranging ways, we work at smoothing out the bumps as best we can. Occasionally, though, the bumps become too high to treat with simple solutions—as happened with the glaring inequality of the 1890s and the 1920s, as well as in the early years of the twenty-first century. In the first two of those cases, preternaturally high levels of inequality combined with economic crashes of major proportions to bring about sweeping reform that directly targeted the rich, whose activities seemed in no small part to have led to the hard times. From being thought of as heroes, they fell to the bottom ranks of public esteem, and thereafter had to live with stiffer regulation of their affairs plus much higher taxes on their wealth.

Could this happen again? The success of Occupy Wall Street in drawing attention to itself and the 1 percent suggests that it might, though Occupy could also turn out to be a flash in the pan. Ultimately, as well, if the push toward reform is to go forward from here, we are likely to have to modify substantially our opinions of the very rich—to understand that (as is true of most people) they tend to care more about their own welfare than they do about ours. There are, to be sure, good people who are rich, and whose generosity is truly impressive, including every one of the individuals whose stories have been told here. Yet, again, neither they nor their generosity are typical of the rich as a whole.

On the contrary, study after study has shown that, as a group, wealthy Americans are less generous than we think. First, however, it should be said that Americans are correctly described as the most generous people on earth. Also, the country's wealthiest citizens are more generous than the rich of any other nation, and they donate a greater share of the nation's total giving by individuals than any other group—roughly 65 percent. Yet a closer look at the details of the larger picture, as provided by a series of exhaustive studies of the philanthropy of high-net-worth Americans, researched and written by the Center on Philanthropy at Indiana University, reveals some interesting trends.

For one thing, the studies show that giving by wealthy individuals varies both across time and for different levels of wealth and income. For example, compared with the 2007 data, in 2009 the group of individuals with the highest net worth (more than $20 million) cut its giving almost in half, reducing the amount from 16.1 percent of income to 8.7 percent. Thus did the economic downturn of those years exact its toll on the generosity of the rich, though a recent article in the *Chronicle of Philanthropy* suggests that lately giving has been going up again. In 2011 the medium total giving for those on the journal's annual list of the fifty most generous Americans was $61 million, compared with $39.6 million the year before. Interestingly enough, too, the *Chronicle* stressed that the increase occurred against the backdrop of "the Occupy Wall Street movement and growing concerns about an economic divide."[7]

But overall the most striking feature of the figures for giving by the rich is how low they are. Until 2007 none of the various groups categorized by net worth in the Indiana University studies even managed to tithe except for the very rich, and again, their giving fell to the point where they too failed to tithe in 2009. The figure for total giving for all of the categories in the studies hovers around 8.5 percent of income, hardly an impressive achievement, especially when millions of other Americans strive to tithe, and many do succeed, despite the obvious fact that the further down the income scale one goes, the greater the sacrifices involved in tithing become. Giving away 10 percent of an income of $1 million leaves a balance of $900,000. If the income is as high as $10 million, the remainder will be $9 million. But giving away 10 percent of an income of $50,000 produces a very different result. In the first two cases no scrimping is required to provide the necessities of life; in the third case it is much less clear that this will be so.

On the other hand, even at the reduced levels of 2009, the percentage of the high-net-worth households in the Indiana University studies that gave to "charity" was definitely higher than that for the U.S. population as a whole (70.5 percent compared to 43.0 percent). Also, the average amount given by such households in 2009 was over $54,000, which could seem like a great deal of money. But that year the median percent of income given by those households was notably lower than the average percentage, which suggests a good deal of variation in individual giving—perhaps a few unusually high cases combined with many other lower ones.

In any event, what does not emerge here is a picture of great generosity as a consistently reliable pattern of behavior among the rich. On the contrary, their giving is much affected by economic and political conditions at particular times. Also, while some wealthy households studied seem to be quite generous, others are much less so, and considering the resources available to wealthy individuals, on average they do not appear to be more generous, in relative terms, than many other Americans. It should be noted, too, that the data for the 2009 Indiana University study consisted of only 1,077 completed twelve-page questionnaires out of a total of 20,000 sent out to randomly selected individuals in "high net worth areas of the United States." Given the low rate of response it seems likely that those who chose to participate had a definitive interest in philanthropy, were likely already actively involved in giving, and indeed may well have been proud of that fact. All of which suggests, in turn, that if anything the Indiana University studies paint too rosy a picture, exaggerating both the giving propensities of rich Americans and the amounts they give.

Also, it appears that even in the case of the truly good (and generous) rich, there is a price we pay, for what they choose to give and what we believe we need can be quite different. Comparing the giving of the rich with that of the general U.S. population, the Indiana University studies yield the following results: as a percent of their total philanthropic outlays, the population at large gives far more to religious causes than the rich do, more also to charities dedicated to fulfilling peoples' basic needs, but less to almost everything else, including the arts, environmental/animal care, health, youth and family services, and education. Thus there exists a clear difference between the philanthropic priorities of the rich and those of the rest of the population. Interesting, too, in this regard is the high proportion of giving by the rich that goes to education, and in particular to elite institutions like Harvard, Yale, MIT, and Stanford, which seems unlikely to reduce the income gap by much. If anything it could actually have the opposite effect by increasing the ranks and wealth of the rich and academically privileged.

From there, as well, it is but a short step to asking whether the tax dollars lost to deductions for charitable giving might be better spent by leaving it to the democratic political process to decide what ought to be done with the money. On this issue it is also instructive that the Indiana University study for 2009 shows that when people were asked what difference it would make in their giving if the income tax deduction for charitable donations were eliminated, less than a third (32.6 percent) said their giving would remain the same, while 48.3 percent said it would decrease "somewhat," and 18.7 percent said it would decrease "dramatically."[8] So not only do the rich give when they want and what they want, their giving also seems to operate in ways not unlike those Robert Keayne laid down in his contract with Boston all those years ago.

By now questions might well be arising as to exactly what the rich do with their money, if they are not in fact so very generous after all. One answer, surely, is that they provide — often with extraordinary openhandedness — for their progeny. Ineluctably, too, dynastic visions creep in, or at a minimum notions about ensuring the "security" of not only children but also grandchildren, as well as generations yet unborn. Then there are all the things money can buy to increase one's comfort and pleasure — the huge cornucopia of delights and luxuries of every kind chronicled in the early twentieth century, with such wit and insight, by Thorstein Veblen in his *Theory of the Leisure Class*. And if more contemporary examples are wanted, perusing the pages of a magazine like *Architectural Digest* can help. Especially useful is the annual issue devoted to homes (invariably the third or fourth residence possessed by their owners) in "exotic places," not a few of which turn out to be so far off the beaten track that they can be reached only by private aircraft.

Other models for expenditures like these are plentiful, particularly if one turns to the past. And there, for all their virtue, a prime example has to be the Rockefeller family, which did indeed provide so lavishly for its progeny that the word "dynasty" is routinely used to describe the result. Nor did the Rockefellers stint on the material aspects of their lives. Despite his announced preference for plain living, John D. Rockefeller owned, in addition to a New York town house, three different country places, each with its own golf course. And to shelter his brood in the city, Junior had Welles Bosworth design what turned out to be the largest private residence in New York (which was torn down once the children were grown, with the site going to the Museum of Modern Art). But of course the Rockefellers did all this while also becoming the most generous family in the nation's history, making them an exceedingly difficult act to follow. But if you could not do it all, economies could be made, and one area where this seems to be done with notable frequency is philanthropy.

Still, while such information may be interesting to have, neither it nor a whole raft of academic studies seems likely to change what Americans think about the giving of the very rich, at least under normal circumstances. For it appears we deeply want to believe that as a group our wealthiest fellow citizens are, and will remain, prodigiously generous. Though it doesn't address philanthropy specifically a recent Gallup poll indicated that 63 percent of the American population believes "the United States benefits from having a class of rich people."[9] And though there are many causes of inequality in the United States, the paradigm that supports the belief in the goodness and generosity of the rich teaches us, as well, that whatever such people did to become rich will ultimately disappear from the equation because, in the end, they will choose to give back to society an ample return for all they owe. To ensure this will happen, too, we make it easy for them with valuable gifts of our own: a marginal tax rate that at present is barely a third of what it was fifty years ago; shelters in which to preserve their wealth; deductions for charitable giving; and gratifying esteem for all we imagine they do for us. Could this change? If Occupy Wall Street has its way it must and will change. A more measured answer might be: "Perhaps. We'll wait and see."

Hidden away in the Medici Palace in Florence is a treasure no tourist should miss. It is a tiny chapel with the walls of its larger room (which one enters first) completely covered by a brilliant fresco depicting a single, long procession winding through a rocky landscape dotted with trees and imposing castlelike buildings, though at every turn the center of attention is the procession itself, filled as it is with dazzlingly attired figures. What particularly attracts notice are three of those figures, all on horseback, all dressed in glittering, fur-trimmed tunics elaborately decorated in gold. In addition they wear stunning hats, each, if one looks closely, incorporating a crown. There are no women in the procession, but around what seems to be its end point groups of angels with golden halos are gathered singing and praying.

If you have a knowledgeable eye you may notice that the clothing worn by the figures in the fresco dates from roughly the middle of the fifteenth century—about the time the Medici Palace itself was built. Or perhaps your guidebook will point this out. So on the basis of the visual evidence, the event pictured in the fresco could easily be something the artist himself had seen. But your guidebook will also tell you that ostensibly the subject of the fresco was the journey of the three Magi, the priest/kings who traveled from the East to Bethlehem bearing gifts for the newborn Christ child. So in effect the artist, Benozzo di Lese, known as Gozzoli, was translating a biblical event—the Adoration—into contemporary times and setting it in all likelihood in the neighborhood of Florence, presumably with the approval—if not indeed at the command—of his patron, Cosimo di Giovanni de' Medici (known as Cosimo the Elder), who had brought to its apogee the Medici family's ongoing rise to great wealth.

Nor was clothing all that linked the fresco to the world of that day, for Cosimo himself actually appears in the procession along with one, or perhaps two, of his sons, one or two of his grandsons, and a nephew, plus several other individuals prominent in the history of Florence. Thus it had both private and public connotations, though the small size of the chapel that contained the fresco suggests it was meant to be a private place. The record also shows, however, that, periodically, lavish reenactments of the Magi's journey in fact staged in Florence. So possibly those, and not the biblical adoration, were the "real" subject of the fresco. Also, toward the end of his life Cosimo used the chapel as an office and received visitors there.

Public and private, then, business and pleasure, power and religious devotion, politics and art: in the Chapel of the Magi they all came together, intricately interwoven with the whole meant to capture the eye, but even more to delight and enrich the imagination. Meanwhile, this was a dangerous time in Florence's history, one full of grinding, sometimes brutal, conflict, in which the Medici played a central role. So perhaps, after all, the chapel was meant to serve as a kind of refuge, with its fresco depicting calm, measured movement forward. But then one looks at the eyes of the figures in it, and startlingly enough they peer about nervously in all directions, full of wary anxiety, as if they expected the whole long, glittering cavalcade to be attacked at any moment.

It is true, of course, that those at the top of any economic and social order are rarely completely comfortable. To possess great power is also to imagine it slipping away in the twinkling of an eye. And so it has been for the rich in America, the world's longest surviving democracy. In Florence life was perpetually awash with conflicting beliefs, systems of authority, and vectors of influence and danger, which shifted kaleidoscopically day by day. By comparison, our own world seems far more orderly and predictable. Yet on the chief issue that has occupied our attention here—the relationship between wealth and democracy—one can discover large swings in direction and, for some people, great opportunities combined with great risks.

If you are rich in America, even more if you become rich, the population at large can see it as a confirmation of the existence of equality of opportunity and thus democracy, or at least a close approximation to it. If, on the other hand, the wealth of a small group of individuals continues to grow and grow while the wealth of others shrinks, it becomes problematic, because at some point it is almost certain to challenge the conviction that the race to become rich is fundamentally fair. Yet if that does occur, ways can still be found to obscure our perceptions of what is happening. For if we believe there are actually benefits that come to us in spite of— indeed because of—the existence of substantial levels of inequality in our midst, perhaps we will mind them less. And this, in turn, is the chief cost of believing, as we do, in the universal generosity of the American rich. Under the influence of that belief we can and do tolerate, even celebrate, the violation of some of our most cherished ideals.

Though again, if our eyes are thus blinkered, it is not the rich who do it: rather we do it to ourselves, because to do otherwise would be to admit that the United States is not, finally, the great bastion of democracy and equality that we want to believe it is. For the rich, however, this remains precarious territory, supported as it is by a willful, albeit optimistic, piece of self-delusion. So like Gozzoli's Florentines elevating themselves to the company of the Magi, our own richest fellow citizens may also be glancing about nervously to see if anyone notices that the spectacle on view is nothing more than a shimmering palimpsest behind which lies a very different reality.

For even in America, history does record moments—like those following the boom years of the 1890s and the 1920s—when the parade was stopped, the veil fell, and people began thinking hard about democracy again.

ACKNOWLEDGMENTS

There are some things in life that are best done alone. Writing a book is not one of them. I am beholden to a number of good people for the generous help they have given me on this project. Joseph Ellis of Mount Holyoke College and Frederick Rudolph, Professor Emeritus of History at Williams College, read and reread jumbled versions of the early chapters, commenting with rigor and insight—often to my considerable discomfort but invariable in ways that forced me to better formulate what exactly I was doing and where it needed to go from there. Also important in this regard was my good friend and colleague in the Williams College History Department, James B. Wood. Whoever passes out such things endowed him with a preternatural intolerance of muddle, which, as usual, helped me a great deal.

I am indebted as well to Williams College for its welcome assistance through sabbatical leaves and generous grants of research funds.

To the good sense and warm support of my agent, Geri Thoma, who never lost faith in the project, I also owe a great deal.

Since I still write in longhand on yellow lined paper, someone has to take those much-erased and constantly scribbled-over sheets and connect them to the wonders of modern technology, which was superbly well done by Margaret M. Weyers, administrative assistant in the Faculty Secretarial Office at Williams College. Linda A. Saharczewski, administrative assistant of the History Department, performed similar magic with the book's illustrations.

My editor at Yale University Press, Christopher Rogers, has been unfailingly kind and thoughtful, even when I was not. I am also grateful to his assistant, Christina Tucker, for keeping the project, and me, on track and to Jeffrey Schier, who copyedited the entire manuscript with impressive skill.

Finally, there is the great debt I owe two members of my family, both fine historians: my son and wise research assistant and editor, Fred Dalzell, and my wife and sometime collaborator, Lee Baldwin Dalzell. At every turn her contributions went way beyond what even the best and most loving of mates could be expected to do in such circumstances. This is a slender volume, but even then "Thank you" sounds like far too slim a reward for your boundless help and support. All I can say is that I mean those words from the bottom of my heart.

NOTES AND SOURCES

In the notes that follow I have provided references for all direct quotations in the text as well as brief discussions, at the beginning of the notes for each chapter, of those sources published and unpublished on which I have particularly relied for information and insight. None of these discussions are in any sense exhaustive, nor were they meant to be. On some of the individuals whose lives are sketched here, for example George Washington and the Rockefellers, complete lists of the available material would doubtless cover more pages than this book itself does. Rather, what I have hoped to do is give the reader a sense of how I would answer—without drawing it out needlessly—someone who asked, "Just where does all this come from? What evidence have you for it?"

And if the imagined interrogator seemed interested in hearing more, I might mention that I have already published books on several of the individuals in question, including, with my wife, Lee Baldwin Dalzell, as co-author, *George Washington's Mount Vernon: At Home in Revolutionary America* (New York, 1998); on the Lawrence brothers in *The Boston Associates and the World They Made* (Cambridge, 1987); and, again with Lee Baldwin Dalzell, in *The House the Rockefellers Built: A Tale of Money, Taste, and Power in Twentieth-Century America* (New York, 2007). A number of the conclusions offered here first saw the light of day in those books, but the world has changed since they were written, and my own interests today differ from what they were then.

On this point I would add that writing history is always a collaborative process. Necessarily we are dependent on what the actors involved chose to reveal about themselves in what they did, said, or wrote, as well as on those good souls who went to the trouble of preserving that evidence. Also—and every bit as important—we stand on the shoulders of a constantly changing company of other historians who have labored to make sense of the same evidence. If, then, one should happen to be crossing for the second time a specific piece of territory, the topography may appear familiar, but invariably collaborating with yourself and others will reveal features of the landscape you missed the first time around, or which—seen from a different angle—prove to be both intriguing and surprising.

Chapter 1. Paradox

SOURCES

A useful and highly readable biography of Andrew Carnegie is Harold Livesay, *Andrew Carnegie and the Rise of Big Business* (Boston, 1978).

Alexis de Tocqueville's *Democracy in America* has been translated into English and published in new editions a number of times over the years. The edition used here was translated by Henry Reeve, with Francis Bowen as editor (Cambridge, Mass., 1864). The best biography of Tocqueville is Hugh Brogan, *Alexis de Tocqueville: A Life* (New Haven, Conn., 2007). See also Arthur Kaledin, *Tocqueville and His America: A Darker Horizon* (New Haven, Conn., 2011), for a nontraditional point of view.

NOTES

1. Carnegie quoted in Livesay, *Carnegie,* 72.
2. Ibid., 188.
3. Tocqueville, *Democracy in America,* vol. 1, 67.
4. Ibid., 64.
5. Ibid.
6. John D. Rockefeller, *Random Reminiscences of Men and Events* (Garden City, N.Y., 1916). The phrase is used there as the title of Chapter VI.
7. Abigail Adams to Isaac Smith, Jr., April 2, 1771, quoted in Joseph Ellis, *First Family* (New York, 2010), 23.
8. Rockefeller, *Random Reminiscences,* 142.
9. Hebert Sandler, quoted in David Whelan, "Billion-Dollar Donors," *Forbes,* October 19, 2009, vol. 184, no. 7, 40.
10. Andrew Carnegie, *The Gospel of Wealth and Other Timely Essays* (New York, 1901), 19.

11. There is no written record anywhere that such an exchange between Fitzgerald and Hemingway ever actually took place.

Chapter 2. Robert Keayne's Contract with Boston

SOURCES

The version of Keayne's last will and testament used here descends from various earlier versions but has been usefully edited for publication as *The Apologia of Robert Keayne: The Last Will and Testament of Mr. Robert Keayne, All of It Written with My Own Hands and Began by Me: Mo. 6, 1653, Commonly Called August,* Bernard Bailyn, ed. (Gloucester, Mass., 1970). Bailyn has also included with the text a helpful introduction of his own, an expanded version of which can be found in his "The Apologia of Robert Keayne," *The William and Mary Quarterly,* Third Series, vol. 7 (Oct., 1950), 568–87. And in addition Bailyn is the author of *New England Merchants in the Seventeenth Century* (Cambridge, Mass., 1955), which provides an invaluable analysis of the broader stage on which Keayne operated as a merchant.

On New England Puritanism, Perry Miller's works remain essential, the most important of them being *Orthodoxy in Massachusetts* (Boston, 1959) and *Errand into the Wilderness* (Cambridge, Mass., 1984). For a fine analysis of Anne Hutchinson's activities and her followers see: John Emery Battis, *Saints and Sinners: Anne Hutchinson and Its Antinomian Controversy in Massachusetts Bay Colony* (Chapel Hill, N.C., 1962).

On Puritan society and politics in general, as well as the way religion interacted with both, no one has written more or more wisely than Edmund S. Morgan. See especially *The Puritan Dilemma: The Story of John Winthrop* (Boston, 1958), though also invaluable are all of the following: *The Puritan Family: Essays on Religion and Domestic Relations in Seventeenth-Century New England* (Boston, 1944); *Puritan Political Ideas, 1558–1794* (Indianapolis, Ind., 1976); *Visible Saints: The History of a Puritan Idea* (Ithaca, N.Y., 1982). Other helpful sources in this respect are Samuel Eliot Morison, *Builders of the Bay Colony* (Boston, 1930); and Keith W. T. Stavely, *Puritan Legacies: Paradise Lost and the New England Tradition, 1630–1890* (Ithaca, N.Y., 1987), and on Boston, Darrett B. Rutman, *Winthrop's Boston: Portrait of a Puritan Town* (Chapel Hill, 1965).

On Anna Keayne Lane Paige's dazzling rise in life see Edmund S. Morgan's

"A Boston Heiress and Her Husbands: A True Story," *Publications of the Colonial Society of Massachusetts,* vol. 26, 409–513. Goody Sherman and her pig are discussed in Bailyn, "The Apologia of Robert Keayne," *William and Mary Quarterly,* 568, and Morison, *Builders,* 92–93.

NOTES

1. Keayne, *Last Will,* 81.
2. Ibid.
3. John Winthrop, "A Model of Christian Charity," *Winthrop Papers* (Boston, 1931), vol. 2, 295.
4. Keayne, *The Apologia,* 9.
5. Winthrop, "Christian Charity," 294.
6. Bailyn, *New England Merchants,* 21.
7. Ibid.
8. Bailyn (Introduction), "The Apologia of Robert Keayne," viii.
9. Keayne, *The Apologia,* 53.
10. Ibid., 57.
11. Ibid., 54.
12. Ibid., 59.
13. Ibid., 61.
14. Ibid., 28.
15. Ibid., 50.
16. Ibid., 56.
17. Ibid., 27.
18. Ibid., 23.
19. Ibid., 6–7.
20. Ibid., 75.
21. Ibid., 76.
22. Ibid.
23. Ibid., 82.
24. Ibid., 27.
25. Records of the First Church of Boston, quoted in Bailyn, "The Apologia of Robert Keayne," 576.
26. Keayne, *The Apologia,* 82.
27. Ibid., 83.
28. Ibid., 84.
29. Ibid., 82.
30. Ibid., 86.
31. Ibid., 87.
32. Bailyn, *New England Merchants,* 98.
33. Keayne, *The Apologia,* 48.

34. *Massachusetts Colony Records,* quoted in Morgan, "A Boston Heiress," 507.

35. Collections of the Massachusetts Society, quoted in ibid., 512.

Chapter 3. George Washington, Revolutionary

SOURCES

A superb edition of George Washington's papers is currently being published in multiple volumes, which began appearing in 1983 as *The Papers of George Washington,* William W. Abbott, ed. (Charlottesville, Va.). Shortly thereafter, with only a few of the volumes published, Lee Baldwin Dalzell and I began our research on Mount Vernon, and the staff of the papers project—the offices of which were located in the Alderman Library of the University of Virginia—were kind enough to give us access to the typescripts that would eventually find their way into print in one or another of the five series of papers project. The citations here will sometimes be to the printed volumes and sometimes to our research notes, though in those cases the information provided can easily be used to locate the appropriate material in the printed volumes. And to fill in the gaps in the *Papers of George Washington,* we also relied on *The Writings of George Washington from the Original Manuscripts Sources,* 30 vols., John C. Fitzpatrick, ed. (Washington, D.C., 1931–44)—an earlier series, which for its time was quite well done. In the case of Mount Vernon a rich trove of sources can also be found in the archives located next door to "the Mansion" in the Mount Vernon Ladies Association House. Another important published source is the *Diaries of George Washington,* 6 vols., Donald Jackson and Dorothy Twohig, eds. (Charlottesville, Va., 1976–79).

The amount of published material on George Washington is immense. Listed here are only those sources that proved particularly helpful in this endeavor. The most recent extensive biography is Ron Chernow's *Washington: A Life* (New York, 2010), which is both eminently readable and judicious in its judgments. However, for the extraordinary wealth of information and detail it provides, nothing equals Douglas Southall Freeman's monumental seven-volume *George Washington: A Biography* (beginning with vol. 1, New York, 1948). More readable but less informative is James T. Flexner's four-volume *George Washington* (Boston, 1965–72).

A good medium-sized biography of Washington is John E. Firling, *The First of Men: A Life of George Washington* (Knoxville, 1988). For several excellent shorter studies see: Marcus Cunliffe, *George Washington, Man and Monument* (Lincoln, 1959); Edmund S. Morgan, *The Genius of George Washington* (New York, 1980); Garry Wills, *Cincinnatus: George Washington and the Enlightenment* (New York, 1984); James MacGregor Burns and Susan Dunn, *George Washington* (New York, 2001); and Joseph Ellis, *His Excellency: George Washington* (New York, 2005).

A book of essays that provide both a variety of insights into Washington's life and character and represent the range of recent scholarly opinion on those subjects is *George Washington Reconsidered,* Don Higginbotham, ed. (Charlottesville, 2001).

Washington's early years have been the subject of a number of books, the best of which is Bernhard Knollenberg's *George Washington: The Virginia Period* (Durham, N.C., 1964). On his role as a military commander much has also been written. Particularly useful are Bernhard Knollenberg, *Washington and the American Revolution: A Reappraisal* (New York, 1941), and Don Higginbotham, *George Washington and the American Military Tradition* (Athens, Ga., 1985). On Washington's presidency two studies rise above a smaller number of titles: Forest McDonald, *The Presidency of George Washington* (Lawrence, Kans., 1974), and Ralph Ketchum, *Presidents Above Party: The First American Presidency* (Chapel Hill, N.C., 1984).

Washington's private life is treated in a number of volumes, including Miriam Anne Bourne's *First Family: George Washington and His Intimate Relations* (New York, 1982) and Elswyth Thane's *Mount Vernon Family* (New York, 1968). On Mount Vernon itself—its building, the people who worked on it over the years, and its multiple ties to Washington's life and character—see Dalzell and Dalzell, *George Washington's Mount Vernon.*

For Washington's will in its entirety see *The Last Will and Testament of George Washington and Schedule of His Property* (Mount Vernon, Va., 1939). A detailed analysis of both the will and the property listed in the schedule can be found in Eugene E. Prussing, *The Estate of George Washington* (Boston, 1927). See also George Washington Nordham, *George Washington and Money* (Washington, D.C., 1982).

On George Washington and slavery—which increasingly troubled him over the years—we are still awaiting a definitive treatment, though François Furstenberg's *In the Name of the Father: Washington's Legacy, Slavery, and the Making of a Nation* (New York, 2008) is a step in the right direction.

In addition to works on Washington, a number of other studies have played a key role in shaping my thinking about him, chiefly through expanding the context in which I was considering his life and career. They are: Edmund S. Morgan, *American Slavery, American Freedom: The Ordeal of Colonial Virginia* (New York, 1975); Rhys Isaac, *The Transformation of Colonial Virginia* (Chapel Hill, N.C., 1982); T. H. Breen, *Tobacco Culture, the Mentality of the Great Tidewater Planters on the Eve of Revolution* (Princeton, N.J., 1985); Allan Kilikoff, *Tobacco and Slaves: The Development of Southern Cultures in the Chesapeake, 1680–1800* (Chapel Hill, N.C., 1986); Fred Anderson, *The Crucible of War: The Seven Years War and the Face of Empire in British North America, 1754–1766* (New York, 2000); Gordon S. Wood, *The Radicalism of the American Revolution* (New York, 1992); Joseph Ellis, *Founding Brothers* (New York, 2000); and Stanley Elkins and Eric McKitrick, *The Age of Federalism* (New York, 1973).

NOTES

1. George Washington, *Last Will and Testament.*

2. Washington, quoted in Freeman, *George Washington,* vol. 3, 22.

3. Washington to William Pearce, Feb. 16, 1794, *Writings of George Washington,* Fitzpatrick, ed., vol. 33, 275.

4. Washington to George William Fairfax, July 25, 1763, *Papers of George Washington,* Colonial Series, vol. 7, 233–34.

5. Washington to Thomas Green, Mar. 31, 1789, *Writings of George Washington,* vol. 30, 262–64.

6. Washington to Lund Washington, June 11, 1783, in ibid., vol. 25, 2.

7. Washington to Lund Washington, Feb. 12, 1783, in ibid., vol. 26, 126–27.

8. Washington to Lund Washington, Nov. 20, 1785, *Papers of George Washington,* Colonial Series, vol. 3, 374.

9. Washington to Robert Cary, April 13, 1761, in ibid., vol. 7, 34.

10. Washington to Robert Cary & Co., May 1, June 12, and Sept. 10, 1759, and Sept. 28, 1760, in ibid., vol. 4, 134, and vol. 6, 317–18, 352–55, 459–64.

11. Washington to Robert Cary, Aug. 10 and Sept. 28, 1760, in ibid., 448–50 and 459–61.

12. Washington to Robert Cary, Aug. 1, 1761, in ibid., vol. 7, 61–62.

13. See, for example, Washington to Robert Cary, May 1 and Sept. 10, 1759, and Sept. 28, 1760, in ibid., vol. 6, 317–18, 352–55, and 459–63.

14. Ibid.

15. Washington to Robert Cary, Aug. 10, 1764, in ibid., vol. 7, 323–31.

16. Quotation, no attribution, Freeman, *George Washington,* vol. 3, 301.

17. Washington, quoted in Ellis, *His Excellency,* 57.

18. Jonathan Boucher, quoted in Flexner, *George Washington,* vol. 1, 303.

19. Washington to George Muse, Jan. 29, 1774, quoted in Freeman, *George Washington,* vol. 3, 342.

20. Washington to John Posey, n.d., quoted in ibid., 179–80.

21. Washington to Bryan Fairfax, Aug. 24, 1775, *Papers of George Washington*, Colonial Series, vol. 10, 154–56.

22. Washington to Lund Washington, Aug. 15, 1778, *Writings of George Washington*, vol. 12, 326–27.

23. Washington to Arthur Young, June 18–21, 1792, in ibid., vol. 32, 65–66.

24. Washington to Lafayette, Apr. 5, 1783, in ibid., vol. 26, 300.

25. Robert Pleasants to George Washington, quoted in Ellis, *His Excellency*, 160–61.

26. Washington to Robert Morris, Apr. 12, 1786, *Papers of George Washington*, Confederation Series, vol. 4, 16.

27. Washington to Anthony Whiting, Oct. 14, 1792, *Writings of George Washington*, Presidential Series, vol. 32, 184.

28. Washington to Anthony Whiting, April 28, 1793, in ibid., 437–38.

29. Washington to Anthony Whiting, Oct. 14, 1796, in ibid., 180.

30. Washington to Tobias Lear, May 6, 1794, in ibid., vol. 33, 357–60.

31. Washington to William Gordon, in ibid., vol. 36, 49.

32. The *Jersey Chronicle*, reprinted in the *New York Argus*, Dec. 26, 1795, quoted in Freeman, *George Washington*, vol. 7, 321, n. 27.

33. George Washington, *Last Will and Testament of Washington*, 4–10.

Chapter 4. The Brothers Lawrence

SOURCES

There is a wealth of unpublished material on the Lawrence family in the collections of the Massachusetts Historical Society. The best published source on Amos Lawrence—and, for that matter, his brother Abbott—remains *Extracts from the Diary and Correspondence of Amos Lawrence, with a Brief Account of Some Incidents of His Life*, Williams R. Lawrence, ed. (Boston, 1855). Beyond that, one should read the essays on the two in *The Dictionary of American Biography* (New York, 1928–96), vol. 11, 46 and 44, and on Abbott Lawrence in the *American National Biography*, John Garraty and Mark Carnes, eds. (New York, 1995), vol. 13, 275. See also Hamilton Hill, *Memoir of Abbott Lawrence* (Boston, 1883).

Samuel Eliot Morison's *Maritime History of Massachusetts, 1783–1860* (Boston, 1921) remains an invaluable treatment of its subject. See also Benjamin Labaree, *Patriots and Partisans* (Cambridge, Mass., 1962); Carl Seaburg and Stanley Patterson, *Merchant Prince of Boston: Colonel T. Perkins, 1764–1854* (Cambridge, Mass., 1971), and Kenneth W. Porter, *The Jacksons and the Lees: Two Generations of Massachusetts Merchants, 1765–1844*, 2 vols. (Cambridge, Mass., 1973).

Two useful sources on the New England textile industry in general are Caroline Ware's *Early New England Cotton Manufacture: A Study in Industrial Origins* (Boston, 1931) and Paul E. River's *A New Order of Things: How the Textile Industry Transformed New England* (Hanover, N.H., 2002), which has the added virtue of being amply illustrated.

On the development of the Waltham-Lowell system in the textile industry Nathan Appleton's *Introduction of the Power Loom and Origin of Lowell* (Lowell, 1858) gives a clear and concise contemporary account, especially when read in combination with Francis W. Gregory's *Nathan Appleton: Merchant and Entrepreneur* (Charlottesville, 1975). Unfortunately there is no biography of Francis Cabot Lowell, but his papers are available at the Massachusetts Historical Society and information on him can be found in Ferris Greenslet's *The Lowells and Their Seven Worlds* (Boston, 1946) and in Robert Sobel's "Francis Cabot Lowell: The Patrician as Factory Manager," in his *Entrepreneurs: Explorations Within the American Business Tradition* (New York, 1974).

My own *Enterprising Elite* seeks to analyze in detail the activities, motives, and values of the group of investors whose capital created the Waltham-Lowell system. The financial returns on those investments are analyzed in Paul F. McGouldrick's *New England Textiles in the Nineteenth Century: Profits and Investment* (Cambridge, Mass., 1968). On labor in the mills see Thomas Dublin's excellent *Women at Work: The Transformation of Worth and Community in Lowell, Massachusetts, 1826–1860* (New York, 1979).

Among the large numbers of studies of textile manufacturing towns in New England two were of particular use here: David B. Cole, *Immigrant City: Lawrence, Massachusetts 1845–1921* (Chapel Hill, N.C., 1963), and Constance Green's *Holyoke Massachusetts: Case History of the Industrial Revolution* (New Haven, 1939). And though its subject is not textile manufacturing in New England, but rather in Pennsylvania, there is no richer, more closely focused analysis of the subject than Anthony C. Wallace's *Rockdale: The Growth of an American Village in the Early Industrial Revolution* (New York, 1978).

Among the sources that shed light on the Lawrences' philanthropic activities are N. T. Bowditch, *A History of the Massachusetts General Hospital (to August 5, 1851), Second Edition, with a Continuation to 1872* (New York, 1872); Frederick Rudolph, *Mark Hopkins and the Log: Williams College, 1836–1872* (New Haven, 1956), as well as the same author's *The American College and University* (New York, 1962); Samuel Eliot Morison, *Three Centuries of Harvard* (Cambridge, Mass., 1936), and Ronald Story, *Harvard and the Boston Upper Class:*

The Forging of an Aristocracy (Middletown, Conn., 1985); Josiah Quincy, *The History of Boston Athenaeum, with Biographical Notices of Its Deceased Founders* (Cambridge, Mass., 1851); and Walter M. Whitehill, *Boston Public Library: A Centennial History* (Cambridge, Mass., 1956).

Three fine books that provide a broader context for considering topics like philanthropy and the life of the mind in the Lawrences' Boston are: Martin Green, *The Problem of Boston: Some Readings in Cultural History* (New York, 1966); Daniel W. Howe, *The Unitarian Conscience: Harvard Moral Philosophy, 1805–1861* (Cambridge, Mass., 1970); and Digby Baltzell, *Puritan Boston and Quaker Philadelphia: Two Protestant Ethics and the Spirit of Class Authority and Leadership* (New York, 1980).

On Massachusetts politics both in general and as they involved the slavery issue there are a number of useful sources, including Arthur B. Darling, *Political Changes in Massachusetts, 1824–1848: A Study of Liberal Movements in Politics* (New Haven, 1925); Kinley J. Brauer, *Cotton Versus Conscience: Massachusetts Whig Politics and Southwestern Expansion, 1843–1848* (Lexington, Ky., 1967); Thomas H. O'Connor, *Lords of the Loom: The Cotton Whigs and the Coming of the Civil War* (New York, 1968); and Ronald P. Formisano, *The Transformation of Political Culture: Massachusetts Parties, 1790s–1840s* (New York, 1983).

Apart from general studies there are a number of biographies that cover the same ground and in several cases carry the story forward to the Civil War and beyond. Among them are David Donald, *Charles Sumner and the Coming of the Civil War* (New York, 1960); Martin B. Duberman, *Charles Francis Adams, 1807–1886* (Boston, 1961); Frank O. Gatell, *John Gorham Palfrey and the New England Conscience* (Cambridge, Mass., 1963); and Robert F. Dalzell, Jr., *Daniel Webster and the Trial of American Nationalism, 1845–1852* (Boston, 1973).

And on other issues shaping the politics of those years see Mary H. Blewett, *Constant Turmoil: The Politics of Industrial Life in Nineteenth-Century New England* (Amherst, 2000).

NOTES

1. Amos Lawrence, *Diary and Correspondence,* 28.
2. Ibid.
3. Ibid., 30.
4. Ibid., 26.
5. Ibid.
6. Ibid., 47.
7. Lawrence to Sarah Lawrence, June 4, 1815, in ibid., 52.

8. Lawrence to Abbott Lawrence, June 7, 1815, in ibid.

9. Ibid., 57.

10. Ibid., 81.

11. Ibid.

12. Ibid., 66–67.

13. For Dickens's discussion of his visit to Lowell see his *American Notes for General Circulation* (London, 1842), vol. 1, 152–63.

14. Appleton, *Introduction of the Power Loom,* 11.

15. The letter, written by James Jackson and John C. Warren and dated Aug. 20, 1810, is reprinted in full in Bowditch, *History of Massachusetts General Hospital,* 3–9.

16. Quincy's address is reprinted in full in ibid., 44.

17. Lawrence to William R. Lawrence, Jan. 31, 1830, quoted in Lawrence, *Diary and Correspondence,* 91–92.

18. Ibid.

19. Lawrence to William R. Lawrence, Nov. 12, 1852, in ibid., 332–33.

20. Lawrence to Robert Trumbull, Nov. 2, 1841, in ibid., 160–61.

21. Lawrence to Mark Hopkins, June 12, 1848, in ibid., 259.

22. Hopkins, sermon of Feb. 21, 1853, quoted in ibid., 348.

23. The quotations are from William R. Lawrence's description of these activities in ibid., 178–80.

24. Ibid.

25. Ibid., 118.

26. Hopkins, sermon, Feb. 21, 1853, quoted in ibid., 349.

27. Amos A. Lawrence, diary, Amos A. Lawrence MSS, Massachusetts Historical Society.

28. Amos Lawrence to [no name, no date], quoted in *Diary and Correspondence,* 257.

29. Amos Lawrence to Abbott Lawrence, June 9, 1847, in ibid., 244–48.

30. Abbott Lawrence to Samuel A. Eliot, June 7, 1847, quoted in Hill, *Memoir of Abbott Lawrence,* 109–14.

31. Ibid.

32. Amos Lawrence, *Diary and Correspondence,* 296.

33. Ibid., 312.

34. Sumner's speech of June 28, 1848, quoted in Donald, *Charles Sumner,* 166.

35. "An appeal to the Good Sense of the Legislative and the Community in Favor of a New Bridge to South Boston," a pamphlet, probably written by Massachusetts Democratic Party leader David Henshaw, quoted in Stanley J. Kutler, *Privilege and Creative Destruction: The Charles River Bridge Case* (New York, 1978), 22.

36. Josiah Quincy, *An Appeal in Behalf of the Boston Athenaeum, Address to the Proprietors* (Boston, 1853).

37. Hopkins, sermon of Feb. 21, 1853, quoted in Lawrence, *Diary and Correspondence,* 348.

38. Robert Winthrop, speech of August 20, 1855, *Addresses and Speeches of Robert Winthrop* (Boston, 1867), 210–12.

39. Williams Lawrence, *Memories of a Happy Life* (Boston, 1920), 418.

40. John D. Rockefeller, quoted in ibid., 140. The remark was reported to William Lawrence in a letter while he was working on his autobiography, but he indicates neither the name of the writer nor the date.

Chapter 5. Rich as Rockefeller

SOURCES

For anyone interested in pursuing sustained research on John D. Rockefeller, the place to begin is the Rockefeller Archive Center in Sleepy Hollow, New York. Its holdings of material relating both to him and to other members of the family are truly vast, and Rockefeller's own papers are open to readers without restrictions. It is necessary to make an appointment before visiting the Center, and any copying of documents must be done by the staff, though they are quite helpful in this regard as well as in other ways.

One of the most interesting and important collections at the Center is a complete run of the correspondence between John D. Rockefeller and his son, John D. Rockefeller, Jr. Available, in print, also is a selection of letters from that collection, *Dear Father/Dear Son,* Joseph W. Ernst, ed. (New York, 1994). And another invaluable resource in print (however murky the details of its authorship) is Rockefeller's autobiography, *Random Reminiscences of Men and Events,* which can be found in several different editions.

Far and away the best biography of Rockefeller is Ron Chernow's *Titan, The Life of John D. Rockefeller, Sr.* (New York, 1998). Full of fascinating details and wise insights, it is thoughtfully balanced throughout. Neither too critical nor too laudatory, it brilliantly captures its extraordinarily complex subject. Other biographies worth consulting selectively are Allan Nevins's *Study in Power: John D. Rockefeller, Industrialist and Philanthropist,* 2 vols. (New York, 1953), as well as an earlier effort by the same author, *John D. Rockefeller: The Heroic Age of American Enterprise,* 2 vols. (New York, 1940).

Two works on family members who played important roles in Rockefeller's life are Clarice Stasz, *The Rockefeller Women: Dynasty of Piety, Privacy, and Service* (New York, 1995), and Raymond B. Fosdick's sympathetic *John D. Rockefeller, Jr.: A Portrait* (New York, 1956).

Information on other individuals who affected Rockefeller's life profoundly, though in very different ways, can be found in a pair of autobiographies: Frederick Taylor Gates, *Chapters in My Life* (New York, 1977), and Ida

Tarbell, *All in a Day's Work: An Autobiography* (New York, 1939). On Tarbell see also Kathleen Brady, *Ida Tarbell: Portrait of a Muckraker* (New York, 1984).

On the history of Standard Oil in its early years a useful source is Ralph W. and Muriel Hidy, *History of Standard Oil Company: Pioneering Big Business, 1882–1911* (New York, 1955). And to locate the company in the unending expansion of the oil industry worldwide nothing surpasses Daniel Yergin's *The Prize: The Epic Quest for Oil, Money and Power* (New York, 1991).

Finally, on Rockefeller's career as a philanthropist there are several solid studies available, including [no author], *The General Education Board: An Account of Its Activities, 1902–1914* (New York, 1930); Richard J. Storr, *Harper's University: The Beginnings* (Chicago, 1966); Richard E. Brown, *Rockefeller Medicine Men: Medicine & Capitalism in America* (Berkeley, 1979); Gerald Jonas, *The Circuit Riders: Rockefeller Money and the Rise of Modern Science* (New York, 1988); and, most important of all, Raymond B. Fosdick, *The Story of the Rockefeller Foundation* (New Brunswick, N.J., 1989).

NOTES

1. Rockefeller, *Random Reminiscences,* 37.
2. Ibid., 58.
3. Rockefeller, quoted in Nevins, *Study in Power,* vol. 1, 135.
4. Rockefeller, *Random Reminiscences,* 65.
5. Ibid., 70.
6. Chernow, *Titan,* 136.
7. Rockefeller, *Random Reminiscences,* 12.
8. John D. Rockefeller to Laura Celestia Rockefeller, January 20, 1872, quoted in Stasz, *The Rockefeller Women,* 73.
9. Rockefeller to Edward Judson, November 29, 1892, quoted in Chernow, *Titan,* 302.
10. William Rainey Harper, quoted in Storr, *Harper's University,* 47.
11. Harper, quoted in Chernow, *Titan,* 327.
12. Rockefeller to Harper, quoted in ibid., 494.
13. Frederick T. Gates to Rockefeller, June 5, 1905, quoted in Fosdick, *John D. Rockefeller, Jr.,* 119.
14. Ida Tarbell, "John D. Rockefeller, A Character Study," *McClure's Magazine,* August 1905, vol. 25, 390.
15. Rockefeller, *Random Reminiscences,* 139.
16. Gates, quoted in Chernow, *Titan,* 342.
17. Rockefeller, *Random Reminiscences,* v.
18. Tarbell, quoted in Chernow, *Titan,* 534.
19. Rockefeller, *Random Reminiscences,* 142.

20. Ibid.

21. Carnegie, quoted in Livesay, *Andrew Carnegie,* 153.

22. Rockefeller, *Random Reminiscences,* 142.

23. Ibid.

24. John D. Rockefeller to John D. Rockefeller, Jr., April 11, 1925, quoted in Fosdick, *John D. Rockefeller, Jr.,* 197.

25. Rockefeller, *Random Reminiscences,* 152.

Chapter 6. Heirs

SOURCES

Many of the sources listed for the previous chapter have been used for this one as well, including: the Rockefeller family materials of the Rockefeller Archive Center; Ernst, ed., *Dear Father/Dear Son;* Rockefeller, *Random Reminiscences;* Chernow, *Titan;* Stasz, *Rockefeller Women;* Fosdick, *John D. Rockefeller, Jr.;* Gates, *Chapters of My Life;* Brown, *Rockefeller Medicine Men;* Jonas, *Circuit Riders;* and Fosdick, *The Story of the Rockefeller Foundation.*

There are two sources on Abby Aldrich Rockefeller, the second one being not only more recent but also more complete: Mary Ellen Chase, *Abby Aldrich Rockefeller* (New York, 1950), and Bernice Kert, *Abby Aldrich Rockefeller: The Woman in the Family* (New York, 1993).

A pair of fine books that deal with the Rockefeller Family as a whole through the first three generations, and in particular with the career of John D. Rockefeller III, are: John Ensor Harr and Peter J. Johnson, *The Rockefeller Century: Three Generations of America's Greatest Family* (New York, 1988), and the same authors' *The Rockefeller Conscience: An American Family in Public and in Private* (New York, 1991). Another excellent source on John D. Rockefeller III, his philanthropic activities, and his relations with the other members of the family is his unpublished diary, which can be found in the Rockefeller family papers at the Rockefeller Archive Center. See especially RFA5.1, B14 F189–192. The only autobiography to have been published by a member of the second or third generation of the Rockefeller family is David Rockefeller's *Memoirs* (New York, 2002).

Several useful studies of Nelson A. Rockefeller are available, including Cary Reich, *The Life of Nelson Rockefeller: Worlds to Conquer 1908–1958* (New York, 1996), and Joseph Persico, *The Imperial Rockefeller: A Biography of Nelson A. Rockefeller* (New York, 1982). There is also a large number of publications dealing with various aspects of his passionate interest in art. To name a few: *Twentieth Century Art from the Collection of Nelson Aldrich Rockefeller,* exhibition catalogue, the Museum of Modern Art (New York, 1969); *Folk Treasures of Mexico: The Nelson A. Rockefeller Collection* (New York, 1990); and Samuel E. Bleeker, *The Politics of Architecture: A Perspective on Nelson A. Rockefeller* (New York, 1981).

On the creation of Kykuit and its gardens, as well as the various family controversies surrounding the place, see Dalzell and Dalzell, *The House the Rockefellers Built: A Tale of Money, Taste and Power in Twentieth Century America* (New York, 2007). And for an inside view of the same subject, accompanied by a great many fine photographs, see Mary Louise Pierson and Ann Rockefeller Roberts, *The Rockefeller Home, Kykuit* (New York, 1998). On Colonial Williamsburg, see Richard Hander and Eric Gamble, *The New History in an Old Museum: Creating the Past at Colonial Williamsburg* (Durham, N.C., 1997), and Anders Greenspan, *Creating Colonial Williamsburg* (Washington, D.C., 2002). And on Rockefeller Center there is Daniel Okrent's splendid *Great Fortune: The Epic of Rockefeller Center* (New York, 2003).

The Museum of Modern Art, on which the Rockefellers lavished so much attention and money, is the subject of several studies, the most useful of them being Sybil Gordon Kantor, *Alfred H. Barr, Jr., and the Intellectual Origins of the Museum of Modern Art* (Cambridge, Mass., 2002), and Harriet S. Bee and Michelle Elligott, eds., *Art in Our Time: A Chronicle of the Museum of Modern Art* (New York, 2004). For a wryly humorous view of modern art see Tom Wolfe's *The Painted Word* (New York, 1975), and on the financial aspects of art collecting: Michael C. Fitzgerald, *Making Modernism: Picasso and the Creation of the Market for Modern Art* (New York, 1994).

Finally, though there has not been a great deal published on the fourth generation of the Rockefeller family, a fair amount of space is devoted to them in Peter Collier and David Horowitz's gossipy if entertaining *The Rockefellers: An American Dynasty* (New York, 1976).

NOTES

1. John D. Rockefeller, Jr., to John D. Rockefeller, June 21, 1905, quoted in Fosdick, *John D. Rockefeller, Jr.,* 119–20.

2. Abby A. Rockefeller, quoted in Chase, *Abby Aldrich Rockefeller,* 28.

3. *Pittsburgh Press,* Nov. 15, 1904, quoted in Fosdick, *John D. Rockefeller, Jr.,* 126.

4. Abby A. Rockefeller to John D. Rockefeller, Jr., Aug. 14, 1903, quoted in Kert, *Abby Aldrich Rockefeller,* 114–15.

5. John D. Rockefeller to John D. Rockefeller, Jr., Apr. 21, 1908, Rockefeller Archive Center, RFA.L. letterbook 223, 109, 129.

6. John D. Rockefeller, as quoted by John D. Rockefeller, Jr., in Fosdick, *John D. Rockefeller, Jr.,* 142.

7. Abby A. Rockefeller to John D. Rockefeller, Jr., Sept. 27, 1915, Rockefeller Archive Center, RFA 1.Z.II, B1 F1.

8. John D. Rockefeller, quoted in Harr and Johnson, *Rockefeller Century,* 145.

9. John D. Rockefeller, quoted in Fosdick, *John D. Rockefeller, Jr.,* 418.

10. John D. Rockefeller to John D. Rockefeller, Jr., Jan. 28, 1915, quoted in ibid., 334; John D. Rockefeller, Jr., to John D. Rockefeller, Jan. 29, 1915, quoted in ibid., 334–35.

11. Ibid.

12. John D. Rockefeller, Jr., "to the author," n.d., quoted in Fosdick, *John D. Rockefeller, Jr.,* 300.

13. Ibid., 329.

14. John D. Rockefeller, Jr., address on the opening of the gymnasium, Rockefeller Center, quoted in ibid., 264.

15. *New York Herald Tribune,* March 31, 1931, quoted in ibid., 268.

16. *Fortune,* December 1936, quoted in ibid., 268.

17. John D. Rockefeller quoted in ibid., 269.

18. The phrase is used as a book title by Harr and Johnson.

19. Abby Aldrich to Nelson Rockefeller, Apr. 14, 1929, Rockefeller Archive Center, RFA2, AA.I, B5 F65.

20. Laurance Rockefeller's daughters, Marion and Laura, quoted in Collier and Horowitz, *The Rockefellers,* 404.

21. Nelson Rockefeller's daughter, Mary, quoted in ibid., 587.

22. John D. Rockefeller III to Nelson Rockefeller, July 15, 1977, Rockefeller Archive Center, RAF4.1, B160 F107.

23. Nelson Rockefeller to John D. Rockefeller III, "Draft," July 18, 1977, in ibid.

24. Abby A. Rockefeller, quoted by John D. Rockefeller, Jr., in a letter to William Welles Bosworth, Oct. 5, 1942, Rockefeller Archive Center, RFA2.I, B21, F195.

25. Laurance Rockefeller, quoted in Pierson and Roberts, *Rockefeller Family Home,* 35–37.

26. John D. Rockefeller, Jr., Commencement Address, Fisk University, June 6, 1928, quoted in Fosdick, *John D. Rockefeller,* 328.

27. Abby A. Rockefeller, quoted in Chase, *Abby Aldrich Rockefeller,* 130.

Chapter 7. Successors

SOURCES

The best way to get a sense of *Forbes*'s "400 Richest People in America" is to see one of the annual issues—published in October—devoted to that subject. The full citations for the two issues of the magazine focused on here are, for October 11, 2010, *Forbes,* vol. 186, number 6, and for October 10, 2011, *Forbes,* vol. 188, number 6. A detailed analysis of how the 400 project unfolded from its inception in 1982 through 2006 can be found in Peter W. Bernstein and Annalyn Iwan, *All the Money in the World: How the Forbes 400 Make—and Spend—Their Fortunes* (New York, 2007).

The most complete account of the origins and early history of the Giving Pledge is Carol J. Loomis, "The $600 Billion Challenge," *Fortune,* June 16, 2010, vol. 162, number 1. For a list of the Pledge signers and their personal statements see the Giving Pledge website, accessed November 23, 2011.

An enormous quantity of information, analysis, and comment—favorable and otherwise—has been published about Steve Jobs over the years. But Walter Isaacson's *Steve Jobs* (New York, 2011) is the first place any thoughtful person should turn to on the subject.

Similarly, a huge amount has been written about Oprah Winfrey, but unfortunately there is as yet nothing close to a definitive biography of her. Until one appears Kitty Kelley's *Oprah: A Biography* (New York, 2010) can be consulted. Less comprehensive but more interesting is Janice Peck's intriguing *The Age of Oprah: Cultural Icon for the Neoliberal Era* (Boulder, Colo., 2008). Ultimately, however, Oprah has had more interesting things to say about herself than others have said about her. See, for example, Bill Alder, ed., *The Uncommon Wisdom of Oprah Winfrey: A Portrait in Her Own Words* (New York, 1997).

NOTES

1. "The Numbers Game," *Forbes,* Oct. 11, 2010, 292.

2. Ibid.

3. *Publishers Weekly* review, accessed via Amazon.com, http://www.amazon.com/All-Money-World-Make-Spend—Their/dp/030727876X/ref=sr_1_1?s=books&ie=UTF8&qid=1335552258&sr=1-1.

4. Bernstein and Swan, *All the Money,* chapter 4.

5. Ibid., 89.

6. "The Richest People in the World," *Forbes,* Oct. 10, 2011, 39.

7. Karen Blankfield, "Mavericks, Ted Turner: The Last Roundup," in ibid., 132.

8. Ibid.

9. Christopher Herman, "Passions: George Kaiser's $10 Billion Bet," in ibid., 132.

10. Victoria Barret, "A Course in Giving," in ibid., 112.

11. Ibid., 114.

12. Ibid.

13. Ibid., 118.

14. Ibid.

15. "A Dedication to Philanthropy," *Forbes,* Oct. 11, 2010, 60.

16. Steve Forbes, "Their Message: Jay-Z and Warren Buffett Talk with Steve Forbes About Wealth, Success and Giving Back," in ibid., 54.

17. Ibid.

18. Quentin Hardy, "In Mark We Trust," in ibid., 81.

19. Ibid.

20. Ibid.

21. Ibid., 86.

22. George B. Kaiser, www.GivingPledge.com.

23. Laura and John Arnold, in ibid.

24. Pierre and Pam Omidyar, in ibid.

25. David M. Rubenstein, in ibid.

26. Sidney Kimmel, in ibid.

27. Lynn Schusterman, in ibid.

28. Michael Bloomberg, in ibid.

29. George B. Kaiser, in ibid.

30. Michael Bloomberg, in ibid.

31. Ray and Barbara Dalio, in ibid.

32. Larry Ellison, in ibid.

33. Michael and Lori Milken, in ibid.

34. David Rockefeller, in ibid.

35. David M. Rubenstein, in ibid.

36. Walter Scott, Jr., in ibid.

37. Bernie and Billi Marcus, in ibid.

38. Ted Forstmann, in ibid.

39. Carl Icahn, in ibid.

40. Lynn Schusterman, in ibid.

41. Eli and Edythe Broad, in ibid.

42. George Lucas, in ibid.

43. Eli and Edythe Broad, in ibid.

44. Ray and Barbara Dalio, in ibid.

45. Harold and Sue Ann Hamm, in ibid.

46. Carl Icahn, in ibid.

47. Michael and Lori Milken, in ibid.

48. Lynn Schusterman, in ibid.

49. Michael Bloomberg, in ibid.

50. George B. Kaiser, in ibid.

51. Eli and Edythe Broad, in ibid.

52. Loomis, "$600 Billion Challenge," *Fortune,* June 16, 2010.

53. Ibid., 92.

54. Andrew Ross Sorkin, "The Mystery of Steve Jobs's Public Giving," *New York*

Times, August 29, 2011, http://dealbook.nytimes.com/2011/08/29/the-mystery-of-steve
-jobss-public-giving/.

55. Isaacson, *Steve Jobs,* 106.

56. Sorkin, "Steve Jobs's Giving," *New York Times.*

57. Ibid.

58. Ibid., accessed November 25, 2011.

59. Kitty Kelley, *Oprah,* 240.

60. Ibid., 400.

61. Kitty Kelley, "No Oprah in the Billionaires Club," Huff Post Impact, www
.Huffingtonpost.com, accessed November 27, 2011.

62. Ibid.

63. Ibid.

64. Oprah Winfrey, quoted in Alder, ed., *Uncommon Wisdom,* 76.

65. Ibid., 246.

Chapter 8. Wealth and American Democracy

SOURCES

For a useful account of the unfolding sequence of events that made up the
Occupy Wall Street protest see "Timeline of Occupy Wall Street," from Wikipe-
dia, http://en.wikipedia.org/wiki/Timeline_of_Occupy_Wall_Street, accessed
December 2, 2011. On the origins of the protest see Mattathias Schwartz, "Pre-
Occupied: A Movement's Past and Future," *New Yorker,* November 28, 2011.

The Web contains innumerable descriptions and analysis of "Occupy." But
some of the most thoughtful reporting on the subject can be found in the *New
Yorker.* See, in addition to the article cited in the paragraph above, Hendrik
Hertzberg, "A Walk in the Park: Will Occupy Wall Street Succeed?," October
17, 2011; Lizzie Widdicombe, "Preoccupied: Occupy Wall Street: A Culture
of Its Own," October 24, 2011; Andrew Marantz, "Mission Control: Occupy
Wall Street, Global Revolution and Vlad Teichberg," October 31, 2011; Hen-
drik Hertzberg, "Occupational Hazards: Protestors and What Lies Ahead,"
November 7, 2011; and George Packer, "All the Angry People: A Man out of
Work Finds Community in Occupy Wall Street," December 5, 2011; all in the
New Yorker, vol. 86, and for a revealing set of photographs see Eliss Curtis,
"Ashley Gilbertson: Finding Occupy Wall Street on Film," November 22, 2011,
in ibid.

On income inequality the two principal documents used here are Janet Yellen, "Speech to the Center for the Study of Democracy, 2006–07, Economics

of Governance Lecture," University of California, Irvine, November 6, 2006, which can be found at www.frbsf.org/news/speeches/2006/1106.html, accessed December 7, 2011; and Congress of the United States, Congressional Budget Office, "Trends in the Distribution of Household Income Between 1979 and 2007," October 2011, http://cbo.gov/publication/42729.

In addition, income inequality in the United States has been the subject of a large number of published studies. For a sampling see: Daniel Cohen, Thomas Piketty, and Gilles Saint-Paul, *The Economics of Rising Inequality* (New York, 1983); Robert E. Kuenne, *Economic Justice in American Society* (Princeton, N.J., 1993); Sheldon Danziger and Peter Gottschalk, *America Unequal* (Cambridge, Mass., 1995); Finis Welch, ed., *The Causes and Consequences of Increasing Inequality* (Chicago, 2001); and Robert H. Frank, *Falling Behind: How Rising Inequality Harms the Middle Class* (Berkeley, Calif. 2007); Timothy Noah, *The Great Divergence: America's Growing Inequality Crisis and What We Can Do About It* (New York, 2012). And for a comparative perspective see also George Irvin, *Super Rich: The Rise of Inequality in Britain and the United States* (Cambridge, U.K., 2008), and for a fuller presentation of Paul R. Krugman's views, see that author's *The Conscience of a Liberal* (New York, 2007).

Studies of philanthropy in the United States are also legion. The one used most extensively here is "The 2010 Study of High Net Worth Individuals: Issues Driving Charitable Activities among Affluent Households," sponsored by Bank of America-Merrill Lynch and researched and written at the Center on Philanthropy at Indiana University in Indianapolis, www.philanthropy.iupui .edu. Though not without its flaws, the study was done with great care and thoroughness and provides an abundance of information on its subject.

The Indiana University studies are also indicative of a steadily growing interest in the subject of philanthropy, which among other things has spawned a number of research centers on the subject like the one at Indiana University, for example, The Center on Wealth and Philanthropy at Boston College. Also, an eminently useful source of information on the subject is the *Chronicle of Philanthropy*.

Among the books on philanthropy the following are some of the most helpful: Robert H. Bremner, *American Philanthropy* (Chicago, 1988); Peter Dobkin Hall, *Inventing the Nonprofit Sector and Other Essays on Philanthropy, Voluntarism, and Nonprofit Organization* (Baltimore, 1995); Charles T. Clotfelter and Thomas Ehrlich, eds., *Philanthropy and the Nonprofit Sector in a Changing America* (Bloomington, Ind., 1999); Mark Dowie, *American Foundations: An*

Investigative History (Cambridge, Mass., 2001); and Stacy Palmer, ed., *Challenges for Nonprofits and Philanthropy: The Courage to Change: Three Decades of Reflections* (Medford, Mass., 2005).

Finally, I should mention a number of books which—though they do not fit precisely in any of the discussions of sources appearing above—have nonetheless contributed to my thinking in a variety of ways. Most are broad studies, some are more narrowly focused. Many I have regularly assigned in courses at Williams College. They are: Thorstein Veblen, *The Theory of the Leisure Class* (New York, 2001); Edward Chase Kirkland, *Dream and Thought in the Business Community, 1860–1900* (Ithaca, N.Y., 1956); Alfred D. Chandler, Jr., *Strategy and Structure: Chapters in the History of American Industrial Enterprise* (Cambridge, Mass., 1969); Nelson W. Aldrich, Jr., *Old Money: The Mythology of Wealth in America* (New York, 1996); Constance McLaughlin Green, *Eli Whitney and the Birth of American Technology* (Boston, 1956); T. J. Stiles, *The First Tycoon: The Epic Life of Cornelius Vanderbilt* (New York, 2010); John Kenneth Galbraith, *The Great Crash, 1929* (Boston, 1955); Andrew Ross Sorkin, *Too Big to Fail: The Story of How Wall Street and Washington Fought to Save the Financial System—and Themselves* (New York, 2009); Roger Lowenstein, *The End of Wall Street* (New York, 2011).

NOTES

1. Schwartz, "Pre-Occupied," *New Yorker.*

2. "Occupy Wall Street," Wikipedia.

3. Quest Post, Friday, January 28, 2011, www.nakedcapitalism.com, accessed December 6, 2011.

4. Yellen, speech of January 6, 2006.

5. Paul Krugman, "The Conscience of a Liberal," blog.nytimes.com/2001/09/18, accessed January 25, 2012.

6. Krugman, "Oligarchy, American Style," *New York Times,* November 3, 2011.

7. Maria Di Mento and Caroline Preston, "As Tensions over Wealth Gap Rise, the Rich Are Giving More," *Chronicle of Philanthropy,* Feb. 6, 2012.

8. Indiana University Study, 2010, 47.

9. Frank Newport, "Americans Like Having a Rich Class, as They Did 22 Years Ago," Gallup, Inc., May 11, 2012, http://www.gallup.com/poll/154619/americans-having-rich-class-years-ago.aspx.

INDEX